CONFERENCE SERIES

innsbruck university press

Mining in European History and its Impact on Environment and Human Societies –

Proceedings for the 2nd Mining in European History Conference
of the FZ HiMAT, 7.-10. November 2012, Innsbruck

Editors:
Peter Anreiter
Klaus Brandstätter
Gert Goldenberg
Klaus Hanke
Walter Leitner
Kurt Nicolussi
Klaus Oeggl
Ernst Pernicka
Veronika Schaffer
Thomas Stöllner
Gerhard Tomedi
Peter Tropper

Forschungszentrum (FZ) HiMAT
Die Geschichte des Bergbaus in Tirol und seinen angrenzenden Gebieten –
Auswirkungen auf Umwelt und Gesellschaft
Universität Innsbruck

The research centre HiMAT is supported by the University of Innsbruck, the Province Tyrol, the Autonomous Province of Bozen-South Tyrol, the Province Vorarlberg, the Province Salzburg and the Department of culture of the Province Tyrol.

© *innsbruck* university press, 2013
Universität Innsbruck
1st edition.
All rights reserved.
Coverphotos: © Mag.ª Barbara Viehweider, Mag.ª Caroline O. Grutsch, DI Michael Moser, Andreas Blaikner
Editorial office, Layout: Mag.ª Veronika Schaffer
www.uibk.ac.at/iup
ISBN 978-3-902936-18-9

Content

Preface 9

Session I
Resource Management

JACEK LECH
    Resource management in prehistoric siliceous rock mining: an archaeological perspective 13

FELICE LAROCCA & CHIARA LEVATO
    From the imprint to the tool: the identification of prehistoric mining implements through the study of digging traces. The case of Grotta della Monaca in Calabria (Italy) 21

CAROLINE O. GRUTSCH, KLAUS-PETER MARTINEK & MATTHIAS KRISMER
    Copper mineralizations in western North Tyrol – In prehistoric times exploited resources? 27

PETER TREBSCHE
    Resources and nutrition in the Urnfield period mining site of Prigglitz-Gasteil in Lower Austria – Preliminary report on the excavations from 2010 to 2012 33

REGULA WAHL-CLERICI
    Três Minas: A discussion of some aspects of the evidence for the use of water in mining 39

CLAUS-STEPHAN HOLDERMANN
    The Highest Abattoir of the Tyrol at the Schneeberg/Moos in the Passeier Valley/South Tyrol 47

Session II
Production & Technology

A. BERNARD KNAPP
    The Social Context of Metallurgical Production and Technological Change: Views from the Eastern Mediterranean 53

SIMON TIMBERLAKE & PETER MARSHALL
    Understanding the chronology of British Bronze Age mines –
    Bayesian modelling and theories of exploitation   59

ERICA HANNING, THOMAS STÖLLNER, ANNETTE HORNSCHUCH &
BEATE SIKORSKI
    Quantifying Bronze Age Smelting Sites in Mitterberg Mining District   67

THOMAS KOCH WALDNER
    Prehistoric copper production in the region of Kitzbühel, North Tyrol -
    mining and smelting   73

DANIEL STEINIGER & CLAUDIO GIARDINO
    Prehistoric mining in central Italy:
    New evidence from the Monti dellaTolfa (Latium)   81

PATRICK ROSENTHAL, DENIS MORIN, RICHARD HERBACH, ADONIS
PHOTIADES, SERGE DELPECH, DENIS JACQUEMOT & LIONEL FADIN
    Mining technologies at deep level in Antiquity:
    The Laurion mines (Attica, Greece)   89

CONSTANTIN CANAVAS
    Mine drainage in medieval Muslim Spain. Continuities and
    discontinuities in a cross-cultural context   97

SUSANNE KLEMM, SUSANNE STROBL & ROLAND HAUBNER
    Mediaeval Iron Smelting in the Area of the Iron Mountain (Steirischer Erzberg)
    at Eisenerz, Styria (Austria)   103

PETRA MÁTYÁS-RAUSCH
    The Life and Mining Work of Felician von Herberstein (1540-1590)   111

DIRK BRANDHERM, ALEXANDER MAASS & EMILIO DIZ ARDID
    Multi-period mining remains from the Sierra de Orihuela (Alicante, SE Spain)   115

Session III
Societal Interaction & Ecology

LARS BLUMA
    The environment approach in German mining: bodies, workplaces and
    hygiene around 1900   123

MARION KAISER
    Influence and Perception. How pit and quarry industry change landscapes   127

VALESKA FLOR
    Living with Lignite. A Glimpse on Lignite-linked Problems in the
    Renish Lignite-Mining Region   133

ANITA FEICHTER-HAID
    The „Pfennwerthandel" in the Mining Region of Kitzbühel   139

MICHAEL KASPAR
    The development of social stratification in the Montafon - transformation of
    a former mining area in the 17th century   145

IVONNE BURGHARDT, CHRISTIANE HEMKER & YVES HOFFMANN
    Medieval mining in Dippoldiswalde (Saxony). New approaches on
    research of mining impact   151

MARTIN ŠTEFÁNIK
    The Role of Italian Businessmen and Entrepreneur in the Beginnings of
    Central Slovakian Metal Mining with special regard to the Productivity of
    Gold in Kremnica in the 1st Half of 14th century   157

ELISABETH GRUBER & IRINA WINDHABER
    Names as Indicators of Mining Activities in the Area of
    Klausen/Villanders (South Tyrol/Italy)   161

TIM MIGHALL, ANTONIO MARTINEZ CORTIZAS, NOEMI SILVA SÁNCHEZ,
SIMON TIMBERLAKE, FRANK M. CHAMBERS & WILLIAM O'BRIEN
    Characterising vegetation changes in former mining and metalworking areas
    during prehistoric and Roman times: Perspectives from Britain and Ireland   167

BARBARA VIEHWEIDER & KLAUS OEGGL
    Reconstruction of the vegetation in the region of Kitzbühel (Tyrol) and the
    impact of different mining phases since the Neolithic   173

UWE MEYERDIRKS
    Neubulach and Freudenstadt: Foundation, development and impact of medieval
    and early modern mining towns in the Northern Black Forest (SW-Germany)   181

WILLIAM O'BRIEN
    Copper Mining in Ireland during the Later Bronze Age   191

Session IV
Data Base, Modelling & Geoinformation supporting Mining Research

IRMELA HERZOG
    Medieval mining sites, trade routes, and least-cost paths in the
    Bergisches Land, Germany   201

MARKUS HELFERT, BRITTA RAMMINGER & REGULA WAHL-CLERICI
    Underground surveying with 3D-laserscanning of the „Galeria dos Alargamentos"
    in the Roman gold mining district of Três Minas and
    Campo De Jales (Northern Portugal)   207

RENGERT ELBURG, FANET GÖTTLICH & THOMAS REUTER
    From the skies into the underground. Remote sensing, survey and documentation
    in a medieval mining landscape in the Ore Mountains   215

KRISTÓF KOVÁCS & KLAUS HANKE
    Spatial Analysis Techniques for Investigation of Tool Marks on
    Archaeological Finds   223

LENA ASRIH
    Airborne laser scans as a tool for historical science? – First methodic
    considerations using the example of medieval mining in the Saxon Ore
    Mountains (Erzgebirge/Germany)   229

List of Authors   235

Sponsors   249

Preface

The exploitation of raw materials, in particular metal ores, was a formative process both for the European Civilisation and the landscape but difficult to understand in its complexity. Decades of concentrated archaeological and historical studies conducted up to now provide solid basic individual knowledge but also accumulated a multitude of research questions for future studies. However, fundamental problems in mining history are of multidisciplinary dimensions and their complexity requires an interdisciplinary approach, and it goes without saying that many of these research questions are solved faster and with better results by mutual networking. Since more than five years we practice such a mutual interdisciplinary networking in our research centre HiMAT which generated novel, innovative key results for the Eastern Alpine mining regions. Consequently we foster the interdisciplinary approach in mining history, and major aims of this conference were to exchange information, to stimulate discussions, to promote international contacts between different disciplines involved in mining history and to encourage similar interdisciplinary attempts in other mining regions.

After three years we convened again in Innsbruck on the occasion of the 2nd Mining in European History Conference to discuss the diversity of mining problems from different points of view of many disciplines. Remembering the conference, one of the most prominent impressions was that this conference is heading towards a leading international platform for ancient mining activities in Europe. For interdisciplinary research an area for intensive scientific exchange and discussions is urgently needed. Therefore the research centre HiMAT is pleased to facilitate cooperation and communication in between interdisciplinary-oriented scholars in history of mining every three years in Innsbruck. With this conference transcript we want to keep this momentum going.

More than 120 scientists from 12 nations have attended the conference. Contributions included archaeological, archaeometallurgical, ethnological, palaeoecological, geological, historical, linguistic and technical aspects of ancient mining activities and ongoing research on these topics adding to the current state of the art in these fields. Comparisons between different mining districts and/or between different phases of mining activities described in these proceedings will hopefully encourage the detection of common patterns, foster new findings, raise new perspectives and questions and contribute to new interdisciplinary ventures. For that purpose we have included a list of contributing authors along with contact information and a brief description of the field of expertise at the end of this conference transcript.

We are very grateful to all authors who contributed to this volume, as well as to all sponsors who have supported the FZ HiMAT and made this 2nd Mining in European History Conference in Innsbruck to a unique event. Last but not least, we are looking forward to see you again in Innsbruck at the "3rd Mining in European History-Conference" in 2015.

On behalf of the editors,

Univ.-Prof. Mag. Dr. Klaus Oeggl
Speaker of the FZ HiMAT

Innsbruck, November 2013

Session I

Resource Management

Resource management in prehistoric siliceous rock mining: an archaeological perspective

Jacek Lech[1]

[1] Cardinal Stefan Wyszyński University in Warsaw, Institute of Archaeology, Poland

Introduction

The systematic exploitation of siliceous rock deposits such as flints, cherts, hornstones, obsidian, rock crystal or radiolarites was the first expression of mining in the history of humankind.

Mining of this type began in the Middle Palaeolithic and lasted until the beginning of the Iron Age. Its most spectacular forms reach back from seven to four thousand years ago and are associated with the development of permanent settlement and the farming economy. Flint mining by prehistoric communities ceased in Europe not quite three thousand years ago.

Some remarks about raw materials

Siliceous rocks were usually easy to knap, sufficiently hard to work and gave sharp edges. They served to produce various implements and weapons. In Europe, in prehistoric times, a variety of siliceous rocks was exploited. Only a small number of them were of interregional importance. The reasons for this importance varied. Sometimes they were technological and depended on the characteristics of the siliceous rock (for instance mining in the Grand Pressigny region in France or Spiennes in Belgium), sometimes they had cultural significance. It is possible to give many examples of siliceous rocks that were popular and distributed interregionally only in one, sometimes quite short period. This was true of obsidian from north-east Hungary and south-east Slovakia. At the time of the Bükk culture, it was distributed in different directions and over considerable distances in the form of small nodules, and even reached northern Poland (Lech, 2003: Fig. 5 and Fig. 6).

Though in Poland it was technologically insignificant, as there were several local good quality raw materials available and mined there. For instance, obsidian was found in a large settlement of the Linear Pottery culture in Olszanica near Cracow. According to Milisauskas (1986:83) Olszanica has probably yielded the largest sample of flint artifacts recovered from a Linear Pottery village in Central Europe. The Olszanica village was a settlement of producers of flint blanks from the Jurassic-Cracow flint and the Olszanica community was engaged in distribution of the raw material (Lech, 2003:22-27). Among the over 42,000 chipped artifacts from the site, obsidian pieces comprise approximately 0.5% (Milisauskas, 1986:145). Blades and flakes of Jurassic-Cracow flint were larger and harder than blades and flakes made of obsidian. Cores, blades and flakes made of obsidian were small and brittle. There was no technological reason for using obsidian at Olszanica, since the same needs could be met using flint.

The presence of obsidian in Olszanica was due to other causes, which can be described as cultural. Among them were aesthetic reasons, and the need for something egzotic; also cosmetic purposes or medical, for which, because of customs or beliefs, the small obsidian blades were considered best. At this time obsidian even reached Lower Silesia, about 400 km from its deposits. For instance it was found in a large settlement in Strachów near Wrocław.

Let us look at another example of cultural influences on the development of flint mining. Striped flint of the Krzemionki type is one of the most important siliceous rocks in Central Europe. The first maps of how *gebänderten Feurstein* was distributed were prepared, independently of each other, by the well known German prehistorians G. Wilke (1917:39, Tafel VI-12) and G. Kossinna (1917:143-150, Abb. 13-16; 1918). They appeared in 1919 in two volumes of the journal „Mannus", nearly one hundred years ago (Lech & Piotrowska, 2009:209-213).

Striped flint was first used on a very small scale by local communities of the Lengyel-Polgar cultural complex living in the direct vicinity of the deposits. The communities of the TRB culture from the Sandomierz Upland were the first to use this striped flint on a wider scale in the second half of the 4th millennium BC (Lech 1991:568-569). At that time, only a limited number of axe-blades was distributed to more distant regions (Lower Silesia, Great Poland, Kuyavia, Chełmno Land).

The role of this flint increased enormously in the period of the Globular Amphora communities in the 3rd millennium BC. Axe-blades of this siliceous rock spread over the whole area of the culture, in the Vistula and Oder river basins and in Pomerania (Lech 1991:568-569). The majority of shafts with developed underground exploitation of the striped flint were dug at this time. But axe-blades made of striped flint had very limited technological significance for the Globular Amphora communities. The absence of wear traces, the careful polishing and the fact that they were frequently placed in the megalithic graves indicate that they were not tools but weapons and symbols of prestige or social position of their owners. It seems that in the case of Krzemionki Opatowskie, flint mining was stimulated by these non-technological motives. The striped flint was one of several raw materials which could be used to make axes and which was available within the oecumene of the Globular Amphora communities, though it had no special technological properties. But it was this attractive material which was preferebly used and axe blades made of it were often placed in graves.

These conclusions are confirmed by the radical change in the importance of striped flint during the Early Bronze Age. Among the Mierzanowice culture communities, the role of striped flint returned to that of technology, and the distribution was more limited than in the TRB culture (Lech, 1991:568-569; 1997:632-634). At the same time, the Vistula river basin found itself within the area where Volhynian flint was imported, while the Oder basin saw an influx of Scandinavian type flint daggers (Lech & Leligdowicz, 2003:286-291).

In the thick chalk beds of north-west Europe there are many layers of flint nodules. It seems that the value of flint was decided not only by its high quality, but also because it came from deep within the earth (Whittle, 1995:252-256; Rudebeck, 1998:322-326; Longworth et al., 2012:120-

121). The recent discoveries, by Walter Leitner and his team from the University in Innsbruck, of prehistoric sites high up in the Alps, where radiolarites and rock-crystal were exploited, indicates that probably also such an origin of raw materials was an important factor in their cultural significance (Leitner et al., 2011). The reason for their long distance distribution was primarily cultural (Lech, 1997:623-635).

About materials and tools used in siliceous rock mines

Together with the development of exploitation methods, prehistoric mining of siliceous rocks developed tools and equipment to facilitate the work. The basic raw materials used in their preparation were of organic origin – animal and vegetable. Of these, only products made of antler and bone, in favourable circumstances, have survived to our time. Utensils, handles of mining tools and safeguards made of wood, other plant material and leather, with a few exceptions, decomposed completely. Sometimes we can reconstruct them on the basis of various traces on the walls of shafts, as in Grimes Graves, or impressions left in the small limestone rubble, as in Krzemionki Opatowskie (Mercer, 1981:20-22, 112; Babel, 2008:103-105).

There is indirect evidence of the wide use of organic raw material in flint mining from the discoveries made at the Bronze Age salt mine at Hallstatt (Kern et al., 2009:46-65). They come from the period when flint mines still functioned in some parts of Europe (Lech & Leligdowicz, 2003:292-297 and Abb. 1; Oliva, 2011:99-101). From among the raw materials used to produce tools for flint mining, most is known about flint and other stones. The most popular tools were hammer-stones of various sizes, and flint or stone blades of picks which have been found in many mines. They were made from raw material found in the mine in Spiennes – Belgium and Rijckholt-St. Geertruid – the Netherlands, as well as material found nearby, as in Casa Montero – Spain and brought in by the miners. Bone tools are less known but these materials were certainly important (Felder et al., 1998:43-49; Collet et. al., 2008:60-62; Capote, 2011; Terradas et al., 2011).

At the radiolarite mine at Vienna-Mauer raw material was extracted from limestone. In the collection of the Naturhistorisches Museum, there were some very worn hammer-stones, as well as levers, a pick and a hammer of red-deer antlers. They all come from the old excavations of Dr. Josef Bayer (Ruttkay, 1970).

Red-deer antler picks were basic tools in the subterranean mines of Grimes Graves. The absolute dominance of such picks for the exploitation of flint from chalk rock was the result of its lithological features. The chalk was quite hard and would split in such a way that antler picks were the most effective tools. Working in chalk to dig and exploit just one shaft needed several hundred antler picks (Mercer, 1981:23-27; Legge, 1981:100-103). Antlers from thousands of animals were utilized there, which means that a system of obtaining them must have existed. Most were shed antlers collected in the forest, some came from hunted or dead animals. The transport of so many antler picks to the mining field was a considerable logistical problem (Clutton-Brock, 1984).

Little is known about the use of wood and other plant materials at Grimes Graves, apart from the fact that they were widely utilized. The scale on which organic raw material was exploited in prehistoric mining is best evidenced by the discoveries made in the Hallstatt salt mine (Kern et al., 2009:46-65).

We have a wide variety of mining tools found at the Krzemionki Opatowskie mine. To work the hard Upper Jurassic limestone, picks with flint blades were used, as well as other hard stones, and tools from red-deer antlers. Roe-deer horns were also used, though less often. Apart from picks, deer antlers also served to make wedges and hammers for separating the flint nodules from the bedrock (Lech, 1981:40-44).

An interesting problem was the means of lighting used for underground work. At the Defensola mine, oil lamps were used. They were found in the exploitation chambers. Seven years ago, A. Galiberti (2005:141-150) published a series of photographs. Galiberti (2005:144) also presented a reconstruction of such a lamp. In many of the mines, there was sufficient daylight coming in from the shaft. The galleries and chambers of the Krzemionki Opatowskie mine were lighted by small resin chips of pine wood, similar to the well known ones from Hallstatt.

About waste dumps

The excavation of galleries and chambers shows evidence of a thought out use of the mining debris of chalk or limestone left on site. According to A. Galiberti and M. Tarantini, in the Defensola A mine, dry stone walls "… represent part of a safety management system inside the mine." There is also a basis to suppose "… that wooden reinforcements were also present." (Tarantini, 2005:93-102; Galiberti & Tarantini, 2005:200). Similar finds are known from the Krzemionki Opatowskie underground chambers. Underground waste dumps were faced with large limestone slabs and traces of wooden strengthening structures were found in the heaps.

The food of prehistoric flint miners

It has not yet been determined what flint miners had to eat. Flint mines do not allow for the reconstruction of miners' meals, as was possible in the Hallstatt mine (Kern et al., 2009:92-95). A symbol of this question of sustenance are the empty vessels sometimes found in the galleries (Muntoni, 2005).

It can be assumed that the Pleistocene hunter-gatherers, leading a nomadic life, visited the siliceous rock deposits during their wanderings. Their diet was directly dependent on the possibilities offered by the natural environment in the vicinity of the mines. In the age of the early farming economies, the mines were located at various distances from the settlements of the communities which exploited them. The question of food for the miners was a function of the distance between the mining field and the miners' settlements, the organization of labour and the resources provided by the natural environment in the vicinity of the mines.

In the galleries and chambers of the Defensola A mine, places where miners had eaten their meals were found with the remains of mainly sheep/goat and sheep (Galiberti & Tarantini, 2005:201).

However, we cannot exclude that the empty vessels discovered underground are the remains of unknown rituals and sacrifices. It seems that that is how the vessels found at Grimes Graves, at the bottom of a shaft excavated by R. Mercer (1981:23-27), could be interpreted.

The mine at Spiennes was located near settlements of the Michelsberg communities who exploited the Spiennes flint. From excavations of the mining field we have numerous remains of camps with fireplaces, vessels, domestic tools and the bones of eaten animals. We can suppose that the animals, before they were consumed were grazed in the mining field by the miners. It seems that in the case of Spiennes and the Rijckholt – St. Geertruid mine, the mining fields were located within the sphere of economic exploitation of at least a few of the settlements. The river La Trouille which flowed through the Spiennes mine provided water (Clason, 1971; 1981; Felder et al., 1998:67; Collet et. al., 2008:69-70).

At times, the water supply was a considerable problem, as in the case of the Sąspów and Krzemionki Opatowskie mines. It was determined that both in Sąspów and in Krzemionki some of the miners' camps were placed near water sources. The Sąspów mine was exploited, among others, by the Lengyel-Polgar community which inhabited the village of Iwanowice, 15 km east of the mine, in a straight line (Lech, 2011:124-126). One of the villages exploiting the Krzemionki Opatowskie flint was Ćmielów, a settlement of the TRB community, located on the edge of the loess upland, 9 km, in a straight line, from the mine (Balcer, 1995). It would seem that in the case of the Sąspów and Krzemionki Opatowskie mines, a large part of the consumed food arrived together with the groups of miners who, on the return trip transported the semi-finished flint products. In the Stone and Bronze Ages, in the case of villages engaged in flint mining, food produced for the whole community also served the needs of the groups of miners. Such settlements may also have supplemented their stocks of food by exchanging it for flint. However, such a hypothesis is difficult to confirm. Flint mining was not a full-time activity, but only a part-time specialization of labour.

References

Balcer, B. (1995): The relationship between a settlement and flint mines. A preliminary study of Eneolithic workshop assemblages from Ćmielów (Southern Poland). Archaeologia Polona 33, pp. 209-221.

Bąbel, J. (2008): The Krzemionki flint mines latest underground research 2001-2004. In: Allard, P.; Bostyn, F.; Gilligny, F.; Lech, J. (eds.): Flint mining in prehistoric Europe. Interpreting the archaeological records. BAR International Series 1891. Oxford, pp. 97-107.

Capote, M. (2011): Working in the flint mine: percussion tools and labour organization at Casa Montero (Spain). In: Capote, M.; Consuegra, S.; Díaz-del-Río, P.; Terradas, X. (eds.): Proceedings of the 2nd Conference of the UISPP Commission on Flint Mining in Pre- and Protohistoric Times (Madrid, 14-17 October 2009). BAR International Series 2260. Oxford, pp. 231-242.

Clason, A. T. (1971): The Flint-mine workers of Spiennes and Rijckholt-St. Geertruid and their animals. Helinium 11, pp. 3-33.

Clason, A. T. (1981): The flintminer as a farmer, hunter and antler collector. In: Engelen, F. H. G. (ed.):

Third International Symposium on Flint, 24-27 Mei 1979 – Maastricht. Staringia 6, pp. 119-125.

Clutton-Brock, J. (1984): Excavations at Grimes Graves, Norfolk 1972-1976. Fascicule 1. Neolithic antler picks from Grimes Graves, Norfolk, and Durrington Walls, Wiltshire: a biometrical analysis. London.

Collet, H.; Hauzeur, A.; Lech, J. (2008): The prehistoric flint mining complex at Spiennes (Belgium) on the occasion of its discovery 140 years ago. In: Allard, P.; Bostyn, F.; Gilligny, F.; Lech, J. (eds.): Flint mining in prehistoric Europe. Interpreting the archaeological records. BAR International Series 1891. Oxford, pp. 41-71.

Felder, P. J. (Sjeuf); Rademakers, P. Cor M.; Grooth, M. E. Th. de; (eds.) (1998): Excavations of Prehistoric Flint Mines at Rijckholt-St. Geertruid (Limburg, The Netherlands) by the 'Prehistoric Mines Working Group' of the Dutch Geological Society, Limburg Section. Archäologische Berichte 12. Bonn.

Galiberti, A.; Tarantini, M. (2005): Conclusions: The Defensola mine in the context of European mining archaeology and the Early Neolithic. In: Galiberti, A. (ed.) (2005): Defensola. Una miniera di selce di 7000 anni fa. Siena, pp. 197-205.

Kern, A., Kowarik, K., Rausch, A. W., Reschreiter, H. (eds.) (2009): Kingdom of salt. 7000 years of Hallstatt. Vienna.

Kossinna, G. (1917): Meine Reise nach West- und Ostpreußen und meine Berufung zu Generalfeldmarschall v. Hindenburg in August 1915. Mannus 9 (1919), pp. 119-195.

Kossinna, G. (1918): Erläuterungen zur Karte der Funde gebänderter Feuersteingeräte. Mannus 10 (1919), pp. 202-206.

Lech, J. (1981): Flint mining among the early farming communities of Central Europe. Przegląd Archeologiczny 28:1981, pp. 5-55.

Lech, J. (1991): The Neolithic-Eneolithic transition in prehistoric mining and siliceous rock distribution. In: J. Lichardus (ed.): Die Kupferzeit als historische Epoche. Saarbrücker Beiträg zur Altertumskunde 55 Bonn, pp. 557-574.

Lech, J. (1997): Remarks on prehistoric flint mining and flint supply in European archaeology. In: Ramos-Millán, A., Bustillo, M. A., (eds.): Siliceous Rocks and Culture. Granada, pp. 611-637.

Lech, J. (2003): Mining and siliceous rock supply to the Danubian early farming communities (LBK) in eastern central Europe: A second approach. In: Burnez-Lanotte, L. (ed.): Production and Managment of Lithic Materials in the European Linearbandkeramik. BAR International Series 1200. Oxford, pp. 19-30.

Lech, J. (2011): Danubian organization of flint mining in the southern part of the Polish Jura: a study from Sąspów near Cracow. In: Capote, M.; Consuegra, S.; Díaz-del-Río, P.; Terradas, X. (eds.): Proceedings of the 2nd Conference of the UISPP Commission on Flint Mining in Pre- and Protohistoric Times (Madrid, 14-17 October 2009). BAR International Series 2260. Oxford, pp. 117-128.

Lech, J.; Leligdowicz, A. (2003): Studien zum mitteleuropäischen Feuersteinbergbau in der Bronzezeit. In: Stöllner, Th.; Körlin, G.; Steffens, G.; Cierny, J. (eds.): Man and Mining – Mensch und Bergbau. Studies in honour of Gerd Weisgerber on occasion of his 65th birthday. Der Anschnitt, Beiheft 16. Bochum, pp. 285-300.

Lech, J.; Piotrowska, D. (2009): Stefan Krukowski (1890-1982) – scholar of prehistoric flint mining in Polnad. A supplement to the book by Professor Stefan Karol Kozłowski. In: Burdukiewicz, J. M.;

Cyrek, K.; Dyczek, P.; Szymczak, K. (eds.): Understanding the Past. Papers offered to Stefan K. Kozłowski. Warsaw, pp. 207-221.

Legge, A. J. (1981): The Agricultural economy. In: Mercer, pp. 79-103.

Leitner, W.; Bachnetzer, Th.; Staudt, M. (2011): Traces of earliest prehistoric flint mining activity in high alpine region of Western Austria. In: Capote, M.; Consuegra, S.; Díaz-del-Río, P.; Terradas, X. (eds.): Proceedings of the 2nd Conference of the UISPP Commission on Flint Mining in Pre- and Protohistoric Times (Madrid, 14-17 October 2009). BAR International Series 2260. Oxford, pp. 91-96.

Longworth, I.; Varndell, G.; Lech, J. (2012): Excavations at Grimes Graves, Norfolk 1972-1976. Fascicule 6. Exploration and excavation beyond the deep mines. London.

Mercer, R. J. (1981): Grimes Graves, Norfolk. Excavations 1971-72: Volume I. Department of the Environment. Archaeological Reports 11. London.

Milisauskas, S. (1986): Early Neolithic Settlement and Society at Olszanica. Memoirs of the Museum of Anthropology, University of Michigan 19. Ann Arbor.

Muntoni, I. M. (2005): La ceramic. Tipologia, attribuzione culturale e funzioni. In: Galiberti, A. (ed.) (2005): Defensola. Una miniera di selce di 7000 anni fa. Siena, p. 111-126.

Oliva, M. (2011): Chert mining in the Krumlov Forest (Southern Moravia). In: Capote, M.; Consuegra, S.; Díaz-del-Río, P.; Terradas, X. (eds.): Proceedings of the 2nd Conference of the UISPP Commission on Flint Mining in Pre- and Protohistoric Times (Madrid, 14-17 October 2009). BAR International Series 2260. Oxford, pp. 97-107.

Rudebeck, E. (1998): Flint extraction, axe offering and the value of cortex. In: Edmonds, M.; Richards, C. (eds.): Understanding the Neolithic of North-western Europe. Glasgow, pp. 312-327.

Ruttkay, E. (1970): Das neolithische Horsteinbergwerk von Mauer (Wien 23). Mitteilungen der Anthropologischen Gesellschaft in Wien 100, pp. 70-115.

Tarantini, M. (2005): I muretti a secco. Tecniche costruttive e tipologie morfologico-funzionali. In: Galiberti, A. (ed.) (2005): Defensola. Una miniera di selce di 7000 anni fa. Siena, pp. 93-102.

Terradas, X.; Clemente, I.; Gibaja, J. F. (2011): Mining tools use in a mining context or how can the expected become unexpected. In: Capote, M.; Consuegra, S.; Díaz-del-Río, P.; Terradas, X. (eds.): Proceedings of the 2nd Conference of the UISPP Commission on Flint Mining in Pre- and Protohistoric Times (Madrid, 14-17 October 2009). BAR International Series 2260. Oxford, pp. 243-252.

Whittle, A. (1995): Gifts from the earth: symbolic dimensions of the use and production of Neolithic flint and stone axes. Archaeologia Polona 33, pp. 247-259.

Wilke, G. (1917): Die Herkunft der Kelten, Germanen und Illyrer. Mannus 9 (1919), pp. 1-54.

From the imprint to the tool: the identification of prehistoric mining implements through the study of digging traces. The case of Grotta della Monaca in Calabria (Italy)

Felice Larocca[1,2] & Chiara Levato[1,2]

[1] Università di Bari "Aldo Moro", Missione di Ricerca speleo-archeologica, Sant'Agata di Esaro (CS), Italy.
[2] Centro Regionale di Speleologia "Enzo dei Medici", Commissione di Ricerca per l'Archeologia delle Miniere, Roseto Capo Spulico (CS), Italy.

Introduction

Sometimes prehistoric extractive contexts can turn out to be rather lacking of digging tools employed by ancient miners. In fact, these implements were left where they were used only occasionally. This happened especially when they broke, becoming useless, or when they were stored away in view of a further return to the mine. Therefore archaeologists working in prehistoric extractive sites have to use also indirect evidence to reconstruct the typology of employed tools. Digging traces are thus one of the most important markers; they are able to give often very detailed information about tools set used during mining activities. The case presented in this contribution concerns Grotta della Monaca in Calabria (Italy), a cave rich in iron and copper minerals and intensely frequented since Prehistory for the exploitation of these sources. Within this mine-cave (see Larocca, 2010; Larocca, 2012 for an overall overview), the occurrence of very soft mineralizations has allowed the perfect preservation of several hundreds of prehistoric digging traces. They show very different shapes that have often allowed to make out the tools used in the site between an advanced phase of Neolithic and the beginning of Copper Age (end of the 5th - beginning of the 4th millennium AC).

The underground site and archaeological researches

Grotta della Monaca, located on the Tyrrhenian slope of northern Calabria, is a karst cave that develops within highly fractured calcareous-dolomitic rocks for about 500m in length. The cavity contains abundant iron hydroxides deposits (goethite and lepidocrocite), occurring in each underground space disguised as veins between rocky bedding. In addition copper minerals, particularly carbonates (malachite and azurite), outcrop in the deepest cave sectors, even though by far to a lesser extent. Iron hydroxides and copper carbonates were mined in different prehistoric times. Archaeological researches carried out from 1997 to 2012 have allowed the identification of three different mining phases: the first and most ancient one dates back at the end of Upper Palaeolithic; the second to a final phase of Neolithic; the third and most recent one to the beginning of Copper Age. These extractive phases, recognized and isolated in different cave sectors, have affected firstly iron minerals (Palaeolithic and Neolithic phases), then copper minerals (Eneo-

Fig. 1: Prehistoric digging traces on soft iron hydroxides left by tools made from different matters as antler, bone and horn (photo by F. Larocca).

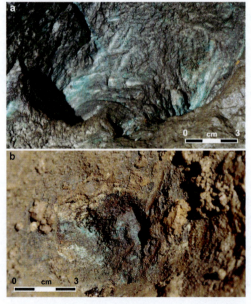

Fig. 2: Prehistoric digging traces on copper carbonates from the deepest cave sectors (photo by F. Larocca).

lithic phase). Palaeolithic mining evidence have been identified only near the cavity entrance (in the so called "Pregrotta"); while Neo-Eneolithic ones are located in the deepest sectors of the cave system ("Sala dei pipistrelli" and "Cunicoli terminali").

Evidence from Pregrotta

Throughout Pregrotta digging traces left by later post-Medieval Period iron hydroxides exploitations (16th-18th century AD) have been long known. Hundreds of these imprints, ascribable to metallic picks, have been identified and recorded. Intense post-Medieval mining activities have disrupted and often deleted the most ancient extractive evidence. For example, Palaeolithic finds, radiocarbon dated to about 20.000 years ago (LTL3580A - 16761 ± 100 BP; 18250-17800 cal AC, 84.6% / 17750-17600 cal AC, 10.8%), only accidentally have reached us: they are attested by a restricted number of flint tools, preserved within a delimited iron deposit saved from next tampering.

During archaeological excavation carried out in Pregrotta loose iron mineral blocks, with stokes traces deeply impressed on their surface, have been often found. These imprints features, with a very irregular shape, have soon excluded the use of metallic picks; in fact they represent a small surviving evidence of most ancient mining activities, certainly dating back to Prehistory. Even though this evidence comes from very disturbed contexts it is comparable with other similar ones found in the innermost cave sector, in which imprints appear both on veins embedded in rock and on loose blocks.

Sala dei pipistrelli and Buca delle impronte

The most significant prehistoric iron hydroxides mining evidence is found particularly in Sala dei pipistrelli. This evidence offers useful data about tools used in extractive activities. Sala dei pipistrelli is a huge completely dark underground place, located in the middle of cave system. Within it several short minor branches open usually near the side walls. One of them is called "Buca delle impronte", literally "Imprints hole": it is the best preserved prehistoric mining context of the whole Grotta della Monaca.

Buca delle impronte is accessible through about a 3m deep shaft, a slight downwards bottleneck opens at its bottom allowing the entrance into an adjoining low and narrow space. Already on the access shaft walls clear digging traces can be observed (*Fig. 1, a*). They appear as stripes mostly with the same orientation and with a slightly curved shape; in their inside, that shows a concave section, are visible scratches parallel in length. These imprints are very similar to those on loose goethite blocks found in Pregrotta as above mentioned. Studies carried out on these imprints show that they were produced by using deer antler picks. This result could be reached thanks to the analysis of the overall imprints shape and above all to the observation of bundles of parallel scratches running lengthwise within stripes. These bundles, displaying a succession of crests and gorges, refer unquestionably to deer antlers outer shape. Other kinds of imprints are visible along the bottleneck walls and particularly in the next narrow and low chamber. Here a thick light yellow goethite vein emerges from calcareous layers. This vein surface is completely covered for all its extension by several digging traces different in shape and size. The high hydration of the hydroxide has allowed their preservation: being soft this mineral has preserved imprints in negative!

Most of digging traces are ascribed to pointed implements; however other imprints imply the use of tools with sharp and flat point. The lacking of lengthwise parallel stripes within pointed imprints refers to small picks made of material different from deer antlers (*Fig. 1, b*). It can be strongly supposed the use of bone but the recourse to horn or wood for suitably shaped and maybe hafted implements is not to be excluded.

In Buca delle impronte there are also digging traces related to tools used as hoes: iron vein surfaces have been affected by several "hoeings", sometimes with a sideways displacement (*Fig. 1, c*). We do not know the exact nature of this tool but it certainly should have had an arched edge, according to the concave imprints left in negative. In other cases mining tools seem to have been used as a kind of chisels, struck deeper and deeper into the mineral by a series of gradual blows received by a percussion tool, according to the "scalariform" arrangement of the imprints.

Some digging traces certainly refer to the use of small bone shovels made from big mammal scapulas. Maybe these shovels were employed especially in presence of very soft mineral and consequently easily extractable through pressure on vein surface. Also in the case of "shovelfuls" it is possible to recognize a scalariform arrangement of digging traces.

Archaeological excavation carried out in Buca delle impronte, within the chamber next to bottleneck, has investigated up to a maximum depth of 90cm a deposit generated by ancient mining activities. Unfortunately, the tools related to imprints have not been found. Probably they were employed elsewhere or maybe they might lie in sectors still not investigated. However the deposit investigation has revealed several goethite blocks with digging traces on their surfaces. These blocks were associated with abundant charcoals, combustion remains of torches used by miners for underground lighting. Archaeobotanical analysis has identified them with Pinus, sylvestris group: therefore mining activities were carried out using light from torches made of small resinous wooden branches. Radiocarbon dating from some of these charcoals set extractive activities in the first half of 4th millennium cal AC (LTL3582A - 4935 ± 45 BP; 3800-3640 AC, 95.4%).

Evidence from Cunicoli terminali

Other evidence comes from "Cunicoli terminali", the most distant places from surface and developing at the end of Sala dei pipistrelli. They are three and the longest passage is over 60m long. Within them it is hardly possible to stand upright and it is necessary to move forward on all fours or crawling. Here mining activities reconstructions are more difficult than those of Buca delle impronte, as in this hypogean sector iron minerals exploitations overlap and get often confused with copper minerals ones. Turning attention first and foremost to iron minerals, ancient diggings evidence has been found here both in situ (that is on veins surfaces) and on loose blocks.

One of the three passages contains on the roof a rich hydroxide vein, tightly embedded in calcareous layers. Its surface is scattered with digging traces: some of them show a plano-convex cross section, other an ovoid one. Plano-convex cross section imprints could be ascribed to bone implement, for example a chisel maybe used with other percussion tools. One of them instead derives from a frontal blow inflicted on vein and seems to be left by a goat horn (*Fig. 1, d*). A fragmented goat horn has been actually found in an adjoining passage, even if it has been not near this imprint. The tool has been radiocarbon dated to the half of 4th millennium cal AC (LT-L3579A - 4684 ± 50 BP; 3540-3360 cal AC, 78.3% / 3640-3560 cal AC, 17.1%), therefore in a phase subsequent to mining activities carried out in Buca delle impronte. This implement is nowadays one of the few mining tools found within the cave.

Digging evidence on loose mineral blocks also comes from Cunicoli terminali. A remarkable sample is represented by an imprint deeply impressed on an iron hydroxide compact mass. The sample has preserved a clear trace – 10cm in length – of a powerful deer antler pick stroke.

During the 4th millennium AC copper minerals exploitation, above all malachite, overlaps with iron mining activities. Malachite appears in Cunicoli terminali as thin greenish layers as on calcareous walls as on small stones scattered on the ground and above all enclosed within sedimentary deposits. In some particular cases, quite infrequently, malachite is deposited as small clots within slight rock fractures. Malachite scraping actions on underground passages walls are attested in the whole Cunicoli terminali. Rock portions green in colour, particularly along some passages walls and roofs, show more clear linear marks ascribable to scraping actions (*Fig. 2, a*). This kind of trace is not easy to recognize and it can be often confused with natural grooves. According to calcareous-dolomitic rock hardness, it can be supposed that cupriferous mineral scraping has been carried out using flint or obsidian tools. This evidence is more easily recognizable when malachite lies on soft iron hydroxide substratum: in this case digging traces are perfectly identifiable and explicable. Within the longest passage of Cunicoli terminali digging traces clearly connected with malachite exploitation have been found in some niches in the rock. Malachite, settled on a soft goethite deposit, appears crossed by linear stripes with half-round section (*Fig. 2, b*).

It seems that a bone awl was used for copper carbonate extraction, as attested by two thin oblique stripes survived with the passing of millennia. The will to retrieve even the smallest copper mineral quantity is clear.

Probably copper minerals exploitation from the cave walls has been an occasional event, also because it was of little advantage compared with the resource amount acquired. Within short time cupriferous minerals were sought on the ground, smashing thick concretionary surfaces with grooved hammerstones: under these calcite layers copper carbonates were substantially more conspicuous than on the cave walls! Cupriferous mineral digging traces turn into massive strippings, often difficult to recognize and archaeologically interpret (Larocca, 2011).

Reference

Larocca, F. (2010): Grotta della Monaca: A Prehistoric Copper and Iron Mine in the Calabria Region (Italy). In: Anreiter, P. et al. (eds.): Mining in European History and its Impact on Environment and Human Societies. Proceedings for the 1st Mining in European History-Conference of the SFB-HIMAT. Innsbruck, pp. 267-270.

Larocca, F. (2011): Grotta della Monaca (Sant'Agata di Esaro - Cosenza). Utensili e tecniche estrattive di età eneolitica per l'acquisizione di minerali di rame. In: VV. AA.: L'età del rame in Italia, Atti della XLIII Riunione Scientifica dell'Istituto Italiano di Preistoria e Protostoria. Firenze, pp. 663-668.

Larocca, F. (2012): Grotta della Monaca (Calabria, Italia meridionale). Una miniera neolitica per l'estrazione dell'ocra. In: Borrell, M. et al. (eds): Xarxes al Neolitic, Actes Congrés Internacional. Gavà, pp. 249-256.

Copper mineralizations in western North Tyrol – In prehistoric times exploited resources?

Caroline O. Grutsch[1], Klaus-Peter Martinek[2] & Matthias Krismer[3]

[1] Institute of Archaeology, University of Innsbruck
[2] Munich
[3] Institute of Mineralogy and Petrography, University of Innsbruck

Introduction

The institutional mining archaeological research in Tyrol of the last years has focused on the „big players" Schwaz-Brixlegg and the Kitzbühel area which without doubt had been of supra-regional importance already in the Bronze Age. But besides these well-known major copper deposits there are many small copper ore occurrences in North Tyrol. These could have supplied at least local demands in prehistoric times as already proved elsewhere, e.g. in Styria (Presslinger & Eibner, 2004).

In western part of North Tyrol, west of the mining district of Schwaz-Brixlegg, more than 70 base metal mineralizations have been documented (for a detailed bibliography see Grutsch & Martinek, 2012). These had been neglected by mining archaeological research so far. In order to gather more information on the potential prehistoric use of copper resources in this particular area the present project was initialized (partially financed by the TWF, Tiroler Wissenschaftsfonds).

The project pursued three main goals: 1) locating any evidence of prehistoric mining in the target region, 2) the mineralogical and geochemical characterization of the copper ores in order to enable the comparison with prehistoric metal products and 3) providing a basis for subsequent archaeological excavations.

Mining archaeological evidence

By well-defined criteria (see Grutsch & Martinek, 2012) 27 out of over 70 ore occurrences have been selected and more than 30 archaeological surveys were carried out during summer 2010. At 21 sites relevant copper mineralizations were found and sampled (*Fig. 1, Tab. 1*).

It has to be noted that in an alpine environment the mining generally proceeded from top to down. The first mining activities (e.g. prehistoric) started upslope at the ore outcrop and subsequent mining (e.g. medieval or modern) took place below, thus preserving remnants of earlier mining activities. This can be observed even in in modern times heavily exhausted mining areas like Schwaz-Brixlegg, Kelchalpe or Mitterberg (Salzburg). Moreover no zoning of the ore body (oxidation zone – cementation zone – primary sulphidic ore), as it is common elsewhere, has been observed in the inner alpine ore deposits, due to extensive erosive glaciation. Usually the

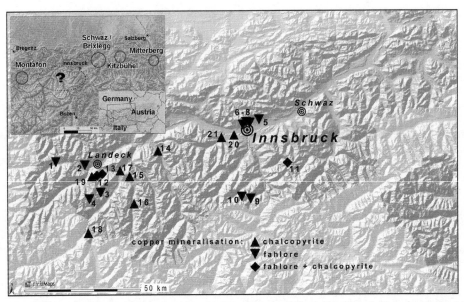

Fig. 1: Mining archaeological research gap in the western part of North Tyrol (top left) and mapping of the surveyed and sampled copper mineralizations during the present study. For the corresponding site names see Tab. 1.

Tab 1: Mineralogical and geochemical characterization of the sampled copper ores from the studied area (Fig. 1).

	site	ore minerals	geochemistry
1	Gand	**tetrahedrite**	Cu, Sb>As, Ag, Hg
2	Flirscher Skihütte	**tennantite**, *pyrite, gersdorffite, siegenite*	Cu, As>Sb, Fe, Zn, Ni, Co, Bi
3	Serfaus Rotenstein	**tetrahedrite**, *gersdorffite, pyrite, siegenite, cobaltite, galenite*	Cu, Sb, As, Fe, Ni, Co, Ag, Pb, Bi, Hg
4	Serfaus Masneralpe	**tetrahedrite**, *chalcopyrite*	Cu, Sb, As, Fe, Zn, Ag, Co, Bi, Hg
5	Rum Enzianhütte	**tennantite**, *galenite, jordanite*	Cu, Pb, As>Sb, Fe, Zn, Ag, Bi, Hg
6	Hötting St. Helena	**tennantite**, *galenite, seligmannite, enargite*	Cu, Pb, As>Sb, Fe, Zn, Ag, Bi
7	Höttinger Graben	**tennantite**, *galenite, jordanite, pyrite*	Cu, Pb, As>Sb, Fe, Zn, Ag, Bi
8	Höttinger Bild	**tennantite**, *galenite, jordanite, pyrite*	Cu, Pb, As>Sb, Fe, Zn, Ag, Bi
9	Obernberg Wildgrube	**tetrahedrite**, *bournonite, galenite, sphalerite*	Cu, Pb, Zn, Sb>As, Ag, Bi, Hg
10	Gschnitztal Gargglerin	**tetrahedrite**, *pyrite, chalcopyrite*	Cu, Sb>As, Fe, Zn, Ag, Bi
11	Navis Knappenkuchl	**tetrahedrite-tennantite**, *pyrite,* **chalcopyrite**, *galenite, gold*	Cu, Sb, As, Fe, Zn, Pb, Bi, Hg, Co, Ni, Sn, Au
12	Tobadill Zirmegg	**tetrahedrite, chalcopyrite,** *arsenopyrite*	Cu, Sb, As, Fe, Zn, Bi, Co, Ni
13	Landeck Knappenhäusl	**tetrahedrite, chalcopyrite,** *arsenopyrite*	Cu, Sb, As, Fe, Zn, Ag, Bi
14	Sautens Haderlehn	**chalcopyrite**, *pyrite, pyrrhotite, gersdorffite*	Cu, Fe, As, Ni, Co
15	Oberfalpetan	**chalcopyrite**, *pyrite*	Cu, Fe
16	Vergötschen Tschingl	**chalcopyrite**, *pyrite, arsenopyrite, gersdorffite*	Cu, Fe, As, Ni, Co
17	near Puschlin	**chalcopyrite**, *pyrite*	Cu, Fe
18	Nauders Mutzkopf	**chalcopyrite**, *pyrite, tetrahedrite, Pb-Bi-sulfosalt, arsenopyrite, gersdorffite, galenite*	Cu, Fe, Pb, Bi, As, Sb, Ag, Ni , Co
19	Tobadill Flathalpe	**chalcopyrite**, *pyrite, cobaltite*	Cu, Fe, As, Co , Ni
20	Axams Knappenhof	**chalcopyrite**, *pyrite, pyrrhotite, galenite, arsenopyrite*	Cu, Fe, Ag, Bi, As
21	Sellrain Schwabenhof	**chalcopyrite**, *pyrite, pyrrhotite*	Cu, Fe

primary sulphidic ore is visible in the outcrops of the deposits showing only minor alteration.

The surveys in the course of these investigations yielded evidence for three potentially prehistoric and one potentially premedieval mining site. The remaining sites are at least post-medieval or modern due to the observed mining technologies and/or written records (*Tab. 2*).

The three potentially prehistoric sites are Navis Knappenkuchl, Serfaus Rotenstein/Masneralpe and Innsbruck Hötting.

The site Knappenkuchl is located in the upper section of the Navis Valley, 2100m above sea level. The limestone crag mineralized with fahlore and chalcopyrite is about 100m long and 50m high and was intensively exploited by fire setting. While mining in modern times has been mentioned by Srbik (1929:99), prehistoric exploitation is indicated by the finds of an eclogite hammer stone on the mine heap and a grooved hammer stone which is displayed in the Bergbaumuseum Brixlegg. A Bronze Age B dagger (Kaltenhauser 1976:205) and a Middle Bronze Age spearhead (in a private collection) from the Navis Valley also show that this area was visited during prehistoric times. The site Navis Knappenkuchl could therefore be an example for one of the small copper deposits, which supposedly had been active from the 9th century BC after the decline of the major deposits (Sperber, 2004:335) like Schwaz-Brixlegg, which is only 25km away.

The potentially prehistoric mining site in Hötting is situated 1.5km north of Innsbruck at about 900m a.s.l. Besides numerous galleries worked with iron tools there is at least one copper ore outcrop which had been exploited by fire-setting. This site is surrounded by a Bronze Age settlement with an urnfield burial ground in the southeast, another Bronze Age settlement in the southwest and Bronze Age ceramic finds at an altitude of 1400m (*Fig. 2*).

The mining sites Rotenstein and Masneralpe above Serfaus at an altitude of about 2000m a.s.l. provide more definite evidence for prehistoric mining activities since several prehistoric mining tools are known (displayed in the Bergbaumuseum Brixlegg). The corresponding workings are very likely to be found at the outcrops of the ore bodies, which are still recognizable.

Even if the evidence (fire-setting, stone tools) indicates possible prehistoric mining activities, exact dating of the mining activities at the three sites is necessary and thus it is highly recommended to obtain datable material in future excavation campaigns.

Mineralogical results

More than 50 polished sections of selected ore samples were studied by ore microscopy and electron microprobe analysis. In addition trace element analysis and determination of lead isotope ratios have been carried out on selected samples. A preliminary qualitative overview of the obtained data is provided in Table 1. The elements mentioned in the column "geochemistry" originate from combined data of neutron activation analysis (NAA), inductively coupled plasma mass spectrometry (ICP-MS) and electron microprobe analysis. The approved sampling and analytical methodology provides representative data of the ore mineralization of a particular site as such and for the raw material potentially exploited in prehistoric times. As it can be expected for early

Tab. 2: *Archaeological evidence at the surveyed sites.*

dating	sites	archaeological evidence
potentially prehistoric	Navis-Knappenkuchl, Serfaus Rotenstein/Masneralpe, Innsbruck-Hötting,	fire setting, opencast, prehistoric hammer stones, undated anvil stones, fall shafts, mine heaps
potentially premedieval	Obernberg-Wildgrube	fire setting, opencast, V-cuts, fall shafts, mine heaps
at least medieval or post medieval	Axams Knappenhof, Flirscher Skihütte, Gand, Innsbruck-Hötting, Landeck Knappenhäusl, Nauders Mutzkopf, Navis Knappenkuchl, Oberfalpetan, Obernberg Wildgrube, near Puschlin, Rum Enzianhütte, Sautens Haderlehn, Sellrain Schwabenhof, Tobadill Flathalpe, Tobadill Zirmegg, Vergötschn Tschingl	galleries worked with iron tools, fall shafts, mine heaps, wooden installations, drill holes, ceramic, tissue and leather remnants, architectural remnants, bones

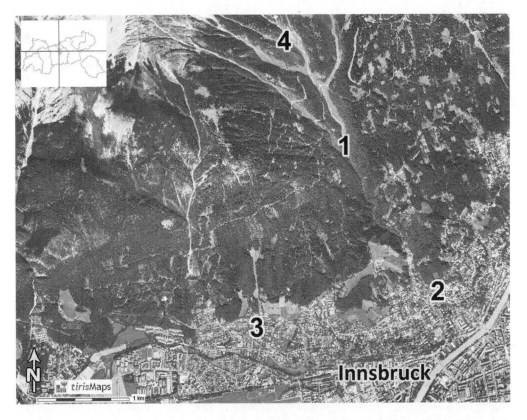

Fig. 2: *1) Fire-setting site in the Höttinger Graben; 2) Bronze Age settlement Hötting with burial ground; 3) Bronze Age settlement Hötting-Allerheiligenhöfe; 4) Bronze Age ceramic finds in the Höttinger Graben.*

smelting technologies neither the fuel (wood or charcoal) nor the crucible or furnace material (clay) contributed significantly to the chemical composition of the produced copper metal. Therefore potentially prehistoric copper metal compositions can be deduced from the ore analysis data.

In the studied area four different types of copper mineralizations can be distinguished:

- In the Verrucano sediments of Permian age fahlores are the predominant copper phases. Smelting these ores would result in a „fahlore-type"-copper (As, Sb) additionally characterized by varying amounts of Ag and Bi and occasionally Ni/Co (*Tab. 1:1-4*).

- The mineralizations in the dolomites of the Brenner Mesozoic (Obernberg, Gschnitztal) and the North Tyrolean Calcareous Alps (Hötting, Enzianhütte) are characterized by fahlores asso-ciated with lead ores (Galenite, Bournonite/Seligmannite). Smelting these ores would also result in a "fahlore-type"-copper (As, Sb, Ag, Bi) additionally characterized by a certain amount of Pb (*Tab. 1:5-10*).

- Fahlore mineralizations in association with chalcopyrite were found in the Tux Alps (Navis Knappenkuchl) and the Silvretta Crystalline Complex (Zirmegg, Knappenhäusl). Smelting these ores would result in a somewhat diluted "fahlore-type"-copper (As, Sb, Bi), sometimes called "mixed copper", further characterized by less Ag and occasionally Ni (*Tab. 1:11-13*).

- In the Ötztal Crystalline Complex chalcopyrite-pyrite-mineralization is predominant (Ober falpetan, Tschingl, Mutzkopf). Smelting these ores would result in a relatively pure copper occasionally comprising impurities of As and Ni similar to "Kelchalm-" or "Mitterberg-copper" (*Tab. 1:14-21*).

Conclusions/Outlook

The present study yielded so far evidence for probably three prehistoric copper mining sites in the western part of North Tyrol. The extracted copper ores were mainly fahlores – the raw material for a characteristic copper metal composition common in the Early as well as in the Late Bronze Age. The Hötting site is of particular archaeometallurgical interest, since the copper ores are associated with lead ores. This could answer the question how lead-rich copper, another typical metal of the Late Bronze Age, was obtained. Due to the relatively small size of the identified copper ore deposits a rather local utilization of these resources must be assumed.

Excavations of the mining sites, the comparison of the now available analysed ores with prehistoric metal products and further surveys for so far unidentified smelting sites should be the next steps of this project.

Acknowledgements

Special thanks to the TWF for funding, to Peter Tropper, University of Innsbruck and Joachim Lutz, Curt-Engelhorn-Zentrum Mannheim for chemical analysis and to Gert

Goldenberg and the other colleagues from the Institute of Archaeologies and Gerald Hiebel, University of Innsbruck; Franz Brunner, Helga Marchhart, Franz Neururer, Andreas Penz and Colonel Zagajsek/TÜPl Lizum.

References

Grutsch, C.; Martinek, K.-P. (2012): Die Nordtiroler Kupfererzvorkommen westlich von Schwaz als Rohstoffpotential der Bronzezeit. In: Oeggl, K.; Schaffer, V. (Hg.): Die Geschichte des Bergbaus in Tirol und seinen angrenzenden Gebieten. Proceedings zum 6. Milestone-Meeting des SFB HiMAT vom 3.-5.11.2011 in Klausen/Südtirol. Innsbruck, pp. 101-106.

Kaltenhauser, G. (1976): Navis, Gem. Navis, BH Innsbruck-Land. Fundberichte aus Österreich 15, 1976 (1977), p. 205.

Presslinger, H.; Eibner, C. (2004): Montanarchäologie im Paltental (Steiermark). Bergbau, Verhüttung, Verarbeitung und Siedlungstätigkeit in der Bronzezeit. In: Weisgerber, G.; Goldenberg, G. (Hg.): Alpenkupfer – Rame delle Alpi, Der Anschnitt Beiheft 17, Veröffentlichungen aus dem Deutschen Bergbau-Museum Bochum Nr. 122. Bochum, pp. 63-75.

Sperber, L. (2004): Zur Bedeutung des nördlichen Alpenraumes für die spätbronzezeitliche Kupferversorgung in Mitteleuropa mit besonderer Berücksichtigung Nordtirols. In: Weisgerber, G.; Goldenberg, G. (Hg.): Alpenkupfer – Rame delle Alpi, Der Anschnitt Beiheft 17, Veröffentlichungen aus dem Deutschen Bergbau-Museum Bochum Nr. 122. Bochum, pp. 303-345.

Srbik, R. (1929): Bergbau in Tirol und Vorarlberg in Vergangenheit und Gegenwart. Sonderabdruck aus den Berichten des Naturwissenschaftlich-medizinischen Vereines Innsbruck, Band 41. Innsbruck.

Resources and nutrition in the Urnfield period mining site of Prigglitz-Gasteil in Lower Austria – Preliminary report on the excavations from 2010 to 2012

Peter Trebsche[1]

[1] Museum of the State of Lower Austria, Asparn an der Zaya, Austria

The Urnfield period copper mining site "Gasteil Cu I" was discovered near the farmstead Gasteil 7 in 1955. It is located in the cadastral area of Prigglitz (district of Neunkirchen) in southeastern Lower Austria. Geographically the site belongs to the Schneeberg mountain region at the easternmost fringe of the Alps. Shortly after discovery, the archaeologist Franz Hampl (Niederösterreichisches Landesmuseum – Museum of the State of Lower Austria) and the geologist Robert Mayrhofer conducted two excavation campaigns in 1956 and 1958. Fieldwork was abandoned after Mayrhofer's death in 1959. Hampl and Mayrhofer published a detailed report on the results of their excavations (Hampl & Mayrhofer, 1963). They found evidence for all stages of copper production, from ore mining to beneficiation and smelting. Hampl and Mayrhofer characterized the place "not so much a settlement but rather a huge work site".

From today's point of view, the interdisciplinary research undertaken was quite forward-looking and progressive for the 1950s. The cooperation between the archaeologist and the geologist formed the core of the project. Additionally, they initiated geoelectrical prospection of the ore deposit, archaeobotanical and archaeozoological analyses as well as spectral analyses of bronze objects.

In the following decades, research at Prigglitz-Gasteil stagnated, until small-scale rescue excavations were prompted by several construction and roadwork projects from 1999 to 2001 (Kühtreiber & Trebsche, 1999; 2001; Lang, 2000). Combining this documentation with the older excavations, it is now possible to outline the settlement area as follows: The maximum extent from North to South is c. 305m, the East-West extent is c. 100-135m (Fig. 1). The mining settlement thus had a total area of at least 3.3 hectares. Thanks to new finds, the chronology of the site can also be defined more precisely. While Hampl dated the settlement only to phase Ha A of the Urnfield Culture and concluded that the settlement had been abandoned at the beginning of phase Ha B (Hampl & Mayrhofer, 1963:71), a bronze vase-headed pin with a small head from the site of Gasteil and a socketed axe with curved decoration from the nearby Klausgraben site show that the settlement continued until the late Urnfield period (phase Ha B2-3) at least (Trebsche & Pucher, in press, Fig. 7).

In 2010, the Lower Austrian Museum of Prehistory resumed systematic archaeological fieldwork at the Prigglitz-Gasteil site. The principal aims of this research project are to document the actual state of preservation of the site and to gain evidence on the organisation of copper ore mining in the Late Bronze Age. The project focuses especially on building structures and technical features

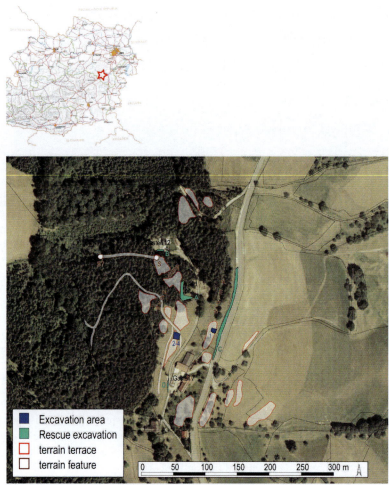

Fig. 1: Topography of the Prigglitz-Gasteil site. 1-4 Excavation areas 2010-2012; A-D Rescue excavations 1999-2001; S shafts (Maps: BEV; NÖGIS).

Fig. 2: Prigglitz-Gasteil: antler tools from excavation area 4 (Photo: Norbert Weigl, Urgeschichtemuseum Niederösterreich).

as part of the mining site. Not only metallurgical aspects, but also the everyday life of Bronze Age miners is being investigated. Where did they live? What was their nutrition like? How were they supplied?

Before the excavations, geomagnetic prospections were conducted in the accessible meadows by Volker Lindinger and Joris Coolen (Austrian Archaeological Institute). Surveying an area of ca. 2 hectares, they discovered numerous magnetic anomalies which indicate furnaces and sunken features, mainly on the settlement terraces.

Together with geologist Günther Weixelberger (Pitten), we mapped micromorphological terrain features such as terraces, dumps, shafts, trackways and sunken roads. From the geological point of view, the site is located at the border between the Greywacke zone and the Limestone Alps. The copper ore occurs in a quartz vein which runs directly west of the mining settlement on the eastern slopes of Gahns mountain. Nowadays, the copper vein is not visible from the surface, and no traces of prehistoric mining activities can be observed. Probably, they are covered by hill scree.

During the first excavation campaign in 2010, a terrace was investigated which was cut into a steep slope (excavation area 1; 8 x 6m). The stratigraphy comprised at least three Urnfield period levels which were clearly separated from each other by dump layers of left-over rock. One level consisted of the remains of a hearth and a roasting furnace. The trampled surface also showed traces of burnt wooden buildings (corner timbering or sill-beam structures). Very few finds were made on the terrace floor. Nevertheless, metallurgical activities can be proven by pieces of fine slag, bronze micro residues and the fragment of a ceramic tuyère.

Excavation area 2 was located on a different terrace about 50m to the west. Here refuse layers were investigated in which the density of finds (ceramics, slag, bone tools, bronze artefacts) was remarkably higher. An assemblage of more than 3000 animal bones is of outstanding interest. According to the archaeozoological analysis by Erich Pucher (Archaeological-Zoological Collection, Museum of Natural History Vienna), the remains of domestic pig account for 63.5% of all identified specimens (Trebsche & Pucher, in press). Such a prevalence of pig is characteristic for Eastern Alpine mining settlements in the Bronze Age. The state of preservation of the faunal remains indicates that the assemblage consists of primary butchering refuse. The range of skeletal parts present is exactly complementary to the pig bone assemblage from Salzberg at Hallstatt which consists of those body parts bearing most of the meat. Therefore the Hallstatt assemblage was interpreted as production refuse of salted pork ham (Pucher, 2010). Evidently, people at Prigglitz employed the same butchering and processing techniques as at Hallstatt. Primary butchering refuse of this specialized technique was found at Prigglitz, while the remains of a further meat processing stage were discovered at Hallstatt.

In the second excavation campaign in summer 2011, area 3 (10 x 5m), located next to area 2, was investigated. Similar to excavation area 1, there were at least four Urnfield period levels, separated by sterile dump layers of different thickness. Some of these layers consisted of coarse non-payable rock; others consisted of fine-grained remains of copper ore beneficiation. Between the deposition of these layers, the terrain was levelled in order to gain space for the construction of timber buildings.

The most important feature in area 3 was a circular working pit with a length of 3.70m, a width of 3.35m and a depth of 1.23m. The multi-layered filling of the pit showed two phases of use. In the first phase, a vertical channel on the western wall of the pit was burnt red by the impact of intense heat. After this, during the second phase, timber boarding was constructed inside the pit. The whole construction burnt down and thus was excellently preserved in the form of charcoal. Several big pieces of charcoal were recovered en bloc for dendrochronological investigation (Michael Grabner, Institut für Holzforschung, University of Natural Resources and Life Sciences, Tulln). The burnt clay structures were sampled for archaeomagnetic dating by Elisabeth Schnepp (Paläomagnetisches Labor Gams, University of Leoben).

During the third excavation campaign in 2012, area 4 (10 x 5.5m) was pegged out so that areas 2-4 form a contiguous surface of about 100m^2. Several post-holes were discovered in the level below the previously mentioned working pit. They had been dug into a thick dark cultural layer. Due to the limited extent of the excavation, no house plans have been recognized until now. However, there is unquestionable evidence of timber buildings on the western terrace. In this season, excavation concentrated on the fourth level, consisting of cultural layers which extended horizontally across the terrace and formed a waste heap on its eastern slope.

A large number of objects were found, particularly in the second and the fourth Urnfield period levels, mainly consisting of animal bones, followed by ceramic sherds, fine slag, some bronze objects and bone and antler tools. The finds from level 4 obviously represent primary refuse which was discarded from the habitation and working platform on the terrace. Voluminous samples were taken from all cultural layers in order to gain charred plant remains, charcoals and micro residues by flotation and wet sieving. Archaeobotanical analyses are coordinated by Marianne Kohler-Schneider and Andreas Heiss (Institute of Botany, University of Natural Resources and Life Sciences, Vienna).

Among the more important bronze finds, are a complete globe-headed pin and several small bronze rings, which once belonged to costume or to chains as grave finds from other regions show. Two socketed arrow heads can be interpreted as weapons, because the analysis of animal bones shows that the miners did not hunt any game at Prigglitz. However, the function of several short bronze sticks with two pointed ends and square cross-section remains unclear. They had been interpreted as small chisels, awls, or tattoo needles. As the specimens from Prigglitz were found among butchering and food residues (animal bones) they could also be considered toothpicks or meat skewers.

A variety of bone tools was also found, for example two sewing needles or several tool handles (for knives or awls). Production refuse shows that carved bone beads were made on site. Among the most remarkable finds are some tools made of red deer antler: A completely preserved hammer shows little usewear, but one side is burnt black. Interestingly, a tool mark in the form of the letter X was carved into the antler (*Fig. 2*). Similar marks are only known from bronze winged axes or picks from the Urnfield period. A second hammer was obviously discarded after very long and intensive use. A third piece of antler with cut-off ends had probably been prepared for the manufacture of a similar hammer. Furthermore, two brow antlers also show traces of heavy use. Both were partially split, and the points were recut or resharpened several times. It seems plausible that the hammers and picks served as miners' tools at Prigglitz. It would certainly have been possible to mine the relatively soft rock with tools made of fresh antler.

In closing, the bronze and ceramic artefacts from excavation areas 1-4 are not very significant in terms of chronology. In 2013, radiocarbon dating will be used to study the overall time span and the chronological relations between the different working terraces of the mining site.

Bibliography

Hampl, F. & Mayrhofer, R. J. (1963): Urnenfelderzeitlicher Kupferbergbau und mittelalterlicher Eisenbergbau in Niederösterreich. 2. Arbeitsbericht über die Grabungen d. NÖ. Landesmuseums 1953-1959. – Archaeologia Austriaca 33, pp. 50-106.

Kühtreiber, T. & Trebsche, P. (1999): KG Prigglitz. Fundberichte aus Österreich 38, pp. 778-779.

Kühtreiber, T. & Trebsche, P. (2001): KG Prigglitz. Fundberichte aus Österreich 40, pp. 599-600.

Lang, R. (2000): KG Prigglitz. Fundberichte aus Österreich 39, pp. 596-598.

Pucher, E. (2010): Hallstatt and Dürrnberg – Two Salt-Mining Sites, Two Different Meat Supply Strategies. In: Anreiter, P. et al. (eds): Mining in European History and its Impact on Environment and Human Societies. Proceedings for the 1st Mining in European History-Conference of the SFB-HIMAT, 12.-15. November 2009. Innsbruck, pp. 193-197.

Trebsche, P. (2010): Wiederaufnahme der Forschungen in der urnenfelderzeitlichen Bergbausiedlung Prigglitz-Gasteil. Archäologie Österreichs 21/2, pp. 18-19.

Trebsche, P. (2011): Die Wiederaufnahme der Forschungen in der urnenfelderzeitlichen Bergbausiedlung Prigglitz-Gasteil. In: Beiträge zum Tag der Niederösterreichischen Landesarchäologie 2010/2011. Katalog des Niederösterreichischen Landesmuseums N. F. 502. Asparn/Zaya, pp. 41-42.

Trebsche, P. (2012): Die zweite und dritte Grabungskampagne in der urnenfelderzeitlichen Bergbausiedlung von Prigglitz-Gasteil. Archäologie Österreichs 23/2, pp. 14-16.

Trebsche, P. & Pucher, E. (in press): Urnenfelderzeitliche Kupfergewinnung am Rande der Ostalpen. Erste Ergebnisse zu Ernährung und Wirtschaftsweise in der Bergbausiedlung von Prigglitz-Gasteil (Niederösterreich). Prähistorische Zeitschrift (in press).

Três Minas: A discussion of some aspects of the evidence for the use of water in mining[1]

Regula Wahl-Clerici[1]

[1] Projecto - Três Minas – Projekt; Universität Hamburg, Archäologisches Institut, Vor- und Frühgeschichtliche Archäologie, Hamburg, Germany.

Três Minas is one of the best preserved Roman mining districts in the Northwest of the Iberian Peninsula (Vila Pouca de Aguiar, Portugal) (*Fig. 1*). In the three primary ore-deposits of Três Minas, Gralheira and Campo de Jales the Romans mined gold, silver and other minerals in the 1st and 2nd century AD. In the area of Três Minas they established an industrial complex with a settlement that included thermae and an amphitheatre (Wahl, 1988; 1993). The presence of the military, as well as of free workmen and women, is proved by inscriptions (Wahl, 1997). The geographical and hydrological situation of Três Minas on the top of the hill demanded a highly elaborated system of water supply (Wahl, 2003).

More than 20 years of survey were necessary to collect all the information on the various components of this system, comprising 12 channels on different levels, dams, tunnels etc. dispersed over a surface of about 120km^2 and in parts heavily disturbed by agricultural and forestry activities (*Fig. 2*). By scrutinizing this system it became possible to follow the aqueducts from their origin to the mining area. It is obvious that they were constructed for different purposes.

The discussion about the use of water in the Roman mines on the Iberian Peninsula is often based on the work of Pliny (n. h. 33:74-78), where he refers to the various systems of mining and the use of water. This text or parts of it have been translated and discussed by many scholars among them philologists, archaeologists and engineers. This paper refers to Domergues (2012) latest translations and reflections on the text in connection with the use of water in Roman mining, as well as his criticism of Pérez González et al. (2008), Birds translation and interpretation (2004), the highly technical approach by the Projektgruppe Plinius (1993) and the excellent edition with translation into German and comments by König et al. (1984).

Plinys text is a strange mixture of descriptions to the point, dubious information and a structure jumping from one item to the other, so that it is often difficult to decide about its homogeneousness. Claude Domergue, after having studied and worked with the text for more than 40 years, emphasizes that Pliny was not a mining specialist and therefore not the author of an essay on its techniques. He suggests that Pliny gives us a general impression of working in the mines, of how hard and painful the conditions were, and also of the economic importance of the gold for the financial procurator (Domergue, 2012:134). To add another item which I think is important, Pliny's information is based entirely or at least partly on direct observation, but we do not know which places he really visited.

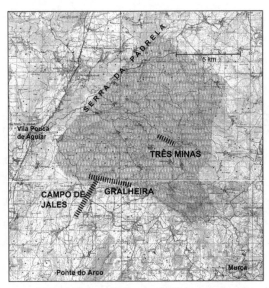

Fig. 1: Roman mining district of Três Minas and Campo de Jales. Broken lines = Ore-deposits of Três Minas, Gralheira and Campo de Jales. Hatched zone = Area of interest for the water-supply for Três Minas. Ponte do Arco = Roman bridge connecting the mining district to the South and the valley of the river Douro. (Carta militar de Portugal Instituto geográfico do Exército 1:50'000. Folhas 6-II (Vila Pouca de Aguiar) and 10-I (Vila Real); draft and realisation: R. Wahl-Clerici.

Fig. 2: Aqueduct cut into the rocks, seen from the North (Photo: J. Wahl).

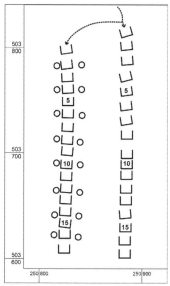

Fig. 3: Situation of the ore-washing facilities. The western line is provided with settling tanks on both sides of every second platform. Dotted line = Aqueducts. Arrows = Direction of water-flow (Draft: J. Wahl; realisation: R. Wahl-Clerici).

It is important to distinguish between the processes of mining and the dressing of the ore, where the use of water was indispensable. Neither fire-setting nor extraction by muscular energy needed water (Wahl, 1998:61-63, Fig. 13-14). It is possible that the Romans substituted the use of vinegar, mentioned by Pliny (n. h. 33:71), with water to intensify the process of wearing down the rocks heated by fire-setting. If this was the case, the quantity of water required was minimal. Water was not indispensable in either crushing or grinding. All the same, the conspicuously smooth surfaces of the cavities in the mortars probably indicate the use of water, although Agricola emphasizes that the so-called wet crushing was only invented after 1512 by Sigismund Maltitz (Agricola, 1994:270). As shown by the about 1000 mortars in Três Minas with their astonishingly constant proportions, crushing-machines were used (Wahl, 1998:65-66, Fig. 13-14), but there is no proof, nor has it ever been mentioned by Wahl, that these machines were activated by water-power (Wilson, 2002:22; Hirt, 2010:35-36). There are various points which make it much more probable that muscular force was used, as e.g. for the lifting devices of the capstan type still visible in the Galeria do Pilar (Wahl, 1988, Abb. 4, Taf. 42a, b).

In any case, water was needed for the process of ore-washing in which the noble metals were separated from the dead rocks (Rosa, 2001). The well known installations consisted of two series of 17 washing platforms, the western ones are complemented by settling tanks on both sides (*Fig. 3*) (Wahl, 1998:66-68, Fig. 15; Wahl-Clerici et al., 2012a:117, Abb. 11a, b). Although detailed research on the ore-washing installations is still lacking, it is obvious that their construction was highly elaborate. The problem was to create a strong enough flow of water to separate the

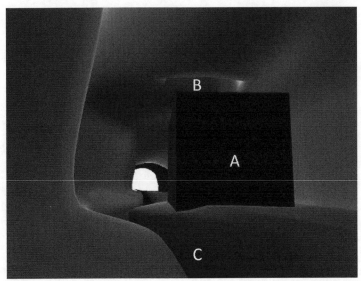

Fig. 4: Galeria do Pilar. Looking south from the entrance towards the end. A = Pillar; B = Pit above the pillar; C = Channel going around the pillar in the enlarged section (Draft: R. Wahl-Clerici; realisation: C. Wahl).

Fig. 5: Galeria do Pilar. Looking north from behind the pillar towards the entrance. Around the pillar the gallery was enlarged towards the East. The channel is visible in the enlargement. The pillar consists of 24 mortars (Photo: C. Wahl).

Fig. 6: Northern hillside of the Corta de Covas seen from the North-East. 1 = Corta de Covas; 2 = Entrance of the Galeria Jürgen Wahl; 3 = Entrance of the pit above the pillar (v. Fig. 5, B); 4 = Entrance of the Galeria do Pilar; 5 = Entrance of the Galeria do Texugo. S = Visible parts of the settlement (Photo and realisation: R. Wahl-Clerici).

valuable components of the ore (especially gold) from the rock, but not too strong, as otherwise all the material including the gold would be flushed away. It seems that these washing platforms were sometimes cut into the mountain, as Jones et al. (1972) suggest for Braña la Folgueirosa (Oviedo, Spain) and Dolaucothi (Wales, UK) (Jones et al., 1972:39-44).

The smelting process: In the area of the "Forno dos Mouros" (Vila Pouca de Aguiar, Portugal) there is a concentration of remains of the ore-dressing processes: mortars, grinding mills and a large heap of ground slag (Wahl, 1988:12, Abb. 1; Bachmann, 1993; Wahl-Clerici et al., 2012 b). Water was supplied by a special aqueduct (Wahl-Clerici et al., 2012b, Abb. 12). For any discussion of how much of this water was needed for which of the processes it will be necessary to excavate the site on a large scale.

It is important to discuss in detail the possibilities of sustaining the extraction-work by water-power. Two alternatives are generally mentioned. One is that already extracted material was transported to the surface by water-power (Domergue, 1990:479). It seems that this sometimes would have been connected to an ore-extracting method (Sánchez-Palencia, 1984/85:356; Sánchez-Palencia et al., 2000b:216). The other is the so-called system of ruina montium, a system to make the mountain collapse (Domergue, 1990, Fig. 25; Domergue, 2008, Fig. 76; Pérez García et al., 2000:183). Both of these systems were largely used at the sites of secondary deposits (e.g. Sánchez Palencia et al., 2000a; Matías Rodríguez, 2006; Matías Rodríguez, 2008). Some authors propose that water-power was also used to attack the mountain at primary gold-deposits, as e.g.

in Dolaucothi (Bird, 2004:62; Burnham et al., 2004:207-223), whereas an unpublished report by Béatrice Cauuet proposes that most of the works were executed by tools and fire-setting (Hirt, 2010:36; confirmed by S. Timberlake in Innsbruck 2012). Another well known example is the spectacular site of Puerto del Palo (Prov. Oviedo, Spain) (Lewis et al., 1970:180-181; Domergue, 1990, Fig. 32) or the already mentioned sites of Braña de la Folgueirosa or Fresnedo (Jones et al., 1972:37-48, Abb. 3. 4).

There are various indications in Três Minas to show that the possibility of water-powered or water-sustained works can be excluded. We will emphasize the situation in the Galeria do Pilar, which was part of the opencast Corta de Covas. Various phases of construction can be distinguished, so the whole length of more than 250m was only established and in use at an advanced stage of the works in the opencast (Wahl-Clerici, 2010).

For the present discussion the emphasis will be on the incline of the gallery, the channel along the Eastern wall and the situation around the pillar. The difference in height between the entrance and the end visible is only 4.5m along the whole length, giving an incline of less than 2%. In fact, this slope and in consequence the speed of flow of water, were not strong enough to move any material.

It is also important to scrutinize the situation around the pillar which, as the circumvention shows, was built before the channel was cut into the soil (*Fig. 4*) (Wahl-Clerici, 2011). Together with the channel narrowing from about 2 Roman ft. to about 1.5 Roman ft. this would have been a serious obstruction for the transport of material by water (*Fig. 5*).

Another important aspect is the position of the various dumps on the surface, which also exclude any water-powered facility for extraction work in the mine, but this would go beyond the scope of this paper and will be discussed elsewhere (*Fig. 6*).

This short discussion shows that without both sophisticated research on the preserved remains of the system of water-supply for the mining district and the discussion of possible traces of their use, the results will remain incomplete.

Endnote

[1] This article is related to the paper „Underground surveying with 3D-laserscanning of the "Galeria dos Alargamentos" in the Roman gold mining district of Três Minas and Campo De Jales (Northern Portugal)" by Markus Helfert, Britta Ramminger & Regula Wahl-Clerici, in this volume.

Bibliography

Agricola, G. (1994): Zwölf Bücher vom Berg- und Hüttenwesen. München.

Bachmann, H.-G. (1993): Zur Metallurgie der römischen Goldgewinnung in Três Minas und Campo de Jales in Nordportugal. In: Steuer, H.; Zimmermann, U.: Montanarchäologie in Europa. Berichte zum Internationalen Kolloquium „Frühe Erzgewinnung und Verhüttung in Europa" in Freiburg im Breisgau vom

4. bis 7. Okt. 1990, pp. 153-160.

Bird, D. (2004): Pliny's Arrugia. Water Power in Roman Gold-Mining. In: The Bulletin of the Peak District Mines Historical Society. Vol. 15, 4/5, pp. 58-63.

Burnham, B.; Burnham, H. (2004): Dolaucothi-Pumsaint. Survey and excavations at a Roman gold-mining complex 1987-1999. Oxford.

Domergue, C. (1990): Les mines de la Péninsule Ibérique dans l'antiquité romaine. Collection de l'École Française de Rome 127. Rom.

Domergue, C. (2008): Les Mines antiques. La production des métaux aux époques grecque et romaine. Antiqua 11. Paris.

Domergue, C. (2012): Les exploitations hydrauliques romaines dans les dépôts alluviaux aurifères du Nord-Ouest de l'Espagne: Las Médulas et le Teleno (Province de León). À propos de publications récentes. In: Bost, J.-P.: L'eau: usages, risques et représentations dans le Sud-Ouest de la Gaule et le Nord de la péninsule Ibérique, de la fin de l'âge du Fer à l'Antiquité tardive (IIe s. a.C. - VIe s. p.C.), Aquitania Suppl. 21, Bordeaux, pp. 111-140.

Hirt, A. M. (2010): Imperial Mines and Quarries in the Roman World. Organizational Aspects 27 BC-AD 235. Oxford.

Jones, R. F. J.; Bird, D. G. (1972): Roman gold-mining in North-West Spain, 2. Workings on the Rio Duerna. The Journal of Roman Studies 62, pp. 59-74.

König, R.; Winkler, G. (1984): C. Plinius Secundus d. Ä., Naturalis Historiae Liber XXXIII. München, Zürich.

Lewis, P. R.; Jones, G. D. B. (1970): Roman gold-mining in North-West Spain. The Journal of Roman Studies 60, pp. 169-185.

Matías Rodríguez, R. (2006): La minería aurífera Romana del Noroeste de Hispania: Ingeniería minera y gestión de las explotaciones auríferas romanas de la Sierra del Teleno (León, España). In: Nueovs elementos de ingenería romana. III Congreso de las Obras Públicas Romans, pp. 211-263.

Matías Rodríguez, R. (2008): El agua en la ingenería de Las Médulas (León, España). In: Lancia 7, pp. 17-112.

Pérez González, M.; Matías Rodríguez, R. (2008): Plinio y la minería aurífera romana: nueva traducción e interpretación de Plin. Nat., 33, 66-78. Cuadernos de Filología Clásica. Estudios latinos, 28, 1, pp. 43-58.

Pliny (n. h.): v. König, R.; Winkler G. C. (1984).

Projektgruppe Plinius (1993): Gold und Vergoldung bei Plinius dem Älteren. Gold und Vergoldung in der Naturalis Historia des Älteren Plinius und anderen antiken Texten mit Exkursen zu verschiedenen Einzelfragen. Tübingen.

Rosa 2001: D. Rosa, Metallogenesis of the Jales Gold District, northern Portugal. Unpubl. Diss. Colorado School of Mines. Golden (Colorado, USA).

Sánchez-Palencia, F.-J. (1984/85): Los „Morteros" de Fresnedo (Allande) y Cecos (Ibias) y los lavaderos de oro romanos en el noroeste de la Península Ibérica. Zephyrus 37/38, pp. 349-359.

Sánchez-Palencia, F.-J.; Pérez-García, L. C., (2000a): La infraestrutura hidráulica: canales y depósitos. In: Sánchez-Palencia, F.-J.: Las Médulas (León). Un paisaje culutral en la Asturia Augustana. León, pp. 189-207.

Sánchez-Palencia, F.-J.; Pérez-García, L. C., (2000b): El lavado del oro y la evacuación de los estériles. In: Sánchez-Palencia, F.-J.: Las Médulas (León). Un paisaje culutral en la Asturia Augustana. León, pp. 208-226.

Wahl, J. (1988): Três Minas. Vorbericht über die archäologischen Untersuchungen im Bereich des römischen Goldbergwerks 1986/87. Madrider Mitteilungen 29, pp. 221-244.

Wahl, J. (1993): Três Minas. Vorbericht über die archäologischen Ausgrabungen im Bereich des römischen Goldbergwerks 1986/87. In: Steuer, H.; Zimmermann, U.: Montanarchäologie in Europa. Berichte zum Internationalen Kolloquium „Frühe Erzgewinnung und Verhüttung in Europa" in Freiburg im Breisgau vom 4. bis 7. Okt. 1990, pp. 123-152.

Wahl, J. (1997): Os Metais. Aspectos da Mineração Romana no Território Português. In: Portugal Romano. A Exploração dos Recursos Naturais, pp. 105-135.

Wahl, J. (1998): Aspectos tecnológicos da indústria mineira e metalúrgica romana de Três Minas e Campo de Jales (Concelho de Vila Pouca de Aguiar). Actas do Seminário Museologia e Arqueologia mineiras. Pub. do Museu do I. G. M., pp. 57-68.

Wahl, J. (2003): Zur Wasserversorgung des römischen Goldbergbaues von Três Minas und Campo de Jales (Vila Pouca de Aguiar, Trás-os-Montes, Portugal). In: Stöllner, T.; Körlin, G.; Steffens, G.; Cierny J.: Man and Mining – Mensch und Bergbau. Studies in honour of G. Weisgerber on occasion of his 65th birthday. Bochum, pp. 495-502.

Wahl-Clerici, R. (2010): Untersuchungen zum Abbaufortschritt in der Corta de Covas (Tagebau A) im römischen Goldbergwerksbezirk von Três Minas (conc. Vila Pouca de Aguiar, Portugal). In: Gorges, J. G.; Nogales Basarrate, T.: Naissance de la Lusitanie romaine (Ier av. - Ier ap. J.-C.). VIIe Table ronde internationale sur la Lusitanie romaine (Toulouse 8-9 novembre 2007), Toulouse/Mérida, pp. 437-458.

Wahl-Clerici, R. (2011): Três Minas. Quelques remarques a propos du pilier dans la „galeria do pilar". Actas del V Congreso Internacional sobre Minería y Metalurgia Históricas en el SE Europeo, León 2008, Madrid, pp. 475-484.

Wahl-Clerici, R.; Wiechowski, A.; Helfert, M.; Ramminger, B. (2012a): Die Golderzaufbereitung im römischen Bergwerksbezirk von Três Minas und Campo de Jales. In: Der Anschnitt 64, Heft 2-3. pp. 109-118.

Wahl-Clerici, R.; Wiechowski, A. (2012b): Der „Forno dos Mouros": ein Aufbereitungs- und Verhüttungsplatz im römischen Goldbergwerksdistrikt von Três Minas und Campo de Jales. In: Ramminger, B.; Lasch, H.: Hunde – Menschen – Artefakte. Gedenkschrift für G. Gallay, pp. 325-338.

Wilson, A. (2002): Machines, Power and the Ancient Economy. In: The Journal of Roman Studies 92, pp. 1-32.

The Highest Abattoir of the Tyrol at the Schneeberg/Moos in the Passeier Valley/South Tyrol

Claus-Stephan Holdermann[1]

[1] Context OG, Archäologie – Bauforschung – Kulturraumanalysen, Ranggen, Austria

On the food supply of the miners during the transition from the Middle Ages to the early modern era.

The SOUTH TYROLEAN MINING MUSEUM has been carrying out archaeological research into the Schneeberg mining complex around Moos in the Passeier valley since 2009. The mining district, which is situated between the Passeier and Ridnaun valleys, is not only one of the oldest and longest-running districts of the Tyrol, but can also be counted among the most spacious of its kind and boasts the most extensive tunnel system of South Tyrol (Stedingk et al., 2002).

The Schneeberg experienced its heyday during the transition from the late Middle Ages to the modern era around the year 1500, after the focus of its production had shifted from silver to lead. The years from around 1450 to 1550 are regarded as the golden age of mining at the Schneeberg. In 1486, around 1000 people were working around the Schneeberg area (for further reading: Sribik, 1928). The mining of silver in the North Tyrolean districts of Schwaz and Brixlegg in the 15th and 16th centuries would not have gained its worldwide recognition without the lead ores from the South Tyrolean deposits in the Gossensaß and Schneeberg regions (for further reading: Haditsch, 1992; Atzl, 1957/58; Baumgarten et al., 1998; Egg, 1992; Mutschlechner, 1993a) The year 1486 is regarded as the climax of mining in the respective district, with 1000 people working in ca. 70 tunnels (Mutschlechner, 1990a).

In the course of the third field campaign of the research project in the year 2011, the so-called "Fleischpankl", the abattoir of the mining district, which can be recognized in the oldest illustration of the district in the Schwaz Mining Book of 1556, was examined. It can be assumed that the miners supplied themselves with products from the neighbouring valleys (Passeier, Ridnaun) and the Sterzing area during the initial years of the mine in the Middle Ages (Mutschlechner, 1993b). Due to the increase of the workforce, provisions for the numerous pitmen largely had to be imported during the transition from the late Middle Ages to the modern era. The range of foods was rather modest and monotonous: flour, lard, bread, cheese, pulses and meat.

Still, many pitmen quit working at the mines because of supply shortages. In order to assure that the mines went on working, the grand entrepreneurs introduced the so-called "Pfennwerthandel" ("penny-value trade", translators note), for which the main entrepreneurs installed several subsidiaries in Sterzing where the miners spent parts of their wages to purchase the required goods at fixed, mostly cheaper prices. Food was bought wholesale by the entrepreneurs, which enabled them to sell at somewhat lower prices. The miners wages were partly or sometimes completely paid in goods like staples, wine, cloth, shoes and various others (Mutschlechner, 1990b).

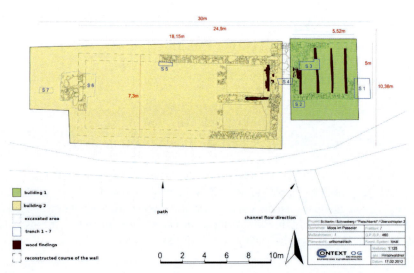

Fig. 1: The "Fleischpankl", abattoir at the Schneeberg/Moos in the Passeier Valley/South Tyrol (CONTEXT OG).

During the transition from the Middle Ages to the early modern era, the miners at the Schneeberg, who also worked in winter, regarded meat as their main food, a diet complemented by staples like rye and wheat porridge, bread and lard. It should be noted that the required quantities of meat could not be covered by the supplies of the Tyrol. As a result, contracts related to deliveries of livestock from Hungary, Salzburg, Carinthia and Styria have been documented for the years 1591, 1597, 1622 and 1659. Herds of up to 300 Hungarian oxen were annually driven up the Schneeberg. The first mentioning (enfeoffment) of the butchers shop at the Schneeberg goes back as early as 1486 and can be found in the book of fees of the Sterzing mining court among the enfeoffments of mining rights (Mutschlechner, 1985; 1987; 1990b; 1990c, 1992; 1993b).

Within the framework of the archaeological investigations of the year 2011, the position and essential aspects of the ground plan of the ensemble as depicted in the Schwaz Mining Book (1556) (Tiroler Landesmuseum Ferdinandeum, Dip. 856) were verified. The butchers shop is situated in the central zone of the so-called "upper mountain". Its position was selected due to the fact that the snow melts early, which makes it easily accessible. All preserved masonry areas were built with lime mortar. These findings not only represent the so far earliest evidence of this building method but also indicate the intention of long-term use. At the present moment it is impossible to assess the original height of the masonry.

The archaeological evidence of the objects in question proves that the "Fleischpankl" ("meat bench", translators note) was an ensemble which originally consisted of two separate buildings. The complete ensemble was 30m long and had a maximum width of 10.38m. The smaller room in the east (5 x 5.52m) can be interpreted as a living area. Its northwestern corner area shows a stone fundament, which was connected with the exterior wall area of the building by means of a butt joint. Stove tiles (flat tiles) prove that this space was originally occupied by a tile stove. Parts of its firemouth are still preserved in the wall substance facing the hallway area. To the south of this area, in the central area of the western wall of the living quarters, lies the door space. Further openings in the wall were situated above the preserved wall substance. The masonry of the living area descends in the northeastern corner, where a massive mortar packet, in which only scattered rests of stone substance can be found, replaces the masonry.

Adjacent to the west of the residential building lies the slaughter room (18.15 x 7.30m). Between both rooms an L-shaped wall section forms a hallway which closes this area to the north. Butt joints connected with both buildings show that this section of masonry was inserted later, thus implying that there once were two separate buildings. The northern half of the building shows a panelled floor reaching as far as the door space of the living area. Individual panels of the same kind can be found in the stratigraphically overlying rubble and indicate that the whole corridor was originally covered with slates. Thus, these partial findings do not represent a hall area but a concluding corridor to the north, which served as a vestibule. The sediment area, which is stratigraphically situated under the panelled floor, the unpanelled sediment of the hallway and the adjoining exterior areas at the same level do not only contain bovine teeth, but also 15th and 16th-century pottery tempered with graphite.

Characteristic features indicating vegetation and relief, as well as construction findings in the south east of the ensemble show that the slaughter room had access to water, which is absolutely necessary for a butchers shop. This access was connected to the conduit system of the mining district and secured the supply of the slaughter room. There is a clearly visible modification in the structure of the eastern wall, where there was a secondary water seal. In the central interior area, the former water inlet continues with a U-shaped wooden gutter, whose direction follows the principal axis of the slaughter room. Remains of the stone wedge trace its course even in the areas without preserved wooden substance, which run as far as the large door space of the western wall (S 6). The function of the central wooden gutter was to dispose of the sewage to the west, through the outlet in the wall.

The frequent occurrence of bovine teeth proves the function of the ensemble as the butchers shop of the mining district, which makes it a unique finding of an abattoir in a mountain area of this altitude. The picture of the "Fleischpankl" in the Schwaz Mining Book (1556) (Tiroler Landesmuseum Ferdinandeum, Dip. 856) shows two construction elements. Due to the perspective, it cannot be judged whether the vestibule connected the two rooms as early as 1556. A further ground plan can be detected in an old map of the district from 1799 from Josef von Senger (after: Tasser, 1994), which depicts two separate buildings. The reason for this might be that the illustrator simply did not include a picture of the vestibule. What the cut does show, however, is that the building still existed at the end of the 18th century. Considering the background of the first shutdown of the mine in the year 1798 (Haller & Schölzhorn, 2008) and the fact that there were only "free diggers" left in the district, it can be concluded that the abattoir was already closed before the turn of the century. This would also explain the sealing off of the inlet pipe on the western side of the slaughterhouse, which suggests a non-water related use of the ensemble.

Finally the ensemble was systematically demolished, which is proven by the large mortar packet in the northeastern corner of the living area, where it descends into the ground without showing a significant percentage of building stone; this conclusion is also supported by the fact that there is no wall rubble in the immediate surroundings of the ensemble. It is not unreasonable to create a causal connection between the demolition of the "Fleischpankl" and the womens house, which was built in the close vicinity of the slaughterhouse in 1896 (Haller & Schölzhorn, 2008). This process might have included a secondary use of wall stones taken from the butchers shop. The present status of the artefact analyses (stove ceramics, pottery, fragments of crown glass, etc.) supports dating the findings from the 15th and 16th centuries to the 19th century.

Bibliography

Atzl, A. (1957/58): Die Verbreitung des Tiroler Bergbaues. Der Anschnitt, Jahrgang 9, Nr. 1/2, pp. 42-48.

Baumgarten, B.; Folie, K. & Stedingk, K. (1998): Auf den Spuren der Knappen. Bergbau und Mineralien in Südtirol. Lana.

Egg, E. (1992): Silber und Blei vom Schneeberg und von Gossensaß. Der Anschnitt, 44. Jahrgang, Heft 3, pp. 80-82.

Haditsch, J. G. (1992): Die Lagerstätte Schneeberg in Tirol. res montanarum, 4, 1994, pp. 18-22.

Haller, H. & Schölzhorn, H. (2008): Schneeberg in Südtirol. Geschichte-Geschichten-Museum. Südtiroler Bergbaumuseum. Meran ², 2008.

Mutschlechner, G. (1985): Ochsen für das Bergwerk am Schneeberg. Der Schlern, 59, 1985, p. 566.

Mutschlechner, G. (1987): Ungarische Ochsen für den Schneeberg. Der Schlern 61, 1987, p. 435.

Mutschlechner, G. (1990a): Bergbau auf Silber, Kupfer und Blei. In: Tiroler Landesmuseum Ferdinandeum (Hrsg.): Silber, Erz und weißes Gold. Bergbau in Tirol. Tiroler Landesausstellung 1990. Innsbruck 1990, pp. 231-267.

Mutschlechner, G. (1990b): Die Versorgung des Bergwerkes am Schneeberg. Der Schlern, 64, 1990, pp. 215-222.

Mutschlechner, G. (1990c): Metzgerbehausung am Schneeberg. Der Schlern 64, 1990, p. 113.

Mutschlechner, G. (1992): Der Schneeberg im Tiroler Landreim (1558). Der Schlern 1992, p. 113.

Mutschlechner, G. (1993a): Schneeberger Erz nach Brixlegg. Der Schlern 67, p. 403.

Mutschlechner, G. (1993b): Der Schneeberg-ein Bergbau der Superlative. Der Schlern 67, 1993, pp. 323-327.

Sribik, R. v. (1928): Überblick des Bergbaus von Tirol und Vorarlberg in Vergangenheit und Gegenwart. Innsbruck.

Stedingk, K.; Baumgarten, B. & Folie, K. (2002): Mineralische Bodenschätze und historischer Bergbau in Südtirol. In: 5. Internationaler Bergbau-Workshop, Ridnaun/Schneeberg, 15.-22. September 2002. Amt für Geologie und Baustoffprüfung, Bozen, pp. 112-137.

Tasser, R. (1994): Das Bergwerk am Südtiroler Schneeberg. Bozen.

Session II

Production & Technology

The Social Context of Metallurgical Production and Technological Change: Views from the Eastern Mediterranean

A. Bernard Knapp[1]

[1] Archaeology, University of Glasgow, Scotland, UK

Bronze Age Mediterranean Archaeometallurgy: A Snapshot

Excavations throughout the Mediterranean have revealed hundreds of mines and smelting workshops as well as the debris associated with the prehistoric extraction of copper from its minerals. Copper ore deposits are found in several regions that flank the Mediterranean, most of which were exploited already in prehistoric times.

In the Levant, rich copper sources are situated around Feinan area in Jordan, and at Timna in Israel. Large-scale mining and smelting of copper ores began no later than the Early Bronze Age at Feinan, which has impressive remains of prehistoric mines and smelting workshops (Hauptmann, 2007): it became one of the most important sources of Near Eastern copper during the third millennium BC (Levy et al., 2002:427). Timna, with its prehistoric mines, copper smelting workshops and settlements, and associated sanctuaries, has been studied extensively and systematically (Rothenberg, 1999). Recent work and a suite of new radiocarbon dates indicate that the peak in copper production at both Timna and Feinan occurred in the early Iron Age (10th century BC) (Levy et al., 2008; Ben-Yosef et al., 2012). Southwest of Timna in the Sinai peninsula lies Serabit el Khadim, an important source of copper that the Egyptians exploited from the third millennium BC onward. Abdel-Motelib et al. (2012) recently reported on 27 Late Chalcolithic to Late Bronze Age mining, smelting and habitation sites in the Sinai and eastern desert of Egypt.

The Aegean region is also rich in copper. The western Cycladic islands of Kea, Kythnos, Seriphos and Siphnos have known sources of copper as well as iron, lead and silver. Evidence for copper mining or smelting activities on Kythnos has been assigned to the earliest stages of the Bronze Age (Bassiakos & Philaniotou-Hadjianastasiou, 2007:47-52). The ores smelted at the Final Neolithic-Early Bronze Age smelting workshop at Chrysokamino on Crete's northeast coast (Betancourt, 2006) most likely came from one of these Cycladic islands. Crucibles from the Early Minoan I cemetery at Aghia Photia suggest not only the production of copper but also the possibility of Cycladic influence (Betancourt & Muhly, 2006:151); lead isotope analyses of copper artefacts from the same site show they are consistent with production from Kythnian ores. On the Greek mainland, copper mineralisation exists at Lavrion in Attica and there are objects and copper ingots made from so-called Lavrion copper (Gale et al., 2009:168-171), but there is still no secure archaeological evidence for the Late Bronze Age mining or smelting of copper ores.

The island of Cyprus is one of the richest countries in copper per surface area in the world (Constantinou, 1992). Because these are sulphide ore deposits, their exploitation came somewhat late in comparison with neighbouring regions. By the Late Bronze Age (after about 1700/1650

Cal BC), however, once the technology of treating such ores became more proficient, Cyprus emerged as one of the most important sources of copper throughout the Mediterranean (Knapp, 2012).

The archaeometallurgical record of the eastern Mediterranean shows a great variety of installations and equipment used to extract copper from its minerals. Different kinds of wind-operated furnace installations were used to extract copper from ores at Early Bronze Age smelting sites on Crete and Kythnos in the Aegean, and at Feinan in Jordan (Betancourt et al., 1999:354, 363; Bassiakos & Philaniotou-Hadjianastasiou, 2007:44-47; Hauptmann, 2007:228-232). During the Middle and Late Bronze Ages, archaeological evidence indicates that tuyères had come to be used widely, along with bellows, to induce a draught into the furnace and raise the temperature required for smelting (Davey, 1979:110; Kassianidou, 2012:102-103). Egyptian tomb paintings depict foot-operated, ceramic pot bellows, the best example coming from a scene in the 15th century BC tomb of Rekhmire (Tylecote, 1992:23).

Mining and Metallurgical Technologies

Technology as a social process involves people's daily practices and abilities, their beliefs and their capacity to negotiate complex economic and political relationships. Metalworking and metallurgical innovation, for example, required not just access to or control over raw material sources, but also a level of political centralisation that could support specialised workshops. Some of the most important innovations in metallurgical production took place in the Levant and Cyprus, where mineral wealth, increasingly centralised power strategies, and a key position in maritime trading systems ultimately came together (Sherratt & Sherratt, 2001:15).

Innovations in metallurgical technology affected not only the environment but also the social practices of those who mined and smelted metals, as well as those who distributed and consumed them. Whilst managers and elites may see technological innovations as progressive and desirable, the people who worked the mines or smelted the ores metals surely saw things differently, often disruptively. Such developments often provide the impetus for social change if not social abuse (Stöllner, 2003:427-429). Galen's description of the conditions in the mines near Soli on Cyprus, the use of child labour in the mining districts of Roman Iberia (Stöllner, 2003:428), and the extreme conditions and short life span of the Christians working in the 4th century AD Roman mines at Phaino (Feinan) in Jordan (Mattingly, 2011:185-199) leave no doubt that the mining and production of metals has severe social consequences that affect and alter people's daily lives.

From individual enterprises to collective operations, the social organisation of production largely determines technological strategies. Indeed, what seems critical in contexts of technological innovation is the organisational complexity involved in setting up specialist workshops, aggregating the output of workers, and documenting or recording what is produced, how it is distributed, etc. Although metallurgical experience and skills developed near the actual ore sources, with the onset of urbanisation (Bronze Age) and the concentration of capital, there developed a conjuncture between local resources and expertise, on the one hand, and on the other capital-intensive technologies and large scale economies, what Sherratt & Sherratt (2001:25) have termed a 'technological dialectic'.

The use of mining or smelting tools such as picks, tongs, hammers, even furnaces, represents both a social and a material phenomenon. Even the most basic use of tools requires some degree of prior knowledge and socialisation. Thus technology involves not just material things but also human actions, which in turn affect social organisation and require the application of knowledge. By identifying technical characteristics or assessing various features of technological design, we can begin to reconstruct not just the production of metals but also the social and spatial organisation that lay behind it.

Archaeometallurgy and Society in the Prehistoric Mediterranean

What can be said about the role and impact of metallurgical production and trade on prehistoric societies in the Mediterranean? By the beginning of the Bronze Age, the production and trade in metals increasingly became key factors in promoting social change. In the Bronze Age eastern Mediterranean, most known metallurgical production sites were located in close proximity to ore deposits, and thus were well isolated from the social, organisational and economic developments that took place in population centres, typically located along the seacoast. This pattern was linked at least in part to the increased production of metals and the development of long-distance trade, itself often propelled by the desire of rulers and elites to acquire imported prestige goods.

From at least the mid-third millennium BC, certain polities in the Levant became involved in the production, bulk exchange and consumption of both ores and finished metal products. The need to produce a final product of standard quality, shape and weight was understood early on and ingot moulds dating to the Early Bronze Age have been found at several sites, both in the Levant (Khirbat Hamra Ifdan – Levy et al., 2002) and on Cyprus (Marki Alonia – Frankel & Webb, 2006:216-217). In the Aegean, metallurgical production flourished – copper on Kythnos; silver/lead and possibly gold on Siphnos – with the emergence of the Cycladic culture and the expansion of interregional trade (Broodbank, 2000). On Cyprus, the third millennium BC was a time of major social change, when indigenous elites and possibly some Anatolian newcomers began to formalise the copper industry that became so critical in all of the politico-economic and social developments of the Middle-Late Bronze Ages (Knapp, 2008).

The circulation of goods, ideas and ideologies across geographic, cultural and economic boundaries may be seen as social transactions that entangled producers, distributors and consumers in wider relations of debt and prestige, dependence and alliance, patronage and privilege (Thomas, 1991:123-124). The growth and spread of metallurgical production, and copper production in particular, promoted greater social distinctions, as certain individuals or groups acquired new wealth.

During the second millennium BC, gold, silver, copper and tin came to represent what Sherratt (2000:83) called 'convertible' value, convertible both economically and literally, inasmuch as these metals could be consumed, stored, redistributed or recycled in various forms and for diverse ends. Documentary evidence from the eastern Mediterranean demonstrates that monarchs, merchants and mariners alike were preoccupied with these self-same metals (Liverani, 1990).

A remarkable series of social and economic changes thus were linked intimately to all the innovative developments in extractive and metallurgical technologies, and to the increasingly widespread production and distribution of metals and metal objects. These changes included:

(1) the proliferation of settlements and the emergence of 'urban' centres;

(2) the development and expansion in interregional trade;

(3) the growth of palatial regimes and city-state kingdoms;

(4) the development and refinement of craft specialisation and the spread of an iconographic koine;

(5) the elaboration of mortuary rituals and burials with large quantities of precious metal goods;

(6) the widespread occurrence of metal hoards and the related trade in recycled and scrap metal. Certain occupational identities came to be focused on metallurgical production and trade, and Cyprus even gave its name to the island's most prominent product: copper ore.

The following Age of Iron itself relied on extractive and smelting technologies developed during the Bronze Age, together with the use of carburisation and quenching, most likely on Cyprus itself (Sherratt & Sherratt, 2001:30). What began as a small-scale by-production of a commodity (iron) regarded as a luxury good elsewhere in the eastern Mediterranean and ancient western Asia resulted in a technological revolution linked directly – albeit over the millennia – to the dramatic social and economic changes that ushered in the Industrial Revolution and the beginnings of the modern era. As Sherratt & Sherratt (2001:31) expressed it: '… these future developments should not overshadow our perception of its beginnings: a logical, even inevitable outcome of the combined processes of economic and technical change, in a context where means, motive and opportunity came together'.

References

Abdel-Motelib, A.; Bode, M.; Hartmann, R.; Hartung, U.; Hauptmann, A. & Pfeiffer, K. (2012): Archaeometallurgical expeditions to the Sinai Peninsula and the Eastern Desert of Egypt (2006, 2008). Metalla (Bochum) 19 (1-2), pp. 3-59.

Bassiakos, Y. & Philaniotou-Hadjianastasiou O. (2007): Early copper production on Kythnos: archaeological evidence and analytical approaches to the reconstruction of metallurgical processes. In: Day, P. M & Doonan, R. C. P. (eds): Neolithic and Early Bronze Age Metallurgy. Sheffield Studies in Aegean Archaeology 7 Oxford: Oxbow, pp. 19-56.

Ben-Yosef, E.; Shaar, R.; Tauxe L. & Ron H. (2012): A new chronological framework for Iron Age copper production at Timna (Israel). Bulletin of the American Schools of Oriental Research 367, pp. 31-71.

Betancourt, P. P. (2006): Chrysokamino I: The Chrysokamino Metallurgy Workshop and its Territory. Hesperia Supplement 36. Athens: American School of Classical Studies.

Betancourt, P. P. & Muhly, J. D. (2006): The sistra from the Minoan burial cave at Hagios Charalambos. In: Czerny, E.; Hein, I.; Hunger, H.; Melman, D. & Schwab, A. (eds): Timelines. Studies in Honour of Manfred Bietak, Volume 2. Orientalia Lovaniensia Analecta 149(2), Leuven: Uitgeverij Peeters en Departement Oosterse Studies, pp.429-435.

Betancourt, P. P.; Muhly, J. D.; Farrand, W. R.; Stearns, C.; Onyshkevych, L.; Hafford, W. R. & Evely, D. (1999): Research and excavation at Chrysokamino, Crete, 1995-1998. Hesperia 68, pp. 343-370.

Broodbank, C. (2000): An Island Archaeology of the Early Cyclades. Cambridge: Cambridge University Press.

Constantinou, G. (1992): Ancient copper mining in Cyprus. In: Marangou, A. & Psillides, K. (eds.): Cyprus, Copper and the Sea, 43-74. Nicosia: Government of Cyprus.

Davey, C. J. (1979): Some ancient Near Eastern pot bellows. Levant 11, pp. 101-111.

Frankel, D., and J.M. Webb (2006): Marki Alonia: An Early and Middle Bronze Age Settlement in Cyprus. Excavations 1995-2000. Studies in Mediterranean Archaeology 123.2. Sävedalen: P. Åström's Förlag.

Gale, N.; Kayafa, M. & Stos-Gale, Z. A. (2009): Further evidence for Bronze Age production of copper from ores in the Lavrion ore district, Attica, Greece. In: Proceedings of the Second International Conference: Archaeometallurgy in Europe 2007 (Aquileia, Italy, June 2007), Milano: Associazione Italiana di Metallurgia, pp. 158-176.

Hauptmann, A. (2007): The Archaeometallurgy of Copper: Evidence from Faynan, Jordan. Berlin, Heidelberg: Springer Verlag.

Kassianidou, V. (2012): Metallurgy and metalwork in Enkomi: the early phases. In: Kassianidou, V. & Papasavvas, G. (eds): Eastern Mediterranean Metallurgy and Metalwork in the Second Millennium BC, Oxford: Oxbow, pp. 94-106.

Knapp, A. B. (2008): Prehistoric and Protohistoric Cyprus: Identity, Insularity and Connectivity. Oxford: Oxford University Press.

Knapp, A. B. (2012): Metallurgical production and trade on Bronze Age Cyprus: views and variations. In: Kassianidou, V. & Papasavvas, G. (eds): Eastern Mediterranean Metallurgy and Metalwork in the Second Millennium BC, Oxford: Oxbow, pp. 14-25.

Levy, T. E.; Adams, R. B.; Hauptmann, A.; Prange Michael, M.; Schmitt-Strecker, S. & Najjar, M. (2002): Early Bronze Age metallurgy: a newly discovered copper manufactory in southern Jordan. Antiquity 76, pp. 425-437.

Levy, T. E.; Higham, T.; Bronk Ramsey, C.; Smith, N. G.; Ben-Yosef, E.; Robinson, M.; Münger, S.; Knabb, K.; P.Schulze, J.; Najjar, M. & Tauxe L. (2008): High-precision radiocarbon dating and historical biblical archaeology in southern Jordan. Proceedings of the National Academy of Sciences 105, pp. 16460-65.

Liverani, M. (1990): Prestige and Interest: International Relations in the Near East ca. 1600-1100 BC. Padova: Sargon Press.

Mattingly, D. J. (2011): Imperialism, Power, and Identity: Experiencing the Roman Empire. Princeton: Princeton University Press.

Rothenberg, B. (1999): Archaeometallurgical researches in the southern Arabah, 1959-1990. Part 2: Egyptian New Kingdom (Ramesside) to early Islam. Palestine Exploration Quarterly 131, pp. 149-175.

Sherratt, S. (2000): Circulation of metals and the end of the Bronze Age in the eastern Mediterranean. In: Pare, C. F. (ed.): Metals Make the World Go Round: The Supply and Circulation of Metals in Bronze Age Europe, Oxford: Oxbow Books, pp. 82-98.

Sherratt, A. & Sherratt, E. S. (2001): Technological change in the east Mediterranean Bronze Age: capital, resources and marketing. In: Shortland, A. (ed.): The Social Context of Technological Change in Egypt and the Near East, 1650-1550 BC, Oxbow: Oxford, pp. 15-38.

Stöllner, T. (2003): Mining and economy – a discussion of spatial organisations and structures of early raw material exploitation. In: Stöllner, T.; Körlin, G.; Steffens, G. & Cierny, J. (eds.): Man and Mining – Mensch und Bergbau: Studies in Honour of Gerd Weisgerber. Der Anschnitt, Beiheft 16, Bochum: Deutsches Bergbau-Museum, pp. 415-446.

Thomas, N. (1991): Entangled Objects: Exchange, Material Culture, and Colonialism in the Pacific. Cambridge: Harvard University Press.

Tylecote, R. F. (1992): A History of Metallurgy. London: Institute of Materials.

Understanding the chronology of British Bronze Age mines – Bayesian modelling and theories of exploitation

Simon Timberlake[1] & Peter Marshall[2]

[1] Cambridge Archaeological Unit, Department of Archaeology, University of Cambridge
[2] English Heritage (Scientific Dating Advisor)

Introduction

A more detailed description of some of the principle Bronze Age mines in Britain was provided in the HIMAT Conference Proceedings for 2009 (Timberlake, 2010). Many of these sites lie close to the western seaboard of Britain with a concentration in North and mid-Wales, especially in mid-Wales where they are associated with lead and copper veins, particularly where the copper mineralisation lies closest to the surface. Most of these mines were identified on the basis of finds of cobble stone tools, the majority of which were collected as beach pebbles along the coast. Only at distances greater than 20km from the coast do we find evidence for the use of river pebbles and glacial erratics, an indication perhaps of a preference for the harder, smoother, unflawed beach stones as tool material.

Given that mining in south-west Ireland began around 2400 AC it would seem reasonable to view the current pattern of sites as representing an eastward migration in copper prospecting following the decline of production at Ross Island (Timberlake, 2009), yet in reality this pattern is far from simple.

On the Isle of Man (IOM) we find evidence of this copper prospection close to one of the shortest sea crossings between Ireland and Britain. Hammerstones have been found associated with mining on the sea cliffs of Bradda Head (Pickin & Worthington, 1989), and also nearby on the Langness Peninsula (Timberlake ibid.).

The copper veins on North and South Bradda Head were described by Lamplugh in 1903 as being 'amongst the most spectacular displays of quartz veining in Europe' (*Fig. 1*). The mineralization here can be seen far out to sea, much as it would have been when Bronze Age peoples crossed in their plank boats or curraghs from Ireland. The presence of this 'metal route' seems all the clearer when we examine the Copper Age/Early Bronze Age metalwork from the island which shows affinities with both Irish and early Welsh and Scottish (Migdale) axes, along with the mixing (or recycling) of Ross Island metal with copper from other sources.

On the north-eastern tip of Anglesey, North Wales, evidence of Early Bronze Age copper mining has been found at least at 4-5 locations underground on Parys Mt. (Jenkins, 1995). The first miners may have been working in opencast drifts to depths of over 20m, mining small shoots of oxidised minerals along faults close to the junction with the sulphide zone. In the 18th century AD when the deposit was rediscovered, lumps of native copper weighing up to 15kg were found within parts of the gossan/supergene zone (Lentin, 1800).

Fig. 2a

Fig. 1   Fig. 2b

Fig. 1: South Bradda Head Mine, Isle of Man, United Kingdom. Stone hammers have been found higher up the cliff above the engine house, near to old opencuts (photo by D. Jenkins, Bangor).

Fig. 2a: Mining pick and hammer tool made of red deer antler. Found within the Comet Lode Opencast excavations on Copa Hill, Cwmystwyth (photo by S. Timberlake).

Fig. 2b: The remains of a kreel-type basket made of hazel (Corylus sp.), probably for carrying ore. Copa Hill, Cwmystwyth (photo by S. Timberlake).

Fig. 3: Two views of a section of the 5m long Early Bronze Age alder wood launder. Copa Hill, Cwmystwyth (photo by S. Timberlake).

Within the dolomitised and partly karstic limestones of the nearby Great Orme's Head Bronze Age miners were working a stockwork of parallel copper veins within the Pyllau Valley. This was mined opencast and by several kilometres of narrow underground galleries, the low water table permitting extraction to depths of at least 30m (Lewis, 1996). Carbonate ores were being extracted using stone and thousands of bone tools. Estimates of Bronze Age copper production ranges from 30 to nearly 1800 tons of metal (Timberlake ibid.).

The only Early Bronze Age copper smelting site in Britain lies less than a km from here at Pentrwyn, on a cliff ledge location on the eastern side of the Great Orme (Chapman, 1997). All that survives of this site today is a layer containing crushed slag, iron oxide, and less than 20g of copper prills. A sherd of Bronze Age pottery was recovered from here in 2011.

The Comet Lode opencast on Copa Hill, Cwmystwyth in mid Wales is a good example of a small to medium sized Early Bronze Age mine, and is unique in terms of its survival and lack of later disturbance. This made it an ideal choice for archaeological investigation. Some 5000 tons of prehistoric mine spoil cover the hillside below the top of this approximately 10m deep opencast, which was partially excavated between 1989 and 2002 (Timberlake, 2003).

The thousands of stone tools recovered or recorded from this mine show a range of utilitarian uses. With the exception of just one or two examples, none of the hammers were grooved, and only 9% showed evidence of modification for the purposes of hafting. However, more than 41% had been re-used, some up to three or four times, and some for a range of different functions. The toolsets included mining hammers, chisels, wedges, crushing stones and ore anvils – and very rarely grinding stones.

The waterlogged conditions on Copa Hill have permitted the survival of many of the objects and tools of daily working life, including antler picks (*Fig. 2a*), rope, hammerstone handles and baskets made of hazel (*Fig. 2b*). The most sensational find however was the discovery of a hollowed-out 5m-long alder log launder, one of the earliest examples of mine drainage known (*Fig. 3*).

Elsewhere Bronze Age miners were mining malachite and azurite within the Triassic sandstones of Alderley Edge in Cheshire, a site close to present day Manchester. A wooden shovel was recovered from this mine during the 19th century, whilst the grooved stone mining hammers from here are unique within Britain (Timberlake & Prag, 2005).

The most recent work has taken place at the Ecton Copper Mines in Staffordshire (Timberlake, 2010). Here ^{14}C dates taken from bone and antler tools were used to model the periodicity and sequence of small-scale Bronze Age mining across the hill; it appears that mining may have shifted from one site (Stone Quarry) to the other (The Lumb), and may only have lasted a few decades, in the period between 1800-1700 AC (report by John Meadows, English Heritage).

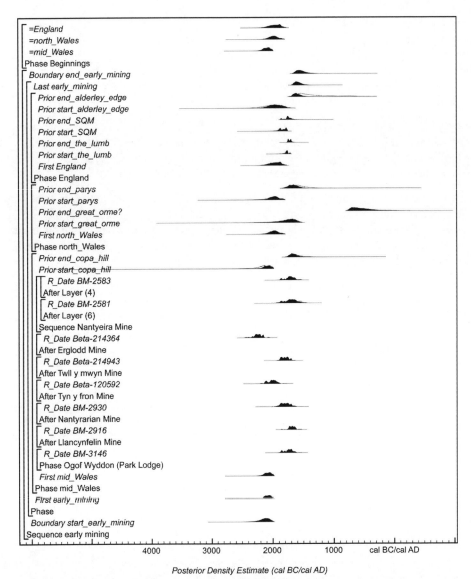

Fig. 4: Probability distributions of dates associated with early mining activity. Each distribution represents the relative probability that an event occurs at a particular time. For each radiocarbon date, two distributions have been plotted: one in outline which is the result of simple radiocarbon calibration, and a solid one based on the chronological model used. The other distributions correspond to aspects of the model. For example, the distribution 'Boundary_start_early_mining' is the estimate for when mining started. The large square brackets down the left-hand side of the diagram and the OxCal keywords define the overall model exactly (P. Marshall).

Bayesian modelling of early mining activity

In order to identify the accurate measurements (ie where the radiocarbon concentration in the sample has been accurately measured) and the accurate dates (ie those accurate measurements from samples with good taphonomic provenance) an assessment of the existing radiocarbon determinations from early mining activity in Wales and England was undertaken.

The three basic criteria for assessing a sample were as follows:

Firstly, was the carbon from the sample in equilibrium with the carbon in the atmosphere when the sample died? The most widespread example of samples that are not in equilibrium are determinations obtained from long lived charcoal – the 'old-wood effect' (Bowman, 1990). Secondly, has the sample been contaminated by a carbon containing material, and thirdly, is the sample securely associated with the archaeological activity that is of interest (Waterbolk, 1971).

A series of site-based Bayesian models (Bayliss et al., 2007) were then constructed for the interpretation of the chronology from the following sites: Alderley Edge, Copa Hill, Mynydd Parys, and the Great Orme (models not illustrated) using the program OxCal v4.1 (Bronk Ramsey, 2009) and the current internationally-agreed atmospheric calibration dataset for the northern hemisphere, IntCal09 (Reimer et al., 2009). However, given uncertainties about the taphonomy of the majority of the samples from other sites in mid-Wales these have not been modelled.

The Bayesian approach

Although the simple calibrated dates are accurate estimates of the dates of the samples, this is usually not what archaeologists really wish to know. It is the dates of the archaeological events, which are represented by those samples, which are of interest. Absolute dating information in the form of radiocarbon dates can be combined with the relative information provided by archaeological context and associations to provide estimates for the dates of the activities.

Fortunately, methodology is now available which allows the combination of these different types of explicit information to produce realistic estimates of the dates of archaeological interest. It should be emphasised that the posterior density estimates produced by this modelling are not absolute. They are interpretative estimates, which can and will change as further data become available and as other researchers choose to model the existing data from different perspectives.

Further details of the Bayesian approach to chronological modelling can be found in Bayliss et al. (2007).

The currency of early mining

A model for early mining activity in Wales and England is shown in Figure 4. This model has been constructed by taking estimates for the start and end of mining activity at individual sites (e.g. Copa Hill – models not shown) and combining them with individual dates from sites with a small number of measurements or where treatment of all of them (for example the dates are treated as a terminus post quos) means they cannot be explicitly modelled.

The prior information in this model is that once mining activity started it was undertaken fairly continuously and relatively constantly over the period of its initial currency (Buck et al., 1992). Evaluation of whether such an assumption is valid will require more precise dating of a wider range of sites than currently available. This prior information is though fairly robust and not making any assumption at all is demonstrably importantly wrong (see Bayliss et al., 2007).

The model has good overall agreement (Amodel=115) between the radiocarbon dates and the prior information (Bronk Ramsey, 2009) and suggests that this activity most probably started in the last quarter of the third millennium cal AC (2315-1995 cal AC; 95% probability; start_early_mining; *Fig. 4*). Although the model produces an estimate for the end of early mining activity, the true nature of such an ending is more difficult to define as it could be argued that such sites do not have definitive endings because they are in many cases re-worked. A good case in point is the estimate for the end of mining activity at the Great Orme, which clearly does not relate to the first wave of mining but much later activity. We have therefore chosen to exclude it from this model - the probability that it is part of the initial phase of dated mining activity is 0%.

More importantly this chronological model allows us to evaluate the sequence and timing of mining activity across England and Wales. An understanding of timing is important as it enables tempo to be understand and it is from this that we can start to seek the underlying social mechanisms that caused the uptake of mining (Whittle et al., 2011). Although the dating of mining activity is far from properly understood and the number of dated sites relatively small we hope that our 'timetable' will serve as a framework for further investigations and modifications in the future.

British mines fall into three spatially distinct groups – mid-Wales (the Plynlimon area), the north Wales coast and north-west central England (Timberlake, 2009) – and by estimating the first dated mining activity in each of these areas (e.g. First mid_Wales; *Fig. 4*) an evaluation of the temporal spread of mining activity can be determined. It is clear that the earliest dated mining activity took place in the mid-Wales group of mines (79.7% probability – *Fig. 4*; Beginnings). The model also provides a most likely order for the start of mining activity in these three areas as follows: Mid-Wales>north Wales coast>north-west central England> = 43.3% probability.

Such an eastward movement from Wales to England of mining activity, over a relatively short period of time, and the similarities in mining methods and tools used suggest that a mutual knowledge and experience linked the miners of mid-Wales and north-west central England.

Summary of current knowledge and ideas

The search for copper

- Prospecting for new copper sources in Britain would appear to predate the decline of Ross Island.
- Central Wales seems to have been one of the first areas of interest.
- Prospectors, or perhaps just the ideas, then spread rapidly (perhaps over a 200 year period) into North Wales and NW England.

- A likely sequence for the onset of mining is as follows: Mid-Wales>north Wales coast>north-west central England. However, this spread from (Ireland) may have come from two different directions; via the IOM and via South Wales.
- The Great Orme was probably an early discovery, yet this mine was only worked on a large scale later on.

The earliest mines
- Small-medium sized mines such as Copa Hill exploited the oxidised zones of sulphide deposits.
- There is a likely to be a Beaker 'association' with the initiation of mining.
- Bronze Age miners were pastoralists, working here in the summer-autumn months. Stone tools were brought from the coast, whilst wood came from the clearance of new pastures.
- Ore concentrate may have been traded for metal, as a means to enter the exchange economy.
- By 1600-1500 AC many of these mines were flooded and abandoned.

Copper mining and production in the Early-Middle Bronze Age
- Great Orme was the main source of British copper between 1600-1400 AC.
- Miners may have lived in or close to this mine – they were supplied with meat and tool material, and the working may have been continuous.
- The deepest workings on the Orme suggest that mining continued into the Late Bronze Age. Metal was now coming from other sources.
- The smelting site at Pentrwyn does not appear to be representative of the main period of metal production.

Metal production
- From 2300-1800 AC the signature of Ross I – sourced metal in British copper-bronze artefacts becomes weaker as the metal is re-cycled and local metal is added (Bray & Pollard, 2012).
- Lead isotopic analysis is problematic as a technique. There is an issue here with the 'pooling of metal' from a variety of different sources.
- Smelting probably took place away from the mines, and may have been undertaken by travelling metalworkers.
- In the absence of archaeological evidence experimental archaeology should be used as a means to understand the smelting process.
- Great Orme metal may have been the source of the Acton Park metalwork (1500-1400 AC).
- New metal from Alpine sources probably reaches the UK as re-cycled scrap from 1400 AC onwards.

Acknowledgments
We would like to thank David Jenkins and Andy Lewis for providing us with the ^{14}C data for Parys Mt and

the Great Orme, and John Barnatt and John Meadows (formerly English Heritage) for the analyses of the Ecton dates in advance of final publication. Alan Williams provided useful discussion on Pentrwyn, and Brenda Craddock on the analysis of hammerstones.

References

Bayliss, A.; Bronk Ramsey, C.; van der Plicht, J; Whittle, A. (2007): Bradshaw and Bayes: towards a timetable for the Neolithic, Cambridge Journal of Archaeology 17.1, supplement, pp. 1-28.

Bowman, S. (1990): Radiocarbon Dating, London.

Buck, C. E.; Litton, C. D.; Smith, A. F. M. (1992): Calibration of radiocarbon results pertaining to related archaeological events, Journal of Archaeological Science 19, pp. 497-512.

Bray, P. J. & Pollard, A. M. (2012): A new interpetative approach to the chemistry of copper-alloy objects: source, recycling, and technology.

Bronk Ramsey, C. (2009): Bayesian analysis of radiocarbon dates, Radiocarbon 51, pp. 337-60.

Chapman, D. (1997): Great Orme smelting site, Llandudno. Archaeology in Wales 37, pp. 56-57.

Jenkins, D. A. (1995): Mynydd Parys Copper Mines. Archaeology in Wales 35, pp. 35-37.

Lentin, A. G. L. (1800): Briefe über die Insel Anglesea (Leipzig, Siegfried Lebrecht Crusias).

Lewis, A. (1996): Prehistoric Mining at the Great Orme: Criteria for the identification of early mining, unpublished MPhil Thesis, University of Wales, Bangor.

O'Brien, W. (2004): Ross Island – Mining, Metal and Society in Early Ireland, Bronze Age Studies 6, Galway, National University of Ireland.

Pickin, J.; Worthington, T. (1989): Prehistoric mining hammers from Bradda Head. Isle of Man. Bulletin of the Peak District Mines Historical Society 10 (5), pp. 274-275.

Reimer, P. J.; Baillie, M. G. L.; Bard, E.; Bayliss, A.; Beck, J. W.; Blackwell, P. G.; Bronk Ramsey, C.; Buck, C. E.; Burr, G. S.; Edwards, R. L.; Friedrich, M.; Grootes, P. M.; Guilderson, T. P.; Hajdas, I.; Heaton, T. J.; Hogg, A. G.; Hughen, K. A.; Kaiser, K. F.; Kromer, B.; McCormac, G.; Manning, S.; Reimer, R. W.; Remmele, S.; Richards, D. A.; Southon, J. R.; Talamo, S.; Taylor, F. W.; Turney, C. S. M.; van der Plicht, J.; Weyhenmeyer, C. E. (2009): INTCAL09 and MARINE09 radiocarbon age calibration curves, 0-50,000 years cal BP, Radiocarbon 51, pp. 1111-50.

Timberlake, S. (2003): Excavations on Copa Hill, Cwmystwyth (1986-1999): An Early Bronze Age copper mine within the uplands of Central Wales. British Archaeological Reports (British Series) 348, Oxford: Archaeopress.

Timberlake, S. (2009): Copper mining and metal production at the beginning of the British Bronze Age, In: Bronze Age Connections (ed. P. Clark), Oxbow, Oxford pp. 956-122.

Timberlake, S. (2010): Geological, Mineralogical and Environmental Controls on the Extraction of Copper Ores in the British Bronze Age. Proceedings 1st HIMAT Conference, Innsbruck 2009, pp. 289-296.

Timberlake, S.; Prag, A. (2005): The Archaeology of Alderley Edge – Survey, Excavation and Experiment in an Ancient Mining Landscape, British Archaeological Reports (British Series) 396, Oxford.

Waterbolk, H. T. (1971): Working with radiocarbon dates, Proceedings of the Prehistoric Society 27, pp. 15-33.

Whittle, A.; Bayliss, A. & Healey, F. (2011): Gathering time: the social dynamics of change. In: Whittle, A; Healey, F; Bayliss, A.: Gathering Time: Dating the Early Neolithic Enclosures of Southern Britain and Ireland, Oxford, pp. 848-908.

Quantifying Bronze Age Smelting Sites in the Mitterberg Mining District

Erica Hanning[1], Thomas Stöllner[2], Annette Hornschuch[2] & Beate Sikorski[3]

[1] Römisch-Germanisches Zentralmuseum, Labor für Experimentelle Archäologie, Mayen, Germany
[2] Deutsches Bergbau-Museum Bochum, Forschungsbereich Montanarchäologie, Bochum, Germany
[3] Ruhr-Univeristät Bochum, Dept of Archeological Sciences, Bochum, Germany

Introduction

In conjunction with the SFB HiMAT, the Deutsches Bergbau Museum in Bochum initiated in 2006 a new series of prospection and excavation campaigns in the environs of the Mitterberg mining district. One of the goals of these activities was to reevaluate almost 150 years of archaeological investigation using modern methods, and to form a chronological, technological and economical model of a major Bronze Age copper production region (see Stöllner et al., 2009; 2011a). The archaeological remains range from mining depressions and dumps from open casts and belowground mining activities, but also remains of ore beneficiation, and smelting activities. This paper is concerned with the last of these metallurgical features. The smelting sites, recognizable by their slag heaps, dot the landscape in a wide arc around the mines, sometimes at a considerable distance to the closest known ore source (*Fig. 1*).

In order to place the smelting sites within the modern landscape, the hand-drawn maps from the literature (e.g., Zschocke & Preuschen, 1932) were georeferenced and integrated into a GIS database (A. Hornschuch, DBM). The database was then used to relocate the sites, pinpoint their exact location within the landscape, to record their degree of preservation and to collect material to date them via radiocarbon dating. Additionally, in order to gain more information about the size and theoretical production output, an intensified prospection program including geophysical prospection and coring was carried out at 6 different smelting sites spread around the Mitterberg main load[1] (*Fig. 1*).

The strong magnetic anomalies created by the metallurgical debris make them ideal candidates for geomagnetic prospection, which was carried out using either a single channel handheld fluxgate gradiometer (B. Sikorski, Ruhr Universität Bochum) or a 6-channel foester FEREX gradiometer mounted on a hand pulled cart (Eastern Atlas GmBH, B. Ullrich). Care was taken to layout the grid, whenever possible, in a relatively wide area around the visible remains in an effort to measure the complete smelting site.

Due to the fact that these Middle to Late Bronze Age smelting sites have an extremely similar organizational plan – not only in the Mitterberg area, but also in many other eastern alpine production centers – it is possible to interpret with relative accuracy in most cases the position of the roasting beds, furnaces and slag heaps from the geomagnetic anomalies (*Fig. 2, left*). In some cases, overlapping of several different phases of furnaces and slag heaps, as well as destruction

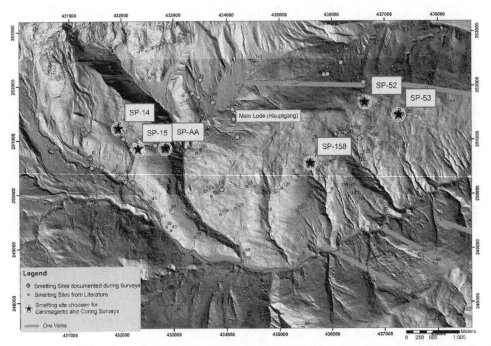

Fig. 1: LiDAR scan of Mitterberg Mining District with smelting sites and ore veins (Photo: DBM, A. Hornschuch).

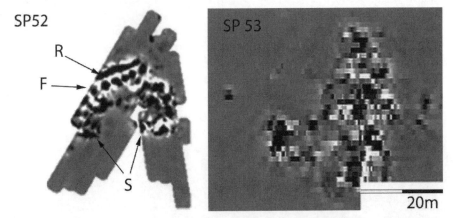

Fig. 2: Two examples of the geomagnetic surveys. At SP 52 (left), the position of the roasting beds (R), furnaces (F) and slag heaps (S) are clearly discernable. At SP 53, destruction and/or overlapping of individual features makes it difficult to locate their position in the geomagnetic anomalies. (Photo: B. Ullirch, Eastern Atlas, B. Sikoriski, RUB).

of the site through subsequent land use makes it impossible to discern the position of the furnace batteries and roasting beds from the geomagnetic anomalies alone (*Fig. 2, right*).

Coring of the features also allowed confirmation of the type and position of the pyrometallurgical installations interpreted from the geomagnetic surveys. Systematic coring and small sondages through the slag dumps was also done in order to calculate the volume of the individual sites, as well as to gain material for further archaeometrical analyses. Two types of corers were used: a hand driven slit corer (= Pürkhauer corer) and a motor driven percussion corer (= Cobra corer). The Pürkhauer corer has the advantage of being relatively light, easily taken into the field. The fine stratigraphy is also preserved without a large amount of compression of the individual layers. It does not do well, however, with coarse material such as large pieces of slag or stone, which are frequent in mining tips and slag heaps and inhibit the passage of the corer. For this reason, the larger Cobra corer was also used, which can literally punch through most material and retain coarse sediment in the sampling chamber. Using alternating Pickhauer- and Cobra coring points, it was possible to gain information about the coarse material in the slag dumps, while correcting the depth and position of the finer stratigraphy.

The core profiles could then by laid on top of the geomagnetic maps in order to give a good estimation of the circumference and depth of the slag heaps (*Fig. 3*). An approximation of the site's size is an important factor for the calculation of the theoretical output of copper metal being produced at the site and in turn being produced in the district as a whole (ex. Stöllner et al., 2011b). In order to gain a better estimate of the amount of slag in comparison to other material (sediment, stone, organic material, etc.) is actually present in the dumps, a vertical sample was taken from the centre of the dump, taking ca. 10 l of material for every 10cm of depth. The total volume of the sample was recorded and was then wet sieved using standardized mesh sizes ranging from 0.25mm up to 22.5mm. Sieve fractions down to 8mm were completely sorted by hand, separating, slag, clay, bone and stone. Remains of poor quality ore and gangue material were also separately recorded. For the sieve fractions between 2 and 8mm, a small representative sample was taken and the slag sorted out by hand. The presence of slag in the sieve fractions below 2mm was checked using XRD analyses by looking for fayalite-like phases which are almost always present in the Bronze Age copper slag from Mitterberg (ex. Viertler, 2011), but not present as mineral in the local rocks. In order to try to develop a typology of the different types of slag in the samples, which could be used to compare and contrast slag from the different sites, all pieces of slag above 22mm were individually recorded in a database, recording their characteristics such as external appearance, size, weight, density, porosity, number of original surfaces, type and size of inclusions, color, and magnetisim. Additionally both XRD and XRF analysis (D. Kirchner, DBM) were done on powdered samples taken from the different sorted sieve fractions to give information of the bulk mineral and chemical content from the different sites.

This very detailed recording of the samples led to some interesting results. One of the sites chosen for the intensified survey program, site SP14, will be used here as an example:

In this case, the slag heap sample was comprised of only ca. 35% slag over 2mm in diameter, while the other 65% was comprised of water, sediment and stone (*Fig. 4*). The determination of

Fig. 3: Smelting site SP 14 with geomagnetic anomalies, sondages, and coring points (Foto: DBM, E Hanning, P. Thomas).

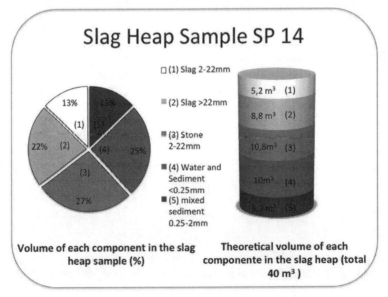

Fig.4: Contents of the sample through the slag heap from SP 14 in vol% and m³ (E. Hanning).

the amount of slag vs. other material is analogous to the "packing factor", which is used in an equation put forward by Bachmann (1982:5) for the calculation of the amount of slag found at a site: *Slag-covered area x depth x specific gravity of the slag² x packing factor = amount of slag (metric tons)*. When the slag density and packing factor are unknown, Bachmann puts forward an average value of $3.5 g/cm^3$ for the slag and a packing factor of 0.8 (i.e. 80% of the slag dump is comprised of slag). Using these theoretical values and a volume of $40 m^3$, as interpreted by the coring profiles and geophysical survey, the amount of slag expected to be at SP 14 would be 112 metric tons. However, when the packing factor is reduced to 0.35 (35% slag in the slag heap) then only roughly $14 m^3$ in the $40 m^3$ slag heap is expected to be slag. The average density calculated from the 210 individually recorded pieces of slag from the SP14 sample was $2.611 g/cm^3$, which is also significantly lower than the average density given by Bachmann. Using these site-specific values, then roughly 36.5 metric tons of slag[3], instead of the 112 metric tons, would be expected to be present – a difference of 75 tons. When the depositional context was not taken into account, there was a significant overestimation of the slag present, which would in turn lead to an overly large theoretical output of metal being produced at the site.

This number must of course also be viewed as an approximation, as the slag heaps are far from homogenous and some material would have been transported away from the site, either by erosion or subsequent use of the land for agriculture or other activities. Ideally the method should be double checked by fully excavating the site and weighing the full amount of slag and sediment present, which is not only extremely time consuming and labor intensive, but would also lead to the complete destruction of the archaeological deposit.

Conclusion

The combination of geomagnetic surveys, systematic coring and sampling of the slag heaps has proved to be an effective way to quantify smelting sites, allowing the efficient investigation of a larger area and creating a more detailed view of a complex copper production landscape. The study has also highlighted the importance of taking the depositional context into account, in order to gauge the amount of metallurgical debris actually present at the site. When morphology and depositional characteristics of the slag heap were not taken into consideration, there was a substantial overestimation of slag at the smelting site, which would in turn lead to a gross overestimation of the theoretical metal production.

Acknowledgements

The study was conducted by the Deutsches Bergbau-Museum Bochum, PP 07 "Der Mitterberg – Ostalpine Erzproduktion in großem Maßstab während der Bronzezeit", within the framework of the SFB HiMAT financed and supported by the Austrian Science Fund (FWF).

Endnotes

[1] The copper smelting remains from Mitterberg are currently being reevaluated as part of E. Hanning's PhD dissertation, Ruhr Universität Bochum.

[2] Bachmann mistakenly refers to the specific gravity of the slag, which is a ratio and is a unitless value. For the calculation of the weight of the slag present at the site, one needs to take into account the density of the slag, which is the amount of mass per volume.

[3] At the time of a previous article written by the authors (Stöllner et al., 2011), the average slag density (2.611 g/cm3) from the site SP 14 had not been calculated, so an average slag value was taken from Bachmann - 3.5g/cm3 (1982:5), leading to a lower estimate of the tonnage of slag at the site.

Bibliography

Bachmann, H. G. (1982): The Identification of Slag from Archaeological Sites. Institute of Archaeology, Occasional Publication no. 6, London.

Stöllner, Th.; Thomas, P.; Maass, A. & Röttger, K (2009): Großproduktion für Kupfer im Raum Mitterberg in der Bronzezeit – Forschungsbericht für die Jahre 2007 und 2008. In: Oeggl, K. & Prast, M. (eds.): Die Geschichte des Bergbaus in Tirol und seinen angrenzenden Gebieten. Proceedings zum 3. Milestone-Meeting des SFB-HiMAT vom 23. - 26.10.2008 in Silbertal. Innsbruck, pp. 231-242.

Stöllner, Th.; Breitenlechner, E.; Eibner, C.; Herd, R.; Keinlin, T.; Lutz, J.; Maass, A.; Nicolussi, K.; Pichler, Th.; Pils, R.; Röttger, K.; Song, B.; Taube, N.; Thomas, P. & Thurner, A. (2011a): Der Mitterberg als Großproduzent für Kupfer. In: Goldenberg, G.; Töchterle, U.; Oeggl, K. & Kren-Leeb, A. (eds.) Forschungsprogramm HiMAT, Neues zur Bergbaugeschichte der Ostalpen. Archäologie Österreichs Spezial 4, pp. 113-144.

Stöllner, Th.; Hanning, E. & Hornschuch, A. (2011b): Ökonometrie des Kupferproduktionsprozesses am Mitterberg Hauptgang. In: Oeggl, K.; Goldenberg, G.; Stöllner, Th. & M. Prast (eds.): Die Geschichte des Bergbaues in Tirol und seinen angrenzenden Gebieten. Proceedings zum 5. Milestone-Meeting des SFB HiMAT vom 07.-10.10.2010 in Mühlbach. Innsbruck University Press. pp. 115-128.

Viertler, J. P. (2011): Mineralogie und Petrologie von prähistorischen Kupferschlacken im Gebiet Mitterberg (Salzburg). Diplomarbeit, Institut für Minerlogie und Petrographie, Universität Innsbruck.

Zschocke, K. & Preuschen, E. (1932): Das Urzeitliche Bergbaugebiet von Mühlbach-Bischofhofen. Wien: Selbstverlag Anthropologischen Gesellschaft in Wien.

Prehistoric copper production in the region of Kitzbühel, North Tyrol - mining and smelting

Thomas Koch Waldner[1]

[1] Institute of Archaeology, University of Innsbruck, Austria

Because of the numerous finds related to the prehistoric copper production, Kitzbühel is one of the best known prehistoric copper mining districts in the Alps.

The research focused specifically on the ore processing heaps in the Kelchalm region, where Richard Pittioni and Ernst Preuschen performed large excavations in the 1930s until the 1950s (Preuschen & Pittioni, 1937, 1954; Pittioni, 1947; Klaunzer 2008). Preuschen and Pittioni located more than 50 ore-processing heaps in the Kelchalm district near Aurach. The archaeological records and discoveries, like stone and wooden tools, found during the excavations enable a reconstruction of the ore processing operation chain. Hammer and anvil stones were used to crush the mix of rock and ore into finely ground particles. Due to the different specific weight of dead rock and ore, these components were separated with water. Some of the most relevant finds related to these wet processing techniques are two troughs with an original size of about 175x80cm as discovered (Preuschen & Pittioni, 1954:20-22, 69, Fig. 10-13 & 36/1). They were made out of fir trunks with diameters of around 80cm. The better preserved trough still has a transversely situated wood lath at the interior. One end of the lath is fixed in a furrow so it was still movable vertically when it was necessary. This construction concept is similar to that from the wet-processing box found on the Troiboden in the Mitterberg district (Stöllner et al., 2011).

Several underground mining sites were found by modern miners during mining activities in the 19th century (Much, 1879:18-36; 1902:1-31). After the modern mining came to an end, the mining entrances broke down. Today none of the prehistoric mining sites are accessible. To gain a picture of the Bronze Age mining, we have to combine different sources, such as historic mining reports, mining maps, and sinkholes on the surface which are related to prehistoric mining activities.

Further information can be obtained by few finds related to the underground mining. Handles for bronze picks (Preuschen & Pittioni, 1937:61; Pittioni, 1947:62-63) and tapers have been found during the excavations on the Kelchalm. The handles are similar in type to those used in the Bronze Age mining district of Mitterberg in Salzburg (Klose, 1918:11, 19, Fig. 29; Eibner, 1998:88; Thomas, 2012:163-169). Even though no bronze picks were found in the region of Kitzbühel, the handles prove that the same socketed picks like those mainly found in Salzburg (Thomas, 2012:237-245) were used for mining in the Kelchalm district.

The significant technological similarities in mining and ore processing with the Mitterberg district suggests a transfer of knowledge or perhaps even a migration from the Mitterberg area to the region of Kitzbühel.

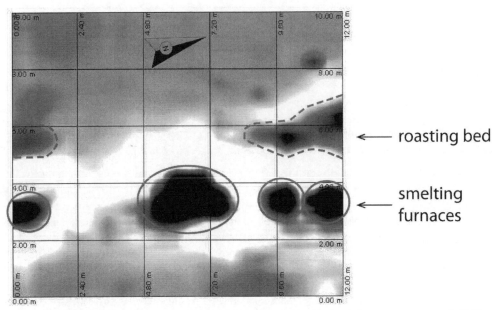

Fig. 1: Magnetic field measurement results from the smelting site WH/SP 3 (Measurement: Koch Waldner & Skomorowski).

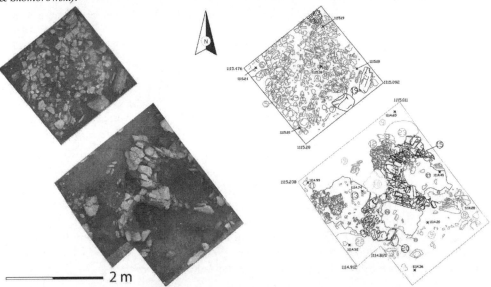

Fig. 2: Photogrammetric and a drawn map of the excavation of the smelting site WH/SP 5. Double smelting furnaces and roasting bed (Foto & Plan: Koch Waldner & Skomorowski).

Smelting sites

Beside the mining and the ore processing features on the Kelchalm, approximately 50 smelting sites have been located in the communal areas of Kitzbühel, Aurach, and Jochberg in the valley bottom as well as on the mountain slopes (Pittioni 1968; Huijsmans, 1993; Krauß, 2004; Goldenberg, 2004; Koch Waldner et al., 2013). Most of the sites investigated are characterized by different slag types such as slag blocks, plate slags, and slag sand. During the investigations in 2011 and 2012 only one smelting site (WH/SP 5) had no evidence of plate slags and processed slags (Koch Waldner et al., 2013).

Although Preuschen and Pittioni had investigated and partly excavated some of these sites in the 1950s until the 1970s, no sufficiently preserved furnaces or similar features were found.

At the smelting site WH/SP 1 four prehistoric furnaces and a mutiphase roasting bed were excavated for the first time in the 1990s (Goldenberg, 2004). These results allow comparisons with smelting plants in other prehistoric mining districts. The site is situated in the area of the Wurzhöhe in the west of Jochberg in a flat area 1305m a.s.l.

In the summer months of 2011 and 2012 additional smelting sites were investigated in this area. WH/SP 2: The smelting site WH/SP 2 is situated above a steep slope 1372m a.s.l., just 280m to the northwest of the site WH/SP 1. Due to excavation work for a small water reservoir, parts of the smelting site were destroyed and many finds like slag fragments, ceramic, and grinding stones came to the surface. Next to the reservoir, an intact part of the slag sand heap was excavated (Koch Waldner et al., 2013). The rest of a wooden construction and an ash dump have been documented. Many quartz fragments with small ore contents were located in a small area of this heap.

WH/SP 3: At the smelting site WH/SP 3 (SP 10: Preuschen & Pittioni, 1955) 1490m a.s.l. many quartz fragments with minimal ore content were found on the surface of a slag sand heap. During a small excavation in autumn of 2011 additional ore residues were found in the heap.

Uphill from the slag sand heap a concentration of furnace stones was documented. By magnetic field measurements in this area, several magnetic anomalies were precisely located and interpreted as four to five furnaces and at least one roasting bed (*Fig. 1*).

The ore residues on several sites in the area of the Wurzhöhe, suggests that in some cases ore was processed at the smelting site. This circumstance might be linked to the fact that some of the smelting plants were situated near ore deposits.

WH/SP 5: Another smelting plant was excavated in the summer 2012. The site WH/SP 5 (SP 27: Pittioni, 1968) is situated 1115m a.s.l., 1km northeast of the site WH/SP 1. Two boarding stones of a roasting bed were visible on the surface. A double furnace and part of a roasting bed were excavated (*Fig. 2*), which were identified through geomagnetic surveys.

The roasting bed was comprised of clay and stone slabs with bigger stones surrounding as a border. The lower parts of the furnaces, about 35cm of the walls, were preserved (*Fig. 3*). The

Fig. 3: Front view of the double Furnace (Foto: Koch Waldner).

bottom of each heating room was an even clay layer with a surface area of 0.5x0.8-1m. Some slag blocks were dumped into two pits on the back sides of the furnaces.

This smelting site is the only site investigated in 2011 and 2012 that did not deliver any slag sand or plate slags. The absence of these slag types shows that some techniques used on the other sites were not used on the site WH/SP 5. This could be explained by an older age of this site. Radiocarbon datings will help to resolve this question.

Slag processing

To extract copper matte, metallic copper, and ore residue from the slag, the blocks of slag were processed to slag sand. The archaeological discoveries from the smelting sites with slag sand heaps suggest that the processing of slags was done with a similar technique as with ore.

In the first step, the slag blocks were crushed and ground to fine particles using anvil and hammer stones. In the second step the copper matte, metallic copper, and ore residue were extracted from the slag with water. Two gutters situated parallelly were excavated on the smelting site WH/SP 4 near the Wagstättalm in the area of the Wurzhöhe (Koch Waldner et al., 2012; Koch Waldner & Goldenberg, 2012). The archaeological investigation has shown that these constructions were used for the wet processing of slag.

Similar constructions for wet processing of slag sand have been found at two smelting sites in the lower Inn valley. The first one is situated in Radfeld near Brixlegg (Goldenberg & Rieser, 2004) and the other in Buch near Schwaz (Klaunzer & Staudt, 2011). The traces of prehistoric mining and smelting activities in the mining district of Schwaz-Brixlegg were dated to the late Bronze Age and early Iron Age (Goldenberg et al., 2012). Another important copper production centre of the late Bronze Age is situated in the Southern Alps in the southeast of Trentino. The results of the investigation of the smelting site Acqua Fredda showed that slag was also processed to slag sand in this late Bronze Age smelting site (Cierny et al., 2004).

The common features of the late Bronze Age smelting sites in different mining districts raise the assumption that the mentioned slag processing techniques are phenomena of the late Bronze Age.

Dating

In the region of Kitzbühel, three smelting sites with slag sand heaps have been already dated. The site WH/SP 1 was dated by ^{14}C-analysis to the 14th/13th century BC (Goldenberg, 2004). Similar results have been gained by analysing charcoal from the site WH/SP 3. The first ^{14}C-sample dates were to the 14th/13th century BC. The calibrated sample GrA-4792_JOVO13 3040 +/- 30 BP has a probability of 95.4% 1410-1210. Further samples will be analysed to get a more precise dating.

Some of the wood chips found in the slag sand processing plant on the site WH/SP 4 have been dated through dendrochronological analyses. Thomas Pichler from the Institute of Geography, University of Innsbruck, was able to reconstruct two tree-ring-series and enabled the first exact dating of a smelting site in this region. According to the results, one tree was cut in the summer of 1272 BC and the other in the dormant season of 1271/70 BC.

Dendrochronological analysis of wooden findings from the Kelchalm dated the processing heaps into the 1250s-1230s BC (Pichler et al., 2009).

Several urn graves were excavated on the prehistoric cemetery in the area of Lebenberg in the city of Kitzbühel (Pittioni, 1952; Eibner et al., 1966; Scheiber, 2011). According to the relative chronology based on the spectrum of finds, this cemetery was used at least from the late 14th until the late 11th BC (Scheiber, 2011:75).

The absolute dating of smelting and mining sites in the 14th/13th century BC combined with the relative dating of the cemetery Lebenberg show that human activities increased in this period.

The archaeological result suggests the assumption that the increase of human activities in the region of Kitzbühel was related to the beginning of an extensive mining industry in the phase of transition from the middle to the late Bronze Age.

Archaeobotanical investigations confirm this theory. The results of the pollen analysis show a continuous curve for grain (Cerealia) since the Late Bronze Age (Viehweider, this volume). This suggests an intensification of agricultural activities which could be explained by permanent presence of a bigger group of people in the upper Leuken valley.

Literature

Cierny, J.; Marzatico, F.; Perini, R. & Weisgerber, G. (2004): La riduzione del rame in località Acqua Fredda al Passo del Redebus (Trentino) nell' età del Bronzo Recente e Finale. In: Alpenkupfer – Rame delle Alpi. Der Anschnitt, Beih. 17., Bochum 2004, pp. 125-154.

Eibner, C.; Plank, L. & Pittioni, R. (1966): Die Urnengräber vom Lebenberg bei Kitzbühel, Tirol. Arch. Austriaca 40, 1966, pp. 215-248.

Eibner, C. (1998): Schaubergwerk Arthurstollen. Arch. Österreich 9/1, 1998, 85-89.

Goldenberg, G. (2004): Ein Verhüttungsplatz der mittleren Bronzezeit bei Jochberg (Nordtirol). In: Alpenkupfer – Rame delle Alpi. Der Anschnitt, Beih. 17., Bochum 2004, pp. 165-176.

Goldenberg, G. & Rieser, B. (2004): Die Fahlerzlagerstätten von Schwaz/Brixlegg (Nordtirol) – Ein weiteres Zentrum urgeschichtlicher Kupferproduktion in den österreichischen Alpen. In: Alpenkupfer – Rame delle Alpi. Der Anschnitt, Beih. 17., Bochum 2004, pp. 37-52.

Goldenberg, G.; Breitenlechner, E.; Deschler-Erb, S.; Hanke, K.; Hiebel, G.; Hüster-Plogmann, H.; Hye, S.; Klaunzer, M.; Kovács, K.; Krismer, M.; Lutz, J.; Maass, A.; Moser, M.; Nicolussi, K.; Oeggl, K.; Pernicka, E.; Pichler, T.; Pöllath, N.; Schibler, J.; Staudt, M.; Stopp, B.; Thurner, A.; Töchterle, U.; Tomedi, G.; Tropper, P.; Vavtar, F. & Weinold, T.(2012): Prähistorischer Kupfererzbergbau im Maukental bei Radfeld/Brixlegg. In: Goldenberg, G.; Töchterle, U.; Oeggl, K. & Krenn-Leeb, A. (Hg.): Firschungsprogramm HiMAT-Neues zur Bergbaugeschichte der Ostalpen, Archäologie Österreichs Spezial 4, 2011, Wien 2012, pp. 61-110.

Huijsmans, M. (1993): Tirol, KG Jochberg, OG Jochberg, VB Kitzbühel. Fundber. Österr. 31, 1992, Wien 1993, pp. 445-446.

Klaunzer, M. (2008): Studien zum spätbronzezeitlichen Kupferbergbau auf der Kelchalm und Bachalm, Bezirk Kitzbühel, Nordtirol. Unpubl. Diplomarbeit, Innsbruck.

Klaunzer, M. & Staudt, M. (2011): Fundchronik Bronzezeit, KG Buch, OG Buch bei Jenbach, VB Schwaz. Fundber. Österr. 49, 2010, Wien 2011, p. 417.

Klose, O. (1918): Die prähistorischen Funde vom Mitterberge bei Bischofshofen im städtischen Museum Carolino Augusteum zu Salzburg und zwei prähistorische Schmelzöfen auf dem Mitterberge. In: Kunsthistorisches Institut der k. k. Zentral-Kommission für Denkmalpflege (Hrsg.): Urgeschichte des Kronlandes Salzburg. Österreichische Kunsttopographie 17. Wien 1918, Beitrag II.

Koch Waldner, T.; Staudt, M. & Goldenberg, G. (2012): KG Jochberg, OG Jochberg. Fundber. Österr. 50, 2011, Wien 2012, pp. 414-416.

Koch Waldner, T. & Goldenberg G. (2012): Charakterisierung der bronzezeitlichen Bergbaulandschaft in der Region Kitzbühel – Ergebnisse und Ausblick. In: Oeggl, K. & Schaffer, V. (Hg.): Die Geschichte des Bergbaus in Tirol und seinen angrenzenden Gebieten, Proceedings zum 6. Milestone-Meeting des SFB HiMAT vom 3.-5.11.2011 in Klausen Südtirol, Innsbruck 2012, pp. 126-133.

Koch Waldner T.; Skomorowski, R. & Grutsch, C. (2013): KG Jochberg, OG Jochberg. Fundber. Österr. 51, 2012, Wien 2013 (in print).

Krauß, R. (2004): Tirol, KG Aurach, OG Aurach, VB Kitzbühel. Fundber. Österr. 42, 2003, Wien 2004, pp. 680.

Much, M. (1879): Das vorgeschichtliche Kupferbergwerk auf dem Mitterberge (Salzburg). Mitt. k. k. Central-Commission NF. 5, 1879, pp. 18-36.

Much, M. (1902): Prähistorischer Bergbau in den Alpen, Zeitschrift des deutschen und österreichischen Alpenvereins 33, 1902, pp. 1-31.

Pichler, T.; Nicolussi, K.; Goldenberg, G. & Klaunzer, M. (2009): Die Hölzer des bronzezeitlichen Bergbaus auf der Kelchalm bei Kitzbühel. Dokumentation und erste Ergebnisse dendrochronologischer Analysen. In: Arch. Korr.bl. 39, 2009, pp. 59-75.

Pittioni, R. (1947): Untersuchungen im Bergbaugebiete Kelchalpe bei Kitzbühel, Tirol (2. Bericht). Mitt. Prähist. Komm. Akad. Wiss. 5, 1947.

Pittioni, R. (1952): Das Brandgrab vom Lebenberg bei Kitzbühel, Tirol, Archaeologia Austriaca 10, 1952, pp. 53-59.

Pittioni, R. (1968): Der urzeitliche Kupfererzbergbau im Gebiete um Kitzbühel. In: Stadtbuch Kitzbühel 2, 1968, pp. 32-102.

Preuschen, E. & Pittioni, R. (1937): Untersuchungen im Bergbaugebiete Kelchalpe bei Kitzbühel, Tirol. Mitt. Prähist. Komm. Akad. Wiss. 3, 1937.

Preuschen, E. & Pittioni, R. (1954): Untersuchungen im Bergbaugebiet Kelchalm bei Kitzbühel, Tirol. 3. Bericht über die Arbeiten 1946-53 zur Urgeschichte des Kupferbergwesens in Tirol. Arch. Austriaca 15, 1954.

Preuschen, E. & Pittioni, R. (1955): Neue Beiträge zu Topographie des urzeitlichen Bergbaues auf Kupfererz in den österreichischen Alpen. Arch. Austriaca 18, pp. 45-79.

Scheiber, E.-M. (2011): Das spätbronzezeitliche Gräberfeld am Lebenberg bei Kitzbühel, Tirol. Unpubl. Diplomarbeit der Universität Innsbruck, 2011.

Stöllner, T.; Fritsch, D.; Gontscharov, A.; Kirchner, D.; Nicolussi, K.; Pichler, T.; Pils, R.; Prange, M.; Thiemeyer H. & Thomas, P. (2011): Überlegungen zur Funktionsweise des mittelbronzezeitlichen Nassaufbereitungskastens vom Troiboden. In: Oeggl, K.; Goldenberg, G.; Stöllner T. & Prast M. (Hg.): Die Geschichte des Bergbaus in Tirol und seinen angrenzenden Gebieten, Proceedings zum 5. Milestone-Meeting des SFB HiMAT vom 7.-10.2010 in Mühlbach, 2011, pp. 141-155.

Thomas, P. (2012): Studien zu den Bronzezeitlichen Bergbauhölzern im Mitterberger Gebiet. Unpubl. Dissertation der Ruhr-Universität Bochum, 2012.

Prehistoric mining in central Italy: New evidence from the Monti della Tolfa (Latium)

Daniel Steiniger[1] & Claudio Giardino[2]

[1] Freiburger Institut für Paläowissenschaftliche Studien F.I.P.S., Albert-Ludwigs-Universität, Freiburg i.Br., Germany
[2] Department of Cultural Heritage, University of Salento, Lecce, Italy

Introduction

Italy plays an important role in the diffusion of early metallurgy in the central and western Mediterranean (Stahm, 1994; Sangmeister, 2005; Cevey et al., 2006). According to new radiocarbon dates we are able to trace back the beginnings of extensive local copper metallurgy in central Italy to the mid 4th millennium BC (Dolfini, 2010). Beside copper artefacts there are many Chalcolithic silver objects known from all over Italy and we also know a good quantity of antimony and antimony-oxide jewellery from Chalcolithic graves in Etruria. Next to copper there are very rich silver and native antimony deposits in this area. All this indicates that Chalcolithic mining can be expected for these resources (Steiniger, 2010; Giardino & Steiniger, 2011). But where is the metal mining in central Italy? By now it is still not possible to identify a precise relation between Chalcolithic metal objects and a specific ore deposit which could lead to the identification of a Chalcolithic mine with the help of lead isotope analysis (Buresta et al., 2006; Cattin, 2008). So far not all copper deposits of central Italy are analysed yet, therefore our team tries to fill this gap with a collection of ores from the missing sites. In the course of a research project funded by the Rome department of the German Archaeological Institute, several indications for prehistoric mining activities have been identified during extensive field surveys in central Italy (Giardino & Steiniger, 2011). Noteworthy in this context is that Late Neolithic/Early Chalcolithic copper mining is well known north and south of central Italy, e.g. in the Grotta della Monaca in Calabria (Larocca, 2005) and in the copper mines of Liguria (Maggi et al., 2011; Pearce, 2011). In the meantime, in the region with the richest metal deposits of all over Italy – the so called Colline Metallifere (translated: ore hills) – there was no direct evidence for prehistoric copper mining so far. Surprisingly we do have quite good indications for the knowledge of mining in central Italy during the Late Neolithic, as it is demonstrated by several pigment mines, e.g. in the Monte Amiata cinnabar mines in Tuscany. Besides stone-hammers, very typical antler tools were collected during modern mining in the last centuries (Grifoni Cremonesi, 1971; Giardino, 1995; Giardino & Steiniger, 2011). Another example is the recently excavated Late Neolithic cinnabar mine of Buca di Spaccasasso near Grosseto (Cavanna, 2007; Cavanna & Pellegrini, 2007), which is currently re-investigated by Nicoletta Volante (University of Siena). The stone-hammers which were used in this mine are of a particular rough type because they were made of a hard sandstone mined closely beside the cinnabar mine itself.

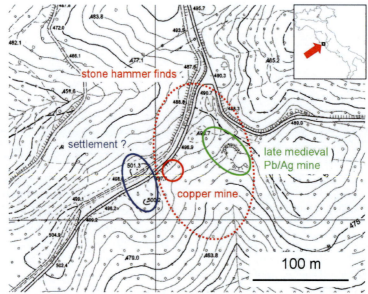

Fig. 1: Map of the mining complex at Poggio Malinverno (Allumiere/Lazio) with schematic indication of stone-hammers, settlement (?) and mining features.

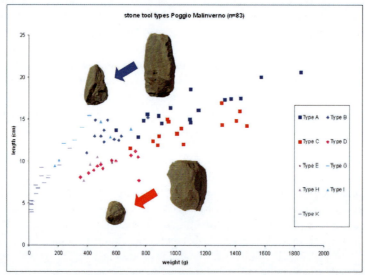

Fig. 3: Length/weight relation of stone-tools from the site of Poggio Malinverno (Allumiere/Lazio). The diagram illustrates the hypothetical steps of fragmentation and reuse during work. Large and heavy stone-hammers (types A and C) loose size and weight during use (types B, D, E - I). Mainly from heavy oval stone-hammers (C) get small round pounders (D). Lateral splitt-off fragments are the lightest group (type K).

Survey

In 2010 surveys started in the Monti della Tolfa, which is the southernmost metalliferous mountain range of Etruria. At a site called Poggio Malinverno (Allumiere, Lazio) a dense concentration of stone-hammers was found next to the road (*Fig. 1*). The stone-hammers from the surface allowed already to distinguish different types, according to size and shape (*Fig. 2*). We propose an interpretation of the fragmentation process and the reuse of bigger fragments illustrated by Figure 3. The long big cylindrical hammers (in the diagram on top) break down to smaller core-like pieces, that were still used until they broke into smaller fragments, indicated on the lower left in the diagram. Another type of stone-hammer can be seen in the lower part of Figure 3; these hammers are thicker, flat and have a round shape. When they broke, some of the remaining core-like pieces seem to be reused as small pounders, which could have been used for small scale work, as "retoucher" to reshape bigger hammer-fragments or for ore treatment. Very similar stone-hammers were recovered at the above mentioned cinnabar mine of Buca di Spaccasasso; the same hard sandstone called "pietra forte" was used as raw material for the hammers from Poggio Malinverno too. The hammers were not made out of pebbles but must be mined somewhere in a quarry. Compared to the Grotta della Monaca or the Ligurian hammers these items are obvious different. One reason can be the use of different raw material. There are no outcrops of magmatic or metamorphic hard rocks that could have been exploited near the two Etrurian mines. The hardest material in the area is the "pietra forte" sandstone of upper Cretaceous-Oligocene age, but this rock does not occur frequently as rounded pebbles in the riverbeds. At Buca di Spaccasasso an outcrop of this rock is just 50m below the mine, where the hammers were produced. Outcrops of "pietra forte" are also located next to the Poggio Malinverno mine.

From a technological point of view we can identify many characteristic similarities between the hammers from the two sites. Some relatively small examples with hafting modifications are noteworthy and discoid, hand held shapes are a common type too. Interesting is that there are mainly notches on the edges instead of proper and deep grooved rills going all around the tools. Some forms were used as wedge or chisel and a portion of them seem to have been shafted with a handle (maybe used as "hammer and pick" but with a wooden "hammer" and a stone "pick"). The distance between the two mines of Buca di Spaccasasso and Poggio Malinverno is less than 90km as the crow flies. A kind of technology transfer between the extraction of cinnabar (pigment mining) and copper (metal mining) in a comparable geological environment seems likely. Before talking about structural relations, technological transfer and socio-economic developments in detail it seem obvious at present that there should be done more research. Due to the current state of research in mining archaeology and our limited knowledge concerning the settlement structure, the organisation of trade routes and the exchange systems it is only possible to start asking questions (for the Alps: Pearce, 2011; for Liguria: Maggi et al., 2011; for central Italy: Giardino & Steiniger, 2011; for Calabria: Larocca, 2005; in this context the flint mining techniques on the Gargano peninsula have to be mentioned too: Galiberti, 2005; Tarantini, 2012).

Fig. 2: Different types of stone-hammers from the surface at the mining complex at Poggio Malinverno (Allumiere/Lazio).

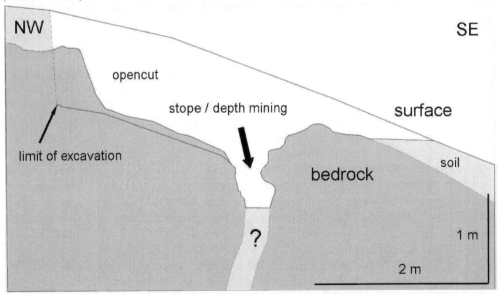

Fig. 4: Schematic drawing of trench 4 profile 5 at Poggio Malinverno (Allumiere/Lazio) mining site excavation 2012. Below a pit-like opencut, a narrow stope follows vertical downwards along the mineralisation. The mining-structures were refilled mainly by dark soil containing several layers of fine crushed minerals. The bedrock consist of partially strongly wheatered, and thus soft, siliceous limestone or massive gangue material (mainly quartz and calcite). In the lower parts the rocks remained fresh and hard.

Excavation 2012

During the first excavation one of the main areas of interest was the dense concentration of hammer-stones along the road. Yet the road constructions have created many distortions and a significant part of the material was dislocated by modern activities. The Poggio Malinverno mining complex is located within siliceous limestone bedrock and contains not only hammerstone finds of old spoil heaps but also large and complex arrangements of late medieval mining dumps, working platforms, probably synchronic or later charcoal production kilns and a big opencast with diverse underground galleries, which belong to an extensive lead and silver mine. Ca. 100m east of the opencast on a small hilltop we presume the existence of a prehistoric settlement due to very coarse and thick pottery that was found in this area by local colleagues as well as during our recent researches.

Between this hilltop and the medieval mine we found a small outcrop of calcite rock, impregnated with azurite and malachite, which displays mining traces that might be interpreted as an ancient or prehistoric copper mine. In the depth quartz appears next to calcite as gangue material and next to copper carbonates primary ores like chalcopyrite, bornite and antimonyfahlores are frequent. Along the northeast side of this rock an opencut or pit-like recess is refilled by partially very dark soil and small crushed mineral debris. On the base of this pit – as always on the last days of the excavation – we discovered that the structure extends vertically downwards in a final narrow trench. We interpret it as a stove which follows the exposed ore vein. After about half a meter depth we had to stop because it got too narrow to follow further downwards without enlarging the trench on one or both sides. Unfortunately it was not possible to dig deeper due to the restricted time schedule, nevertheless is it a very promising spot to continue the excavation. On the southwestern side of the calcite rock we found a shaft-like structure that continues probably deeper. We were able to collect a few pieces of charcoal of the superior layers that filled the shaft; the radiocarbon results are 360 - 30 BC (cal 2 sigma, 2124 ± 45 BP, LTL12808A). The intensive use of the road nearby (only about ca. 5m off) and a dense settlement pattern in the area during Roman Republic times is well documented and therefore we do not interpret the dates of the layers next to the surface as an indication of a Roman mining phase at the site (although that cannot be ruled out). A few meters downhill we have found another trench-like opencut, running in a perpendicular direction to the small underground structure. In the dark layers of the large pit alongside the big rock we recovered few prehistoric pottery sherds in situ. They were without a specific decoration or shape that would determine a special chronological classification. Similar material was also discovered on the hilltop nearby, presumably this provides an evidence for a settlement or cemetery. It is probably that the layers in the pits and shafts represent some spoil or dump coming from that area a few meters up the hill.

Local context

In general the Monti della Tolfa show a dense pattern of Middle and Late Bronze Age sites (Giardino, 1995:109-114), but up to now, only a few non-metallic stray finds were known for the Chalcolithic, without proper context. This situation changed when we relocated two unpublished copper daggers and a Mirabella Eclano type copper axe in the museum of Allumiere. As nearly all Chalcolithic copper daggers in Italy are from graves, it can be expected that these are from the same context and therefore we maybe do not have a Prehistoric copper mine only, but also proper indications for two Chalcolithic cemeteries in the environs. The interesting point is that these daggers are exactly from the mountain ridge that runs from the highest peaks of the Monti della Tolfa down to the sea. Along this path lies the mine, the settlement, and the presumed two graveyards. With these finds the Prehistoric evidence in the Monti della Tolfa increased considerably; and therefore we hope that we can continue the excavation in the mine and our field research during the next years.

Supplementary notes

During fieldwork in summer 2013 we gathered further chronological data for the Poggio Malinverno site. In the area described previously in the paper to be a probable settlement, we have discovered grave finds of typical Proto-Villanovian and Etruscan style in situ, indicating a Late Bronze and Iron Age cemetery (ca. 11-10th and 6th cent. BC). As some of the graves were placed on top of mining debris layers, this gives a terminus ante quem for older mining activity. Although we cannot date the stone-hammers precisely, they most probably predate the Late Bronze Age.

Special thanks for supporting our research to

Deutsches Archäologisches Institut Rom, Università del Salento Lecce, Fritz Thyssen Stiftung Köln, Soprintendenza per l'Etruria Meridionale Roma, Museo Civico di Allumiere, Università Agraria di Allumiere, Comune di Allumiere, Università di Siena, Università di Napoli, Simon Timberlake and Alexander Maass.

We are also grateful to the organisers of the HiMAT-Conference Innsbruck.

Bibliography

Buresta, E.; Giardino, C.; Gaggi, C. (2006): Indagini archeometallurgiche su reperti preistorici dalla Val di Chiana: lo sfruttamento dei giacimenti toscani nelle prime fasi delle età dei metalli. Rivista di Scienze Preistoriche 56, pp. 273-292.

Cattin, F. (2008): Modalités d'approvisionnement et modalités de consommation du cuivre dans les Alpes au 3e millénaire avant notre ère: apport des analyses métalliques à la connaissance des peuplements du Néolithique final, du Campaniforme et du Bronze ancien. Dép. d'anthrop. et d'écologie de l'Univ. (Thèse de doctorat: Faculté des sciences. Section de biologie; Archéol. préhist.; Sc. 4019), unpublished doctoral thesis, Genève.

Cavanna, C. (2007): Spaccasasso: una cava di cinabro. In: Cavanna, C. (ed.): La preistoria nelle grotte del parco naturale della Maremma. Atti del Museo di Storia naturale della Maremma, Supplemento al numero 22, Grosseto, pp. 207-220.

Cavanna, C. & Pellegrini, E. (2007): La Buca di Spaccasasso: ricerche 2000-2004. In: Cavanna, C. (ed.): La preistoria nelle grotte del parco naturale della Maremma, Atti del Museo di Storia naturale della Maremma, suppl. al n. 22: 117-136.

Cevey, C.; Günther, D.; Hubert, V.; Hunger, K.; Hildbrand, E.; Kaeser, M.-A.; Lehmann, E.; Müller-Scheessel, M.; Wörle-Soares, M.; Strahm, C.; Van Willigen, S. (2006): Neue archäometallurgische Untersuchungen zum Beginn der Kupfermetallurgie in der Schweiz. Archéologie Suisse t. 29, 1, pp. 24-33.

Dolfini, A. (2010): The origins of metallurgy in central Italy: New radiometric evidence. Antiquity 84(325), pp. 707-723.

Galiberti, A. (2005): Defensola. Una miniera di selce di 7000 anni fra. Siena.

Giardino C. (1995): Il Mediterraneo occidentale fra XIV e VIII secolo a.C. Cerchie minerarie e metallurgiche. The West Mediterranean between the 14th and 8th Centuries BC. Mining and metallurgical spheres. BAR International Series 612, Tempus Reparatum, Oxford.

Giardino, C. & Steiniger, D. (2011): Evidenze di miniere preistoriche nell'Etruria Meridionale. In: C. Giardino (ed.): Archeometallurgia: dalla conoscenza alla fruizione. Atti del Workshop, 22-25 maggio 2006 (Cavallino (LE), Convento dei Domenicani). Beni archeologici - conoscenza e tecnologie, Vol 8. Bari, pp. 289-292.

Grifoni Cremonesi, R. (1971): Revisione e studio dei materiali preistorici della Toscana. Atti della Società toscana di Scienze naturali. Memorie, s. A 78, pp. 170-300.

Larocca, F. (2005): La miniera pre-protostorica di Grotta della Monaca (Sant'Agata di Esaro - Cosenza). Roseto.

Maggi, R.; Campana, N.; Pearce, M. (2011): Pirotecnologia e cronologia. Novità da Monte Loreto. In: C. Giardino (ed.): Archeometallurgia: dalla conoscenza alla fruizione. Atti del Workshop, 22-25 maggio 2006 (Cavallino (LE) Convento dei Domenicani). Beni archeologici - conoscenza e tecnologie, Vol. 8, Bari, pp. 281-287.

Pearce, M. (2011): Le evidenze archeologiche di estrazione mineraria preistorica in Italia settentrionale. In: Giardino, C. (ed.): Archeometallurgia: dalla conoscenza alla fruizione. Atti del Workshop, 22-25 maggio 2006 (Cavallino (LE), Convento dei Domenicani). Beni archeologici - conoscenza e tecnologie, Vol. 8. Bari, pp. 253-266.

Sangmeister, E. (2005): Les débuts de la métallurgie dans le sud-ouest de l'Europe: l'apport de l'étude des analyses métallographiques. In: Ambert, P.; Vaquer, J. (eds.): La première métallurgie en France et dans les pays limitrophes. Actes du colloque international, Carcassonne 2002, Mém. Société Préhistorique francaise, XXXVII, pp. 19-25.

Steiniger, D. (2010): The relation between copper and flint daggers in chalcolithic Italy. In: P. Anreiter (ed.), Mining in european history and its impact on environment and human societies: Proceedings for the 1st Mining in European History-Conference of the SFB-HiMAT, 12.-15. November 2009, Innsbruck. Innsbruck, pp. 151-156.

Strahm, C. (1994): Die Anfänge der Metallurgie in Mitteleuropa. Helvetia Archeologia 25, pp. 2-39.

Tarantini, M. (2012): A view from the mines. Flint exploitation in the Gargano (South-Eastern Italy) and socio-economic aspects of raw materials procurement at the dawn of metal production. In: Conati Barbaro, C. & Lemorini, C. (eds.): Social, economic and symbolic perspectives at the dawn of metal production. BAR international series 2372. Oxford, pp. 53-63.

Mining technologies at deep level in Antiquity: The Laurion mines (Attica, Greece)

Patrick Rosenthal[1], Denis Morin[2], Richard Herbach[2,3], Adonis Photiades[4], Serge Delpech[5], Denis Jacquemot[5] & Lionel Fadin[6]

[1] UMR CNRS 6249 Laboratoire Chrono-environnement, Université de Franche-Comté, France
[2] UMR CNRS 5608 Laboratoire TRACES, Travaux et Recherches Archéologiques sur les Cultures, les Espaces et les Sociétés, Université de Toulouse-le-Mirail, France
[3] Université de Technologie de Belfort-Montbéliard (UTBM), France
[4] Institute of Geology and Mineral Exploration (IGME), Attica, Greece
[5] Equipe Interdisciplinaire d'Etudes et de Recherches Archéologiques sur les Mines Anciennes et le Patrimoine Industriel (ERMINA), Besançon, France
[6] French school at Athens (EFA), Greece

The silver mines of Laurion (Attica, Greece) were the most important mining district of ancient Greece during the fifth and fourth century AC. This source of wealth highly contributed to the power of Athens (Ardaillon, 1987; Conophagos, 1980; Domergue, 2008). Mining, and metallurgical remains were scattered on an area extending almost 150km^2.

In 1865 started the mining resumption of Laurion, first by the treatment of the ancient slags and waste (Ledoux, 1874) and quickly by reopening of the mines (Cordella, 1869; Cambrésy, 1889; Conophagos, 1980). Therefore, more than one hundred years of extracting of lead, zinc and silver singularly led to the rediscovery, to the use, and sometimes to the destruction of ancient works. Contemporary mining works closed in 1977. Since these last operating phases, these researches as described are the first systematic underground deep exploration and survey ever carried out between Spitharopoussi plateau and Megala Pefka valley (*Fig. 1*).

Geological mapping, field investigation, and survey (surface, shafts and galleries), and underground explorations lead to a revision of the lithostratigraphic subdivision (Morin & Photiades, 2005). This new data allows to specify the geometry of the enclosing beds (*Fig. 2*) and provides substantial details about ancient mining technologies.

Geology

The Lavreotiki peninsula is located in the northwestern Attic-Cycladic metamorphic complex; it belongs to the median metamorphic belt of the Hellenides and is built up of various alpine tectonic units (Photiades & Carras, 2002; Photiades et al., 2004). In this context, rich deposits of zinc, lead and silver have concentrated (Leleu, 1966; Voudouris et al., 2008; Bonsall, 2011; Berger et al., 2013).

The study area is mainly composed of metamorphic rocks with (bottom to top) Lower and Upper Kamariza marbles (80 to 100m thick) interpreted as opposite Triassic-lower Jurassic limbs of a

90   Session II: Production & Technology

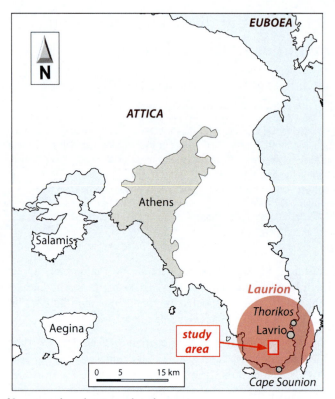

Fig. 1: Location of Laurion silver district and study area.

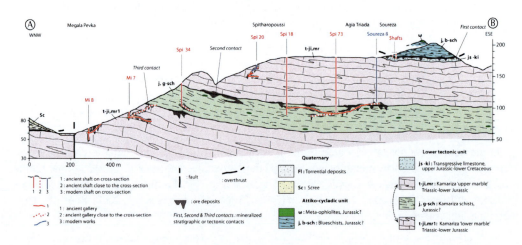

Fig. 2: Geological cross-section with mineralized contacts, ancient mining shafts and networks.

recumbent syncline with hinge made of Jurassic Kamariza schist (15 to 40m); the Transgressive calcareous formation (Jurassic) overlaying locally upper Kamariza marble and finally, the Laurion blueschist unit (Jurassic) with meta-ophiolite overthrusted on previous layers (*Fig. 2*).

The ancient miners managed to separate lead and silver from ores as galena and cerussite (Conophagos, 1980). They developed an impressive complex of absolutely vertical shafts (Morin et al., 2013) and mining network through marbles and micaschists up to deep level.

An upper ore occurrence is related to the tectonic contact between the Laurion blueschist unit and the Transgressive calcareous formation or the Upper Kamariza marble. It includes oxides with calcite-fluorite matrix and lead, zinc and silver sulphides speckled in porous carbonate of the Transgressive calcareous formation. It has been called first contact by the nineteenth century miners.

Near the contact between Upper Kamariza marble and Kamariza schist, a cerussite ($PbCO_3$) and smithsonite ($ZnCO_3$) occurrence in a more or less brecciated matrix with fluorite and quartz, forms the so called second contact of the nineteenth century miners.

A lower occurrence connected with the interface between Kamariza schist and Lower Kamariza marble contains filled cavities with cerussite and iron oxide in a calcite-fluorite-quartz matrix, that is the so called third contact of the nineteenth century miners (*Fig. 2*).

Working methods suitable to the geological setting

Tools

In hard rock as marble, progress in the shafts, galleries and stopes was almost exclusively performed using hammer and handpick (Löhneiss, 1617; Waelkens, 1990). In the schist, more friable, miners used pickaxes, mattocks and iron wedges.

Two scenarios emerge according to the depth and position of the ore deposits:

Mineralized outcrops and shallow deposits

They were initially operated from the surface and deeply by winzes and drifts. The miners extracted the ore from the surface from cracks and joints and often starting from karstic hole, more rarely by sinking shafts from the surface (Spi 15 upper network). Some shallow joints were opencast mined.

In order to progress the miners dug sideward horizontally small section galleries, to probe the size of the mineralization. Working galleries were often deepened after an initial stoping. The inclined extraction was done from the main gallery, by digging the floor. It is therefore common to see the different marks of working faces and drifts at the top of large stopes (Mi 7, Spi 15) (*Fig. 3*). They represent the first step of underhand stoping, initial phase of a generalized lateral robbing.

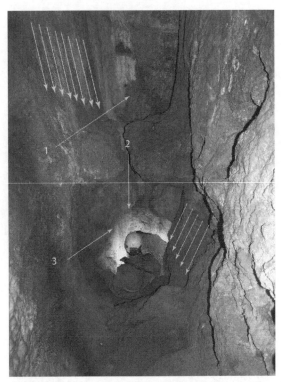

Fig. 3: Mining in marble (Spi 15): Inclined extraction from the main gallery, by digging the floor – conceptual schema.

Some of these works present adjacent exploratory drifts which sometimes are intersecting or coalescent and can be real maze. They look like an anastomosed network which develops into three dimensional ways. Subsequently, this initial framework can be enlarged by stoping walls, roof and floor (Mi 7).

In the Spi 15 shaft upper network, which is close to the first contact, a blind shaft cut from bottom to top was found; such a structure exists in the lower part of the Spi 5 network to provide an access to a higher level.

Deep mineralizations

Two kinds of access toward deep mineralizations can be distinguished according both to geomorphology and to the occurrence layer.

- **Beneath the plateau**, stoping works are linked to the main shafts sunk from Upper Kamariza marble by narrow quadrangular section galleries. Stoping works extend along the axis of a drift through Kamariza schist or in lower Kamariza marble. From there, miners proceeded by cutting working faces (Gruner, 1922) or cells more or less equidistant, while continuing exploitation toward the drift. On either side of it, 5 to 15m long stopes were opened. In the Megala-Pefka-Spi 18 underground network, the height of the drifts ranges from 0.80m to 2.80m. The survey carried out accurately reproduces the morphological characteristics of this kind of network connected up, at the third contact (- 80m), by one of the deepest vertical shafts (101.50m).

The waste (ecvolades) lies directly on the floor, the larger blocks were crushed or carrefully stacked in low walls along the pathways to contain smaller fractions.

This working method made the roof more secure by preserving residual pillars. The stopes were backfilled to get a sufficient height to carry on the works; therefore only mineralized rocks were hoisted to the surface.

- **On the western slope of the plateau**, the bottom of the shafts sunk from Kamariza schist outcrop often opens in the main gallery or in a stope after an eastward offset of axis. Due to the poor stability of the schist, this voluntary offset improved miner's safety at this connecting level. The average orientation of the main gallery is then parallel to the slope. Stopes are developed mostly towards the plateau (Spi 63 network). The quadrangular section main gallery cut in the rock or embanked in stopes partially walled, goes from one stope to another. Stopes are 30 to 40m of horizontal development and 0,80m to a few m high.

The heterogeneous texture of the schist layers prevents cutting it as accurately and securely than marble. Fracturing is a key factor for working options. Except a few pillars, the lack of support induces the collapse of large slabs from the roof. When mineralization goes deeper, miners opened inclined works by digging from the main gallery. Stoping was realized on both sides of these level galleries. The ore was carried outside on men's backs or by dragging.

Mining chronology – first results

Most explored ancient mines seem to fit with a single operating phase. They do not appear to have been a subject to resumption of work except for some networks opened in Lower Kamariza marble (Mi 7) and some others close to surface (Spi 20), easily accessible where the old works can be seen among more recent stopes mostly dated from the nineteenth century. In Megala Pefka – Spi 18 network carried out on the third contact, one can wonder about widenings forming real stoping, the succession of several operating phases has to be considered.

Age dating

According to historical and archaeological data (Ardaillon, 1897; Healy, 1978; Hopper, 1968; Kalcyk, 1982; Lohmann, 2005) complemented by the observations of mining engineers (Cordella, 1869; Conophagos; 1980), a full mining activity in the Laurion area is known during the fifth and fourth century BC and a short recovery during the second century BC.

Fragments of oil lamps found during explorations confirm the fourth century BC data, and indicate roman and byzantine operational phases too in some networks (Blondé, 1983; Butcher,

1982). Several radiocarbon ages on charcoal from small fire places confirm these three main periods.

A short mining portion located at the end of the Spi 18 shaft network shows very narrow galleries and working faces typically worked by fire setting. Charcoal remaining from fire setting places provides a first radiocarbon age (fifth to sixth century AD; 2 sigma cal AD 411: cal AD 542; Poz-47265/Spi18-M5) that could date byzantine mining works.

Acknowledgements

This study was supported by TRACES Laboratory, University and CNRS, Toulouse; Chrono-Environment Laboratory, University of Franche-Comté; University of Lorraine; Lavrion Technological and Cultural Park; Municipality of Lavrio; French School at Athens (EFA); PERSEE Association; Fenzy-Honeywell Safety Products France. We are grateful to the members of the ERMINA National Association whose endurance was severely tried and tested during the underground explorations.

Bibliography

Ardaillon, E. (1887): Les mines du Laurion dans l'Antiquité. Paris.

Berger, A.; Schneider, D. A.; Grasemann, B.; Stockli, D. (2013): Footwall mineralization during Late Miocene extension along the West Cycladic Detachment System, Lavrion, Greece. Terra Nova, 25, pp. 181-191

Blondé, F. (1983): Greek lamps from Thorikos. Miscellanea Graeca, Gent, 6.

Bonsall, T. A.; Spry, P. G.; Voudouris, P. C.; Tombros, S.; Seymour, K. S.; Melfos, V. (2011): The Geochemistry of Carbonate-Replacement Pb-Zn-Ag Mineralization in the Lavrion District, Attica, Greece: Fluid Inclusion, Stable Isotope, and Rare Earth. Economic Geology, 106, pp. 619-651.

Butcher, S. A. (1982): Late Roman lamps from a mine gallery at Thorikos, in Spitaels: Studies in South Attica, 1, Miscellanea Graeca, Gent, 5, pp. 137-48.

Cambrésy, A. (1889): Le Laurion, Revue universelle des Mines, Liège (3),6, pp. 109-128; (3), 7, pp. 76-102, 175-217; (3), 8, pp. 01-17.

Conophagos, C. E. (1980): Le Laurium antique et la technique grecque de la production de l'argent. Athènes.

Cordella, A. (1869): Le Laurium. Marseille.

Domergue, C. (2008): Les mines antiques: la production des métaux aux époques grecque et romaine. Paris.

Gruner, L. E. (1922): Cours d'exploitation des mines. Méthodes d'exploitation en carrière et souterraine. Livres III. Paris.

Healy, J. F. (1978): Mining and metallurgy in the greek and roman world. New York.

Ledoux, C. (1874): Description raisonnée de quelques chemins de fer à voie étroite. Première partie: Chemin de fer d'Ergastiria, Annales des Mines, Paris, (7), 5, pp. 329-427.

Hopper, R. J. (1968): The Laurion mines: A reconsideration, Annual of the British School at Athens, 63, pp. 293-326.

Kalcyk, H. (1982): Untersuchungen zum attischen Silberbergbau: Gebietsstruktur, Geschichte und Technik. Dissertation. München.

Leleu, M. (1966): Les gisements plombo-zincifères du Laurium (Grèce). Sciences de la Terre, Nancy, 9, 3, pp. 293-343.

Lohmann, H. (2005): Prähistorischer und antiker Blei-Silberbergbau im Laurion. No. 124, Der Anschnitt, Bh. 18, pp. 105-136.

Löhneiss, G.E. (1650): Bericht vom Bergwerck. Online-edition, Sächsischen Landesbibliothek – Staats- und Universitätsbibliothek. Dresden.

Morin, D.; Herbach, R.; Rosenthal, P. (2012): The Laurion schafts, Greece. Ancient ventilation systems and mining technology in Antiquity. Historical Metallurgy, 46, 1, pp. 9-18.

Morin, D.; Photiades A. (2005): Nouvelles recherches sur les mines antiques du Laurion (Grèce). Mines et métallurgies dans l'Antiquité. Etat des recherches. Pallas, Toulouse, 67, pp. 327-358.

Photiades, A.; Carras, N. (2002): Stratigraphy and geological structure of the Lavrion area (Attica, Greece), Bull. Geol. Soc. Greece, XXXIV/1, 103-109.

Photiades, A.; Mavridou, F.; Carras, N. (2004): Geological map of Greece "Lavrion sheet" in scale 1:50 000. IGME.

Voudouris, P.; Melfos, V.; Spry, P. G.; Bonsall, T. A.; Tarkian, M.; Solomos, C. (2008): Carbonate-replacement Pb-Zn-Ag±Au mineralization in the Kamariza area, Lavrion, Greece: Mineralogy and thermochemical conditions of formation. Mineralogy and petrology, 94/1-2, pp. 86-106.

Waelkens, M. (1990): Tool Marks and Mining Techniques in Mine. No. 3. in Mussche, H.F. et al.: Thorikos IX – 1977-1980, Gent, pp. 115-143.

Mine drainage in medieval Muslim Spain. Continuities and discontinuities in a cross-cultural context

Constantin Canavas[1]

[1] Faculty of Life Sciences, Hamburg University of Applied Sciences, Germany

A major challenge for mining practice has been the water drainage. The implementation of efficient technologies for removing water became increasingly important with increasing mine depth. In this sense, development and implementation of appropriate hydraulic technologies can be regarded as a determining factor for the spread of mining activities in greater depths and the formation of specific mining patterns.

The present study focuses on evidence considering the practice of mine drainage in medieval Muslim Spain (al-Andalus). The questioning of the study is framed by the consideration of continuities and discontinuities in mining practice in regions under changing political and societal frame. In the case of the medieval Muslim dominion we have good reasons to assume a background of hydraulic knowledge of ingeniously Arab-Islamic origin possibly influenced through practices during the Hellenistic era and Roman Late Antiquity, as well as through Iranian knowhow. However: Did mine engineers in al-Andalus *continue* the Roman mine drainage tradition, or did they implement *different* (Iranian or novel) drainage techniques? What factors might have influenced the drainage technological choices?

Similar questioning can be addressed at the transition from the Muslim to the Catholic dominion. Indeed, in many places there existed repeated ore exploitation, sometimes even since the Roman period, throughout the Muslim into the Catholic era. What continuities or discontinuities, and what changes can be testified with respect to the drainage technology?

In this context written sources, as well as older and recent archaeological evidence are revisited. Information about mining in medieval Muslim Spain is mostly available through Arabic geographies or travelling reports. The results of this cross-checking are then compared with the general record of hydraulic knowledge and practice in Muslim Spain, as well as with mine drainage evidence from the former (Roman) and the next (Christian) periods in the Peninsula and in medieval Central Europe, in order to trace (dis)continuities and changes. The scope of the study is embedded into the perspective of history of technology. Its aim is to systematise questioning and appropriate methodological instruments.

Water in mining practice

Water is involved in various ways in mining practice through mining history. Mine drainage is a necessary prerequisite to maintain underground access to the ore whenever the ground water level is touched. On the other hand, water intrusion (flooding) is a long-term natural consequence of abandoning a working mine.

Mining in the Iberian Peninsula: a controversial subject of medieval historiography?

Metals exploitation as part of economic activities in medieval Muslim Iberian Peninsula has been treated by only few modern scholars (see e.g. Dubler, 1943; Lombard, 1974; Constable, 1994). According to the Arabic sources all seven metals known in the Late Antiquity were found and exploited in Muslim Iberian Peninsula: gold, silver, copper, lead, tin, iron, and mercury. This assertion is based on information provided by geographers and travellers writing in Arabic, such as Ibn Ḥawqal (10th century), al-Bakrī (11th century), al-Idriīsī (12th century), M. al-Ḥimyarī (13th or 15th century?), or scholars such as al-Hamdānī (9th-10th century). A compilation of the historical record was provided by al-Maqqarī in the first half of the 17th century. (For a detailed presentation of the Arabic historical evidence on metals in the medieval Muslim Iberian Peninsula see Dubler, 1943:11-16.)

It should be noted that the information provided by Arab geographers refers to the Christian (Northern) part of the Peninsula too – a peculiarity of special importance for assessing the reliability of the evidence in times of intense Muslim-Christian rivalry (Constable, 1994:xix ff.). Some of this evidence can be checked through references in the Christian archives, in a similar way like in the comprehensive studies of Thomas Glick on irrigation in medieval Valencia (Glick, 1970). A further source of evidence on mining activities are some names of places, such as Almaden (from the Arabic word *al-ma-din*, "mine"), Constantina "of iron" and Castillo del Hierro (Firrīš).

Mining in periods of transition: the cross-ethnical context

The historical frame of the medieval Iberian Peninsula is dominated by transition periods: from Roman/Visigoths to Arab- and Berber-Muslim rulers, later to Christian kings. Manifold questioning raises from this background: In what extent did mining practice during the Muslim rule was related to similar practice during the Roman period? Was the need for mine drainage in al-Andalus similar to that during the Roman period? Is there any evidence of know-how transfer with respect to Greco-Roman Late Antiquity hydraulics – or of ingeniously Muslim hydraulic techniques developed in the Eastern Mediterranean or in al-Andalus? Finally: Did the drainage practice in Muslim al-Andalus find continuation in the Catholic dominion, or in medieval Central Europe?

The issue of mine drainage in Arabic sources

The work in the mines seems to be an issue of minor interest in the Arabic sources (Ben Romdhane, 2008:7). Some problems related to underground water in the mining practice are mentioned in the encyclopaedic work of al-Hamdānī, who lived in the 9th-10th century AD in South

Arabia (al-Hamdānī 10th century AD / ed. Toll, 1968:150-151), though no information on using specific drainage techniques is given by the author. The treatise reflects the mining practice (especially in respect with gold and silver) in Muslim Arab societies (al-Hamdānī), with a specific focus on South Arabia. Some important details in his accounts concern evidence and references regarding pre-Islamic mining activities (pp. 148-149), as well as the presence of migrant Iranian specialists in South Arabian silver mines (pp. 144-145). The latter detail is an implicit indication of knowhow transfer from Iran to South Arabia and even beyond – possibly considering several aspects of mining practice, including drainage. Similar thematic references on drainage could not be found in the sources of mining practice in al-Andalus.

Mine drainage during the Roman period

There is rich evidence on Roman mining activities in the Iberian Peninsula till the 3rd century AD. Various drainage techniques are testified through archaeological or historical evidence: non-flooded underground galleries, man-carried pots, man-driven windlass, rotating devices with endless chains for raising water from deep wells, men-driven tread-wheels with clay, wooden or copper buckets (like the ones mentioned by Vitruvius), Archimedean screws (like those mentioned by Vitruvius), and even pumps. For more details see Domergue, 1990:434 ff., 443 ff., 450 ff.; see also Craddock, 2008:100 for evidence on regulations regarding the maintenance of Roman mine drainage systems, as well as pp. 113-114 for indications on the use of several drainage techniques in Roman mines in the Iberian Peninsula. In one of these techniques, the counter-excavation technique, tunnels are driven from two sides of a shaft, e.g. in the gold mine of Três Minas. For a similar technique, the *qanāt*, in the Roman context see Grewe 2008:322-324. See also Hodge, 1992:20-24 for considerations on Iranian *qanāt*, Etruscan *cuniculi* and mine drainage in the Roman context.

Some of these hydraulic techniques are also known in the general Arab Muslim context, e.g. *sāqiya* (lever), *noria* (rotating device with endless chains), as well as the *qanāt* technique of underground canals. The description provided by al-Hamdānī (al-Hamdānī 10th century AD / ed. Toll, 1968:150-151), a system of perpendicular shafts and underground tunnels which link them, resembles somehow to the *qanāt* technique (Ben Romdhane, 2008:11); however, it contains no explicit reference to the term.

What happened after the Muslim conquest? Archaeological evidence

Till now there is no archaeological evidence of medieval use of the Archimedean screw, neither of *qanāt* for mining drainage in the Iberian Peninsula. Three types of ceramic pots, presumably used for raising water (man-carried, or belonging to an animal- or water-driven *noria*?) were found in a mine at Mirabuenos (Villaviciosa) in the Province of Córdoba dating from the Muslim period; they belong to finds excavated by Antonio Carbonell Trillo-Figueroa in 1945, and they are kept in the Archaeological Museum of Córdoba (Grañeda Miñon, 2008:28; 25, Fig. 3/1: c-d-e).

A peculiar find kept in the Museum of Granada is an acid-resistant high-temperature burned tube with lead-tube extension and chalk-based seal of the junction between clay and lead tube. It was found near Sevilla; presumably it was necessary when chemical substances (e.g. ferric sulphates) were used in mining to render the soil brittle. The special tube met the need of removing the acid aqueous solution from the mine (Dubler, 1943:30ff.). It is not clear, however, what kind of techniques were used to press the acid liquid to the earth surface.

Central European developments – links to Muslim Iberian practice?

In a medieval Central European context we have iconographic evidence of animal-driven (horse, ox) windlass or *noria* with endless chain and buckets or leather balls for raising water from deep wells in the Bohemian mines of Kutna Hora / Kuttenberg dating from 1490 (Winkelmann, 1958:72, Fig. 36). Further evidence indicates the use of man- and water-driven water raising machines (Braunstein, 1983). Despite the comparability between water machines used for drainage in medieval Central European underground excavations and water technological developments in Andalusí irrigation, we cannot trace transmission paths between al-Andalus and medieval Central Europe in respect with drainage technology in mines.

Conclusions

One plausible explanation for explaining discontinuities in the mine drainage techniques is the long time gap between the abandoning of Roman mines and Muslim mining activities in the Iberian Peninsula. Although the drainage techniques used during the Roman period belong to the repertoire of hydraulics in medieval Muslim societies, the evidence of their application in Muslim Iberian peninsula is still poor; systematic archaeological evidence concerning Muslim mines is still missing!

In contrast to the Roman practice of controlling mining activities through the state, the organisation schemes for mining and metallurgy in Muslim al-Andalus followed diversified schemes: silver, gold, and mercury mining was controlled centrally by the Muslim state, whereas iron production seems to have been rather decentralised and based on family or tribal structures. Could that account for different drainage techniques – i.e. when depending on communal water management schemes?

Muslim mines were presumably abandoned before the Christian conquest. Metallurgy in the transition from the Muslim the Christian dominion can be traced only in singular cases. Sufficient evidence on possible continuity in drainage techniques is still missing.

References

Al-Hamdānī, al-Hasan Ibn Al-mad (10th cent. AD): Kitāb al-Ǧauharatain [The Two Precious Metals Gold and Silver]. Arabic text and German transl. ed. by Toll, E., Uppsala 1968.

Ben Romdhane, Kh. (2008): Exploitation des métaux précieux au Mghreb médieval: l'apport des sources écrites. In: Canto García, A. & Cressier, P.: Minas y metalurgia en al-Andalus y Magreb occidental: explotación y poblamiento. – Casa de Velázquez, Madrid, pp. 1-18.

Braunstein, Ph. (1983): Innovations in Mining and Metal Production in Europe in the Late Middle Ages. The Journal of European Economic History, 12/3, pp. 573-591.

Constable, O. R. (1994): Trade and traders in Muslim Spain. The commercial realignment of the Iberian Peninsula, 900-1500. – Cambridge University Press, Cambridge.

Craddock, P. (2008): Mining and Metallurgy. In: Oleson: J. P. (2008): The Oxford Handbook of Engineering and Technology in the Classical World. – Oxford University Press, Oxford, pp. 100.

Domergue, Cl. (1990): Les mines de la péninsule Ibérique dans l'antiquité romaine. – École Française de Rome.

Dubler, C. (1943): Über das Wirtschaftsleben auf der iberischen Halbinsel vom XI. zum XIII. Jahrhundert. Beitrag zu den islamisch-christlichen Beziehungen. – Librairie E. Droz, Genève / E. Rench Verlag, Zürich.

Glick, Th. (1970): Irrigation and Society in Medieval Valencia. – Harvard University Press, Cambridge, Massachusetts.

Grañeda Miñon, P. (2008): La explotación andalusí de la plata en Córdoba. In: Canto García, A. & Cressier, P.: Minas y metalurgia en al-Andalus y Magreb occidental: explotación y poblamiento. – Casa de Velázquez, Madrid, pp. 19-36.

Grewe, K. (2008): Tunnels and Canals. In: Oleson: J. P. (2008): The Oxford Handbook of Engineering and Technology in the Classical World. – Oxford University Press, Oxford, pp. 322-324.

Hodge, A. T. (1992): Roman Aqueducts and Water Supply. – Duckworth, London.

Lombard, M. (1974): Les métaux dans l'Ancien Monde du Ve au XIe siècle. – Mouton, Paris.

Winkelmann, H. (1958): Der Bergbau in der Kunst. Glückauf, Essen.

Mediaeval Iron Smelting in the Area of the Iron Mountain (Steirischer Erzberg) at Eisenerz, Styria (Austria)

Susanne Klemm[1], Susanne Strobl[2] & Roland Haubner[2]

[1] Austrian Academy of Science (ÖAW), Institute for Oriental and European Archaeology (OREA), Vienna, Austria
[2] Institute of Chemical Technologies and Analytics, University of Technology Vienna, Austria

Introduction

Austria's largest iron mine, called Steirischer Erzberg or Iron Mountain, at Eisenerz, Styria, has a long tradition of mining going back to the Middle Ages. Nowadays, Steirischer Erzberg survives as an open pit mine. The destruction of the original surface of the mining area and the inaccessibility of the remaining historical galleries prevent archaeological investigations of the mine at present.

In 1889 two iron smelting sites were discovered at the eastern ridge of the mine. One of these sites, now called 'Feisterwiese 1' was partly excavated in 1929. Since then, a further 27 archaeological sites, where iron slag has been found, have been recorded (Klemm, 2003; Klemm et al., 2012). Based on analogy with the finds (pottery sherds, slag types and ^{14}C-dating) from the Feisterwiese 1 site we date these sites in general to the Mediaeval Period (*Fig. 1*).

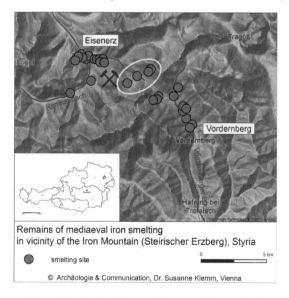

Fig. 1: Mediaeval iron smelting sites in the vicinity of the Iron Mountain (Steirischer Erzberg), Styria; (Graphics: S. Klemm).

Historical written sources demonstrate that mining at Steirischer Erzberg started at the latest in the 12th and 13th century AD, though the earliest mining could go back as far as the Early Middle Ages, probably as early as the 8th century AD (Klemm et al., 2012).

The Archaeological Evidence

In 1889 two iron smelting sites were discovered in an area called 'Feisterwiese' at the eastern ridge of the mine. The first archaeological investigations of one of these sites, now named 'Feisterwiese 1', took place in July 1929 by the Styrian archaeologist Walter Schmid and the engineer Walter Schuster (Schmid, 1932). Archaeometallurgical analyses by Gerhard Sperl and others followed in the late 1970s (Sperl, 1980). The remains of three furnaces were found and were first dated to the Roman Period by Walter Schmid. This early date was later revised to the 14th to 15th/early 16th century AD by a radio-carbon date (Sperl, 1980) as well as by Late Mediaeval pottery sherds found with the slags and other remains of iron smelting (Klemm el al., 2012).

All analysed finds are single or surface finds from the slag dumps of iron smelting sites. This means that the analysed items are random samples. One of the sites is located in a narrow valley called Gerichtsgraben (FP 60108.001) just beside a small stream at 1100m.a.s.l., the other two sites are located on Polster, the steep mountain opposite Steirischer Erzberg.

The site FP 60108.003 is situated beside a small mine and a quarry from a later period (FP 60108.002) at 1530m.a.s.l. on a very steep slope. The steep slag dump covering an area of 25 x 15m lies below a small, flat area of 12 x 6m. The site FP 60108.009 consists of a flat area of 16.5 x 10m and also a very steep slag dump (Klemm, 2003).

Archaeometallurgical analyses

Samples of iron ore, slag and a furnace wall were analysed from the archaeological sites FP 60108.001, 60108.002, 60108.003 and 60108.009 (*Fig. 2a, e; 3a-g*). The samples were prepared for metallographic analyses by light optical microscope (LOM) and scanning electron microscope (SEM). To obtain a general survey of the elemental composition of the samples, X-ray fluorescence analysis (XRF) and energy dispersive X-ray analysis (EDX) in the SEM were used. Selected samples were also investigated by X-ray diffraction (XRD) and differential thermo analysis (DTA).

The iron ore sample:

In Figure 2a an iron ore sample is shown (FP 60108.002-1.2). XRF analysis showed 91 wt.% Fe_2O_3, 5 wt.% SiO_2, 1 wt.% Al_2O_3 and 2 wt.% MnO. The concentrations of other elements were below 1 wt.%. XRD analysis showed goethite – FeO(OH) as crystalline phase only. After metallographic preparation, a layered structure on the surface of the ore became visible when examining it by LOM (*Fig. 2b*). In the SEM the core was quite inhomogeneous with many pores

Session II: Production & Technology 105

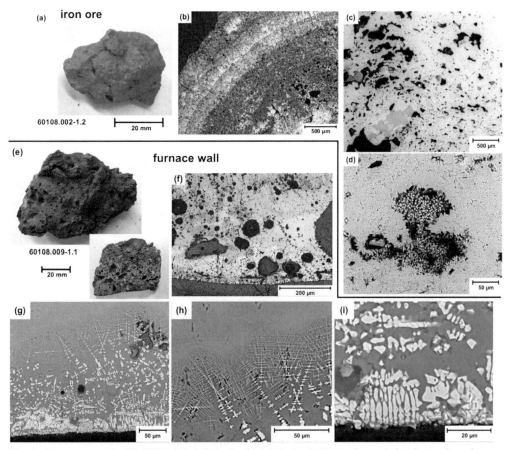

Fig. 2: Iron ore sample FP 60108.002-1.2 (a-d), (b) LOM, (c, d) REM; slagged clay lining from furnace wall FP 60108.009-1.1 (e-i), (f) LOM, (g-i) REM; (Photos: R. Haubner).

(*Fig. 2c*) and a dark-grey Mn-enriched spot (EDX-analysis) was observed on the left side. A large pore with goethite crystals is shown in the centre of Figure 2d.

Sample of slagged clay lining from the furnace wall:

Figure 2e shows the original fragment and a cross section after cutting the sample for metallographic preparation (FP 60108.009-1.1). XRF analysis yielded in 68 wt.% SiO_2, 14 wt.% Al_2O_3, 10 wt.% Fe_2O_3, 3 wt.% Na_2O and 3 wt.% K_2O. In Fig. 2f (LOM) a cross-section through the porous slagged clay lining of the furnace wall can be seen. A narrow band of the reaction zone of the furnace wall is visible at the bottom of Figure 2f. Figure 2g-i (SEM) shows the reaction zone of the clay lining in more detail. There are long dendrites growing from the surface into the clay lining. The Fe-enriched dendrites are thought to be fayalite (Fe_2SiO_4) as indicated by

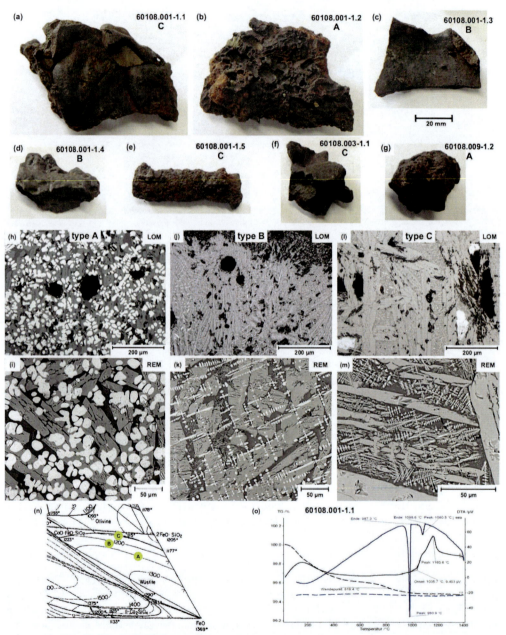

Fig. 3: Slag samples FP 60108.001-1 to 5, 60108.003-1, 60108.009-1 (a-g); metallographic pictures of slag solidification types A, B, C (h-m); FeO-SiO$_2$-CaO phase diagram containing the rough compositions of the solidification types (n); DTA measurement (o); (Photos: R. Haubner).

EDX analysis. We assume that the fayalite-rich slag penetrates the clay lining of the furnace wall during the reduction process.

The metallurgical slag samples:

A classification of the slag into three solidification types (Type A, B, C) is possible from the metallographic investigations and XRF data. Figure 3a-g show the original slag samples, all of them are coarse slags except Figure 3e which is a so-called 'Schlackezapfen'. In Figure 3h-m characteristic microstructures of the three solidification types are shown.

The criterion is the crystallisation sequence of the different phases from the melt. From the XRF data, the compositions of the slags are calculated and plotted into a FeO-SiO_2-CaO phase diagram (*Fig. 3n*). Due to the complexity of the slag composition the melting temperatures in the phase diagram may differ from the actual melting temperatures. To verify the melting behaviour of the slags DTA was carried out using an inert Ar atmosphere. One of these DTA-diagrams is shown in Figure 3o. During the heating process, the weight (TG/% – dashed lines) decreased slightly because of the evaporation of water and because, at higher temperatures, hydroxides and carbonates decomposed. The DTA-signal (DTA/µV – continuous line) showed a melting peak at 1160°C during the heating process. The cooling curve showed a small peak at 1080°C and a large peak at 980°C due to the solidification of the molten slag.

These data show that this slag was created in a bloomery furnace or a furnace of a similar type because the slags melt at higher temperatures during blast furnace processes. Again, there are differences in the crystallisation behaviour of a slag depending on its composition. Generally, one phase crystallises followed by another or by two other phases simultaneously and finally the eutectic composition (ternary eutectic) solidifies. The following phases were identified: wustite (FeO, white), fayalite (Fe_2SiO_4, light-gray) and glass phase (amorphous silicates, dark-gray).

Solidification type A (*Fig. 3h, i*) has a high amount of dendritic wustite, which crystallises first followed by the fayalite and the glass phase (*Fig. 3n*, isothermal curve A). The wustite dendrites are coarse because during the eutectic solidification wustite precipitates on already solidified crystals. The high amount of wustite in the slag is thought to be a result of an interrupted reduction process.

Solidification type B (*Fig. 3j, k*) has a lower amount of wustite compared with type A. The iron reduction process is nearly complete. The composition of the melt is close to the liquidus curve on the wustite side and the melting temperature is about 1200°C (*Fig. 3n*, isothermal curve B). The long, thin dendrites are typical of the wustite microstructure. Wustite solidification is followed by that of fayalite and the glass phase. The slag did not move during solidification resulting in large wustite dendrites with lengths of about 200µm.

Solidification type C (*Fig. 3l, m*) again has a chemical composition close to the liquidus curve on the fayalite side. The melting temperature is approximately 1100°C (*Fig. 3n*, isothermal curve C). First, large fayalite crystals up to 1 mm in size crystallize, and then during the progressive cooling process an eutectic mixture of small, fine-grained wustite dendrites, fine-grained fayalite and glass phase forms. The large pores in the microstructure are the result of a volume decrease during solidification.

Microanalytical measurements indicated some differences in the chemical composition of the various slags. In the fayalite phase Mn and Ca concentrations vary and in the glass-phase the contents of Ca and K differ. The Mn and Ca differences can be explained by the use of inhomogeneous iron ores. K_2O was introduced by charcoal which is used as a reduction and heating source. Higher Al_2O_3 concentrations can be explained by the dissolution of the clay lining (Oelsen, Schürmann, 1954).

Conclusions

The archaeological and archaeometallurgical research into Mediaeval iron smelting in the vicinity of Steirischer Erzberg is still in its initial stages despite there having been archaeological research in the area for more than 120 years. The smelting processes in bloomery furnaces have been described by several authors (Johannsen, 1925; Sperl, 1984; 1988; Straube, 1986; Strobl et al., 2010). Anomalies in the metallurgical process itself as well as in the composition and quality of the ore and charcoal cause inhomogeneous slag compositions. The slag analyses in this study can be compared to the analyses by Gerhard Sperl (1980). Furthermore there can be differences in the slag composition depending on the stage of reduction at which the slag was removed from the furnace.

The three solidification types of iron slag as described above are able to be created in one furnace. The fayalite-rich slags analysed confirm that bloomery processes took place at these iron smelting sites but it is not possible to describe the differences in the process parameters used. Finally another issue remains open for discussion: that of whether a simple bloomery process was carried out by means of a Rennofen or by the Stückofen or Stuckofen which was developed later.

Acknowledgements

Our thanks go to our colleagues from the Institute of Chemical Technologies and Analytics, TU-Wien, for their contribution in measuring various samples: Dr Johannes Zbiral for XRF, Dr Erich Halwax for XRD and Dr Christian Gierl for DTA analysis. We also like to thank Horst Weinek and Hubert Wörnschiml of Eisenerz who were responsible for discovering the iron smelting sites in question.

References

Johannsen, O. (1925): Geschichte des Eisens. Düsseldorf, 5-59.

Klemm. S. (2003): Montanarchäologie in den Eisenerzer Alpen, Steiermark. Mitteilungen der Prähistorischen Kommission 50. Wien, 1-205.

Klemm, S.; Strobl, S.; Haubner, R., (2012): Archäologische Funde mittelalterlicher Eisenverhüttung und Holzkohlenproduktion im Nahbereich des Steirischen Erzberges. In: res montanarum, Sonderband, 69-81.

Oelsen, W.; Schürmann, E., (1954): Untersuchungsergebnisse alter Rennfeuerschlacken. In: Archiv Eisenhüttenwesen 25/11/12 (1954), 507-514.

Schmid, W. (1932): Norisches Eisen. Beiträge zur Geschichte des Österreichischen Eisenwesens, Abt. I, Heft 2, 1-60 (167-226).

Sperl, G. (1980): Über die Typologie urzeitlicher, frühgeschichtlicher und mittelalterlicher Eisenhüttenschlacken. Studien zur Industrie-Archäologie VII. Wien, 1-68.

Sperl, G. (1984): Die Technologie der direkten Eisenherstellung. In: Erz und Eisen in der Grünen Mark. Graz, 95-108.

Sperl, G. (1988): Möglichkeiten zur Rekonstruktion der urgeschichtlichen Hüttenprozesse des Kupfers und Eisens aus Schlackenuntersuchungen am mittelalterlichen Beispiel Feistawiese. In: Jahrbuch des Römisch-Germanischen Zentralmuseums Mainz 35, 639-641.

Straube, H. (1986): Kritische Gegenüberstellung der Theorie über die Metallurgie des Rennfeuers. In: Ferrum 57, 20-28.

Strobl, S.; Haubner, R.; Klemm, S., (2010): Metallographic investigations of a historical bloom found in Styria – Austria. In: Longauerová, M. (ed.): Special Issue, 14th International Symposium on Metallography, Acta Metallurgica Slovaca Conference 1, 655-660.

The Life and Mining Work of Felician von Herberstein (1540-1590)

Petra Rausch-Mátyás[1]

[1] Hungarian Academy of Science Research Centre for the Humanities, Institute of Hitory, Komló, Hungary

Introduction

The aim of this study is the life and mining-work of Felician von Herberstein in the Kingdom of Hungary and in the Austrian hereditary provinces, which was carried out in the course of the authors Ph.D. Thesis. He was employed as a mining expert by the king of Poland and prince of the Principality of Transylvania (István Báthory) to innovate mining techniques and miners support (Rausch, 2007; Rausch-Mátyás, 2012).

His Background, Family and Activiy

His family was a noble, distinguished and aristocratic family from Styria; the estate's centre was in Guttenhag and Herberstein. His father was Andreas von Herberstein, who was head of the Styrian cavalry and a seneschal of the Habsburg archduke Ferdinand. Felician's uncle, Sigismund von Herberstein, was a well-known traveller and diplomat. Sigismund von Herberstein wrote about Russia (the Principality of Moscow) for the first time in second half of the 16th century. His work is an excellent description about this hitherto unknown country. Information about Felician's life and activity can be gained form the funeral oration written by David Reuss, who was a court-pastor of the family of Herberstein. David Reuss wrote this oration about Felician and his son, Raimund. He died in 1591 and this funeral oration was later published in 1595 which survived in a few copies in the National Library of Hungary and the Austrian State Archives (Finanz- und Hofkammer, Alte Hofkammer). The members of this line of descent were Lutherans, and they successfully championed Lutheran church protection, especially during the reign of the archduke Charles. Felician von Herberstein after his move to Nagybánya (now Romania, County Maramures, Baia Mare) not only protected the local Lutheran church but also helped the primary school, and supported the local temple's restoration. He was buried in this temple in 1590, but it was destroyed by fire in the 18th century and only the church tower remained. In the local museum there is a brief description of his life and professional activities, where he lead the mining-administration and the local mint for more than ten years, and in the course of this activity he obtained excellent results.

Felician von Herberstein was born in 1540; he spent his youth in the imperial and royal centre in Vienna in the service to the Court. He carried on with university studies in the newly-founded University of Graz. During these years he dealt with natural science subjects outside the university studies. He could speak more than four foreign languages and after he finished the studies he continued diplomatic services in Malta, France and in the Ottoman Empire. During this diplomatic service his political carrier was starting despite the fact that his main objective was to innovate his mining expertise. In order to achieve this goal he travelled around the metal mining districts, and salt mines in the Austrian hereditary provinces to examine mining technologies and modes of production. He was especially interested in solving the problems of deep mining, which lie in providing fresh air and transport of waste materials away from the shafts. During this time he was member of the War Council (Hofkriegsrat), so he could travel around the Hungarian mining districts to learn about Hungarian mining traditions. In the course of this activity he visited the most important cities, which dealt with deep mining in Highland (now Slovakia). These cities were Selmecbánya, Körmöcbánya and Besztercebánya. In mines the miners exploited gold, silver and copper in very high quality (Bobory, 2005). At this time these mines represented the most developed metal-mining district in the Kingdom of Hungary. Felician von Herberstein was an innovator and therefore he wanted to rent the risky metal-mining district of Szatmár (now Romania, county Maramures), at the border between the Principality of Transylvania and the Kingdom of Hungary. The centre of the mining-district of Szatmár was Nagybánya, which represented the site of the chamber (administration) and the mint. The leader of the chamber guided the mining-administration, in mint produced high-quality gold and silver coins. Although there were three other settlements that belonged to this district, which contained many mines, but the most important mine in the area was in Nagybánya, the so-called Királytáró or Nagyverem, which was rented by Felician von Herberstein. This region was in the possession of the Hungarian king until 1585, and after that it belonged to the Principality of Transylvania. Since Felician von Herberstein dealt with exploiting ores before, he moved with his family to Nagybánya, because his friend, a member of the well-known Hungarian aristocratic noble family Batthyány, Boldizsár Batthyány, obtained permission from the Hungarian king to open a metal-mine in his own estate. In the course of this enterprise he asked Felician von Herberstein for help, so the Styrian noble man could enter the mining business. After this he moved on to Nagybánya and contacted the Transylvanian government in order to rent the mining-district of Szatmár.

During this time the prince of Transylvania was István Báthory who was at the same time the king of Poland too. Since he wanted to support local metal-mining he looked for a suitable specialist in this field. For this reason Felician von Herberstein visited him in Poland, and so this Styrian noble man became in charge of conducting a study tour to survey the sites of Transylvanian metal-mining and Herberstein visited many Transylvanian metal-mining-districts in 1585. After that he wrote a detailed account in Latin. This account allows to extract important information about Transylvanian precious metal-mining's techniques. Herberstein described in detail deep underground mining, gold washing and open cast mining. In this time the most profitable mode of metal mining were gold washing and open cast mining, because deep underground mining demanded highly specialized craftsmanship and significant financial investment. Due to this survey the Herberstein family was on good terms with the princes of Transylvania (family Báthory) and so Felician von Herberstein was allowed to rent the noble metal mines in the county of Szatmár. Since he wanted to develop deep underground mining in this region he had to borrow money from various investors for carrying out his plans. He started mining activities in Feketebánya. This settlement belonged to Nagybánya and due to the nature of the promising gold and silver mines miners had to start deep underground mining to obtain the ores. In the course of these activities shafts, beams and air shafts were being rebuild, and the mining facilities constructed by János Thurzó in 1522 (he was a business partner of the Fugger family) such as the furnaces and pulping mills were restored. In addition he ordered new furnaces and pulping mills to be built due to the increasing productivity. He also was responsible for building a new mint with new coin-manufacturing machines because the new coins had a wider surface and he purchased the new machine from credit (Bobory, 2005; Huszár, 1996). Since Felician von Herberstein was a very good innovator he refined the modes of ore purification and therefore he imported lead for this process from Poland. He was greatly appreciated by his workers since they got high salaries and their employer operated a private grocery, where the workers were charged lower prices, than in the other groceries. He hired a lot of German miners and gave them accommodation too. Since Felician von Herberstein provided not only a good primary school and rental flats for his workers they were very loyal and faithful to him.

He had two sons, the firstborn was Raimund, but he died in 1591. The second son, Friedrich von Herberstein would have continued his father's enterprise, but since he had to cope with a lot of problems he gave it up and moved to Poland in 1597. The developments of Felician von Herberstein had a very important influence in this region over the years and the building of the mint still stands.

Acknowledgement

The project was supported by OTKA PD 108877 scholarship. (Hungarian Scientific Research Fund, postdoctoral scholarship).

Bibliography

Rausch, P. (2007): Adalékok az erdélyi nemesérc-bányászat történetéhez a 16. század második felében. Egy bányászati reformer élete és munkássága: Herberstein Felician (1540-1590), Pécs. Respectively Rausch-Mátyás, P. (2012): A szatmári bányavidék története a Báthory korszakban (1571-1613). A nemesérc-bányászat művelése és igazgatása, Pécs.

Bobory, D. (2005): Felician von Herberstein (1540-1590) stájer főúr rövid életrajza és magyar kapcsolatai David Reuss gyászbeszéde alapján, Lymbus, Magyarságtudományi Közlemények, Budapest, pp. 5-26.

Huszár, L. (1996): Erdélyi éremművesség a 16.-18. században, Kolozsvár, pp. 67-70.

Multi-period mining remains from the Sierra de Orihuela (Alicante, SE Spain)

Dirk Brandherm[1], Alexander Maass[2] & Emilio Diz Ardid[3]

[1] School of Geography, Archaeology and Palaeoecology, Queen's University Belfast, UK
[2] Freiburger Institut für Paläowissenschaftliche Studien, c/o Albert-Ludwigs-Universität, Freiburg, Germany
[3] Museo Arqueológico Comarcal, Orihuela, Spain

Over the course of two four-week fieldwork campaigns conducted in the summer months of 2010 and 2011 the authors carried out an extensive survey of mining remains on the northern margin of the lower Segura valley, straddling the border between the modern-day provinces of Alicante and Murcia. This work followed on from some earlier site visits and from a cursory survey undertaken during a single week in June 2007 (Brandherm & Maass, 2010).

The original aim of our survey project was to identify evidence for prehistoric mining activities in the Sierra de Orihuela and Sierra de Callosa, ca. 50km to the north of the well known Cartagena-La Unión mining district (cf. Bocamina, 2005), to assess the role any such activities would have played within the economy of local communities, and to determine their potential impact on overall settlement patterns in the region (Brandherm et al., 2011).

Particular emphasis was placed on identifying possible remains of 3rd and 2nd millennium AC copper mining operations, due to the previously recorded presence of Bronze Age pottery on what at the time were believed to be prehistoric spoil heaps at the aptly named Cerro de la Mina (*Fig. 1 left*), and of suspected ore-crushing or mining hammers from Early Bronze Age habitation sites in the study area (Brandherm & Maass, 2010:17-20). It was hoped that our fieldwork would produce the first direct evidence for Bronze Age copper mining in south-east Spain, helping to resolve the ongoing debate about the societal backdrop of Early and Middle Bronze Age metal production in this area (Maya, 2003; Montero Ruiz & Rodríguez de la Esperanza, 2004).

From early on during our first full survey campaign, however, it became increasingly clear that as a consequence of the extensive transformation the landscape had suffered from later, mainly post-medieval mining operations, a much broader approach would be required. Accordingly, over the remainder of our fieldwork we set out to compile a complete inventory of all mining-related sites in the Sierra de Orihuela and Sierra de Callosa, revealing a much more extensive and much more varied mining heritage than originally expected.

As an outcome from our survey, more than 100 extraction sites and a number of other mining-related structures have been recorded across the study area. The vast majority of these are located on the southern face of the Sierra de Orihuela. While most of the respective sites are of post-medieval date, some earlier workings could also be identified.

Fig. 1. Left: Cerro de la Mina, modern shafts and spoil tips on slope in foreground, likely evidence for EBA ore processing has been identified on slopes of Cerro in the centre; top right: anvil crushing stone; bottom right: hammer stones.

Fig. 2. Left to right: Plan of LIA/Roman iron mine with intrusive modern workings; shaft entrance with tool marks left by stone mauls; LIA/Roman stairwell; LIA/Roman gallery with intrusive modern workings.

Fig. 3. Horno de Santa Matilde, late 19th century mercury distillation furnace situated next to Virgen del Carmen cinnabar mine.

Contrary to our initial expectations, direct evidence for Bronze Age mining so far has failed to materialize. The aforementioned spoil heaps which originally had been deemed to be of prehistoric date, upon closer examination were identified to comprise a mix of modern mining spoil and redeposited prehistoric settlement material. Clear proof of prehistoric copper mining in the study area thus remains elusive, but an intensive walkover survey of the Early Bronze Age settlement on the Cerro de la Mina, whence the redeposited material derived, recorded more than 500 hammer stones and several anvil slabs of a type usually associated with ore processing (*Fig. 1 right*). Their find spots cluster in different sectors of the site, and part of our survey work focused on mapping their varying concentration, originally in the hope that this would provide clues regarding the location of possible Bronze Age mines.

It soon became clear, however, that the hammer stones from this site do not represent the full range of differently sized tools one would expect to find in a prehistoric mining operation. It now seems that, rather than dealing with evidence for on-site ore extraction, we may be looking at a work camp where ore potentially mined elsewhere was crushed in preparation for smelting. This comes with the caveat that extensive modern spoil tips at the site might still hide traces of earlier mining activity.

In any case, it seems unlikely that the activity in which these implements were employed would have been a casual pursuit. The vast majority are made from metabasite not occurring locally, but which had to be quarried and brought to the Cerro de la Mina over a distance of several kilometres. These hammer stones seem to have been used unshafted, being of a very different type from the grooved stone hammers previously published from two other significant Early Bronze Age settlements in the study area, San Antón and Las Laderas del Castillo (Simón García, 1998:Figs. 14, 1; 23, 1. 2). The latter pieces turned out not to be mining or ore-crushing tools at all, but likely metalworking implements. They thus have to be viewed in the context of much later stages in the chaîne opératoire of metalwork manufacture, together with other sporadic instances of evidence for metalworking from nearby Bronze Age settlements sites (Bocamina, 2005:171 No. 22; Simón García, 1998:42 Figs. 14, 2. 3; 22, 15).

To help determine the role of local ore bodies as sources for raw material in this chaîne opératoire, ore samples from a number of sites surveyed as part of our project are currently being analysed for their trace-element composition and lead-isotope signature. The results from this programme will then be compared to corresponding analyses of Bronze Age metalwork from the area, to see if a match can be established.

Another outcome from our fieldwork has been the identification of a multi-period iron mining operation on the northern outskirts of the modern town of Orihuela (*Fig. 2*). Some of the workings at this site can tentatively be dated to the Late Iron Age or Early Roman period (2nd -1st centuries AC), based on layout, tool marks and some fragments of Late Iberian pottery. As evidence for pre-Roman iron mining in southern Iberia remains limited to date, and as prior research on Roman mining activity has focussed mainly on the Cartagena-La Unión mining district and on the Iberian pyrite belt further to the west (Domergue, 1987; 1990; Arboledas Martínez, 2010), this new discovery makes both an unexpected and most welcome addition to our corpus of data.

Fig. 4. Left to right: Remains of modern mining operation and abandoned stockpiles of iron ore on the north face of the Sierra de Orihuela.

In the 19th and early 20th centuries AD this mine was reopened, causing the destruction of some of the earlier galleries. Tool marks in one of the shafts at this site also betray the use of stone mauls, indicating extraction activity predating the Late Iron Age, probably for the procurement not of iron ore, but of high-quality volcanic rock to be used for manufacturing querns (*Fig. 2 centre left*).

Modern mining operations in the study area have also targeted gold and mercury deposits, with a rare single-chamber late 19th century mercury distillation furnace remarkably well preserved (*Fig. 3*). Except for a broadly similar, but double-chamber furnace in Almadén de la Plata, this would seem to be the only surviving installation of its kind in Western Europe. The cinnabar ore processed in this furnace came from the nearby Virgen del Carmen, Cueva Montero and La Colón mines, which today are largely inaccessible.

A limited number of extraction sites also were identified on the north face of the Sierra de Orihuela. The most extensive of these is an iron mine operating into the first half of the 20th century, when ore extraction in the Sierra de Orihuela ceased to be an economically feasible activity. Stockpiles of iron ore left behind right next to the adits are testimony to the sudden end of the operation (*Fig. 4*).

With these outcomes from our survey work, focus of the project has shifted from trying to address research questions relating exclusively to prehistoric mining activity on the lower Segura to a diachronic long-term perspective that also looks at evidence left by mining operations during later periods.

The ultimate aim of the project, though, remains unchanged: to establish a sound empirical basis that will allow for a better understanding of changes in the social organization underpinning mining operations in the study area, and also a better understanding of the effects mining here may have exerted on the wider landscape over the last few millennia, from its beginnings to the cessation of extraction activity in the 20th century. At different times, different mineral resources were being targeted by the local population, with significant lacunae during certain periods, most notably later Antiquity and the Middle Ages.

On a final note, apart from serving research objectives, the information gathered in our survey is also being used by the local council in its campaign to promote interest in the forgotten mining heritage of the Sierra de Orihuela among the wider public, signposting some of the more easily accessible remains while restricting access to unsafe sites.

Acknowledgements

Special thanks go to María Manuela Ayala Juan (Universidad de Murcia) for her liberal sharing of unpublished information, José Luis Simón García (Generalitat Valenciana) for moral and administrative support, and to Milena Kreft (Ruhr-Universität Bochum) for her untiring commitment and stirling work. The project was generously funded by a small projects grant from the British Academy's Albert Reckitt Archaeology Fund and a startup research grant from Queen's University Belfast.

References

Arboledas Martínez, L. (2010): Minería y metalurgia romana en el sur de la Península Ibérica, Sierra Morena oriental. BAR International Series 2121. Oxford.

Bocamina (2005): Bocamina: patrimonio minero de la Región de Murcia. Del 8 de sept. al 6 de nov. de 2005, Museo de la Ciencia y el Agua. Murcia.

Brandherm, D. & Maass, A. (2010): Copper Mining, Settlement and Society in the Earlier Bronze Age of Southeast Spain: prospects for new research in the Lower Segura valley. In: Mining in European History and its Impact on Environment and Human Societies – Proceedings for the 1st Mining in European History Conference of the SFB-HIMAT, 12.-15. November 2009, Innsbruck. Innsbruck, pp. 17-22.

Brandherm, D.; Maas, A.; Diz Ardid, E. & Ayala Juan, M. M. (2011): Surveying for Early Mining Remains in Southeast Iberia. PAST – The Newsletter of the Prehistoric Society 67, pp. 13-14.

Domergue, C. (1987): Catalogue des mines et fonderies antiques de la péninsule ibérique. Publications de la Casa de Velázquez – Série Archéologie 8. Paris.

Domergue, C. (1990): Les mines de la péninsule ibérique dans l'Antiquité romaine. Collection de l'École Française de Rome 127. Roma.

Maya, J. L. (2003): La minería del cobre durante el Calcolítico y Bronce Final en la Península Ibérica. In: Mata Perelló, J. M. & González Pérez, J. R. (eds.): Actas del Primer Simposio sobre la Minería y la Metalurgía Antigua en el Sudoeste Europeo, Centre d'Arqueologia d'Avinganya, Serós (Segría, Catalunya, España), del 5 al 7 de mayo del 2000, Vol. 1. Madrid, pp. 87-116.

Montero Ruiz, I. & Rodríguez de la Esperanza, M. J. (2004): Der prähistorische Kupferbergbau in Spanien. Ein Überblick über den Forschungsstand. Der Anschnitt 56, pp. 54-63.

Simón García, J. L. (1998): La metalurgia prehistórica valenciana. Servicio de Investigación Prehistórica – Serie de Trabajos Varios 93. Valencia.

Session III

Societal Interaction & Ecology

The environmental approach in German mining: bodies, workplaces and hygiene around 1900[1]

Lars Bluma[1]

[1] Deutsches Bergbau-Museum Bochum, Bochum, Germany

Introduction

This article tries to analyse how medical and hygienic experts gained momentum in determining the perception and practice of coal mining at the Ruhr around 1900. As a consequence, mining no longer appeared as a pure unit of production but as a spatial, social and hygienic environment. Medical experts, engineers and sanitarians now addressed mining in terms of the hygienic movement with the aim to examine and with it to configure the relationship between miners and their workplace environment. Although the hygienic problems of the industrialized Ruhr area (esp. the outbreak of different infectious diseases like typhoid or cholera) were discussed since the middle of the 19th century in terms of environmental regulations, my thesis is that the reflection on mining as a problem of environment started not until a single but dramatic event took place: the hookworm epidemic at the Ruhr in the late 19th century, which affected solely miners.

The hookworm epidemic at the Ruhr

In 1892 two cases of hookworm infection were diagnosed at a pit of the Ruhr area (Zeche Graf Schwerin). The responsible health insurance of the miners, the Allgemeine Knappschaftsverein zu Bochum, immediately started an examination of the pit staff concerned, especially of miners with visible anaemic symptoms (Martin, 2000:430). Together with physicians of the Knappschafts-Berufsgenossenschaft, the German occupational insurance association of mining, the excrements of the miners were analysed with microscopes and hookworms were found in 18 samples (Löbker, 1896:19).

As a result the royal mining authority in Dortmund commissioned the medical head of the Knappschafts-Berufsgenossenschaft, Ferdinand Löbker, to give his expert opinion on the extent of the worm illness in the Ruhr area and the necessary action to combat the epidemic. Löbker suggested several measures that were immediately implemented at the infected coal mine. Because the infection was strictly limited to miners working underground, the medical experts focused their actions against the epidemic on the mining workplaces there, and especially the unhygienic circumstances were examined. But all these medical and hygiene instructions controlled by the mining authority could not prevent the outbreak of an epidemic, which grew to a serious threat to mining on the Ruhr.

Löbkers suggestions were obviously inadequate. This was partly due to the fact that he and the physicians of the Knappschaft, but also the whole international community of medical and hygiene experts, knew only little about the spreading and the way of distribution of the hookworm in the miners body and its environment. However, it is more important that Löbker, and with him the head of the medical department of the Knappschaft, August Tenholt, thought that it was sufficient to examine only miners with visible anaemic symptoms (Langenfeld, 1981:68-70). By doing so, the physicians ignored the large number of worm carriers who still showed no visible signs of illness. Consequently only the anaemic workers received a de-worming treatment. The miners who showed no symptoms, but were already infected with the hookworm, were not removed from work and could still spread the parasite underground.

Tenholt was convinced that the fight against the hookworm should basically only be fought with hygienic and technical means, by installing toilets underground, the draining of wet areas of the mine and the improvement of the ventilation to regulate the temperature (Tenholt, 1903:7-13). However, these preventive measures required not only technical realisation, but also a change in the habits of the miners. They had to use the toilets underground, but this was not self-evident and the necessary behavioural changes were not easy to achieve (Langenfeld, 1981:56).

Tenholt developed a medical-hygiene action programme which was aimed less at the body of the miner, but rather at the environmental conditions in the pit which he defined as a principal intervention place in the fight against the parasites: "The contagion does not occur by transmission from a sick worker to his close neighbour, as we can see by infectious diseases, but through the pit" (Tenholt, 1903:17). Tenholts target was a readjustment of the workplace as a techno-natural environment. Three measures especially were in the centre of his next plan: the lowering of the temperature underground to 22 degrees, the draining of the coal clearances and their disinfection.

Until then the different groups, like Knappschaft, the miners, the mining authority and the mining companies worked together with only little friction. But with the outbreak of an actual epidemic, scathing criticism of Tenholt's plan was heard and the mining companies expressed their dissatisfaction emphatically. In 1902, the pit owners demanded the addition of a new agent, the Institut für Hygiene und Bakteriologie in Gelsenkirchen, to fight the disease (Bruns, 1904a:3). The institute had been founded following the advice of the famous scientist and microbiologist Robert Koch who had investigated a typhoid epidemic in the Ruhr district in 1901 (Wüstenberg, 1977). The institute was responsible for supervising the canalisation and water supply of the local authority districts in the Ruhr area and to set up an epidemic guard.

The head of the institute, Hayo Bruns, then proposed a catalogue of measures which was contrary to Tenholts plan. In committees and at scientific conferences, partially initiated by the German Reichstag and therefore on top of the political agenda, Bruns promoted a bacteriology oriented control of the hookworm epidemic analogous to the fight against typhoid, cholera, dysentery etc. (Bruns, 1904b:21-22). What Bruns wanted was a systematic microscopic examination of excrements from all miners at the Ruhr who were endangered by hookworm disease. For him it did not matter if a miner had anaemic symptoms or not. Important was, and this is the basic message of the bacteriological approach, the infection with the worm. Consequently, he demanded that all worm infected miners, regardless of visible signs and symptoms or ability to work, should be removed from their workplaces and immediately de-wormed. The former individual diagnosis, which had been based on external, visible symptoms, was to be substituted by a complete microscopic serial examination. Bruns wanted to attack the hookworm in the body of the miners, a clearly defined location. In contrast, Tenholt and the Knappschaft intended to fight the hookworm at the miners' workplace underground by a slow transformation of hygiene standards. And this was anything but a clearly defined battlefield.

Now the opponents of this conflict tried to support their theories with intensive research. The miners workplace was converted to a medical experimental ground. The physicians and microbiologists examined the pits with regard to temperature, air humidity, soil conditions and ventilation to specify the ideal breeding conditions for the hookworm. The mines were searched thoroughly for hookworm eggs and larvae to track down possible paths of infection, and at the same time the hookworm was investigated experimentally in the medical laboratories of the Knappschaft and the Institut für Hygiene und Bakteriologie (Tenholt, 1903; Bruns, 1904b). This intensive research produced new knowledge about the hookworm and with it also a new understanding of the body of the miner and its interrelation with the workplace environment (Bluma, 2009:319-320).

The production of scientific facts was important, indeed, but it was not crucial for the final success of Bruns bacteriological approach because the medical knowledge among the two opponents was nearly identical and the two different strategies derived from this knowledge were both rational and logical. What really helped Bruns concept was the formation of a new network and the social compatibility of his approach with the main players. The pit owners for example were not really interested in a slow project to establish hygiene and medical standards underground at that time. Although the mining authority and the coal mining companies were convinced that the hygienic transformation of the workplace was an important measure to prevent further epidemic hazards in the long run, they now wanted a quick and definite solution for the hookworm problem there and then because, in 1903, the epidemic led to considerable disturbances in the coal production. And Bruns could offer such a solution. By contrast, Tenholt could only offer an uncertain plan whose targets could only be met in the remote future. Thus the crucial point for the success of Bruns intervention was not an advance of medical knowledge but an advance in effectiveness.

In the end the bacteriological approach of Bruns supported by the mining companies was successful. The comprehensive microscopic examination of underground miners on the Ruhr and the systematic de-worming of all infected miners caused a rapid reduction of the hookworm illness after 1903 (Bruns, 1914:398). Nevertheless, after this quick success, the long-term project of a hygienic transformation of miners workplaces became a major paradigm in the German mining industry to prevent further risk of infection of any kind.

Summary

To sum up, there are some fundamental changes the hookworm epidemic caused for mining at the Ruhr. First of all we can see the rise of a new modern dispositive that linked industrial coal mining with the gathering of new medical knowledge about the miners body, its productivity and vulnerability at the workplace. Therefore the hookworm was responsible for a long-lasting process of a hygienic and bacteriological transformation of the miners workplace. The examination of miners excrements to avoid further hookworm epidemics remained for example a common practice in German mining until the 1970s. Furthermore, hygiene in mining became a comprehensive concept integrating quite different fields of action: the fight against typical occupational diseases like hookworm, nystagmus and silicosis, the prevention of explosion hazards, the provision of a medical and first aid infrastructure, the installing and organisation of toilets in the pits, as well as hygiene outside the workplace, embedding housing conditions and all parts of urban infrastructure.

Endnotes

[1] A detailed version of this article will be published in European Review of History, Vol. 20 (2013).

Bibliography

Bluma, L. (2009): Der Hakenwurm an der Ruhr. Umwelt, Körper und soziale Netzwerke im Bergbaus des Kaiserreichs. Der Anschnitt: Zeitschrift für Kunst und Kultur im Bergbau 61 5/6, pp. 314-329.

Bruns, H. (1904a): Die Bekämpfung der Wurmkrankheit (Ankylostomiasis) im rheinisch-westfälischen Ruhrkohlenbezirk. Separatadruck aus der Münchener medizinischen Wochenschrift 15 & 16.

Bruns, H. (1904b): Versuche über die Einwirkung einiger physikalischer und chemischer Agentien auf die Eier und Larven des Ankylostoma duodenal, nebst Bemerkungen über die Bekämpfung der Krankheit im Ruhrkohlengebiet. Jena.

Bruns, H. (1914): Die mikroskopische Untersuchung der Fäzes in ihrer Bedeutung für die Bekämpfung der Ankylostomiasis. Ein Bericht über den Stand der Wurmkrankheit im Ruhrkohlengebiet nach 10jähriger Bekämpfung. Seperat-Abdruck aus der Zeitschrift für Hygiene und Infektionskrankheiten 78, Leipzig.

Langenfeld, H. (1981): Die Ankylostomiasis im Ruhrgebiet: ein Beitrag zur Geschichte der medizinischen Parasitologie. Frankfurt a. M./Bern.

Löbker, F. (1896): Die Ankylostomiasis und ihre Verbreitung unter den Bergleuten im Oberbergamtsbezirk Dortmund. Wiesbaden.

Martin, M. (2000): Arbeitsschutz und Arbeitsmedizin im Ruhrbergbau 1865-1914. PhD diss., Ruhr University Bochum (microfiche).

Tenholt, A. (1903): Die Ankylostomiasis-Frage. Zusammenfassende Uebersicht. Jena.

Wüstenberg, J. (1977): 75 Jahre Hygiene-Institut des Ruhrgebiets Gelsenkirchen. Gelsenkirchen: Verein zur Bekämpfung der Volkskrankheiten im Ruhrkohlengebiet.

Influence and Perception. How pit and quarry industry change landscapes

Marion Kaiser[1]

[1] Deutsches Bergbau-Museum, Bochum, Germany

The production and use of natural stone (including sand and gravel) deserves much more attention among historians than it currently does. Only a few regions have been studied more intensely, and this branch of mining is often handled like 'unwelcome relatives' (Bartels & Klappauf, 2012:231). Stone-Extraction and the use of its products characterize many landscapes. Environmental history often mentioned a special conflict, which resulted from such activities: the historical movement to protect the Siebengebirge near Bonn. It is taken for an initial event of the landscape-protection movement in Germany (Ludwig, 2006). But to only look at the conflicts would be one-sided. The relationship between human society and the pit and quarry industry are manifold, and they include, e.g., former productive areas now forming sites under protection as natural habitats.

Economic importance and changes due to industrialization

In regions such as the Siebengebirge or the Eifel Mountains large quantities of stone were quarried since ancient times. Most of the stone was used near the mining sites, but some more valuable stones have been transported over long distances, e.g. millstones from the Eifel Mountains. They had special properties or were found close to important transport routes, like the river Rhine (Schaaff, 2008).

During the 19th century natural stone craft developed into an industry. Stonemasons and quarrymen started to use machines, larger companies and new products developed. Some parts of the branch grew enormously. The growth of cities and the construction of traffic infrastructure required large amounts of stone. But some industrial branches, too, like iron and steel production demanded stone materials. An important double effect resulted from the uprise of the railways. First limestone is needed to produce steel for construction purposes, as well as gravel for roadbeds, secondly railways made transport easier and cheaper.

A good example of the development in such a region is the Westerwald Hills. Here people had used basalt for buildings since medieval times. But the relevance of basalt grew enormously since the beginning of the 19th century. The stone was used to develop the road-infrastructure, for example as paving stones or, since the end of the 19th century, as gravel for railway-lines. At the beginning deposits situated next to the river Rhine became highly important. But later on railways reached the Westerwald Hills and their deposits became profitable. The biggest basalt mining area extends near Enspel at former "Stöffel" hill. Actually it is a crater. In 1903, when

Fig. 1: The basalt quarry "Stöffel" near Enspel in the Westerwald (M. Kaiser).

Fig. 2: The castle of Bad Bentheim. The oldest parts of it are built in the 12th century (M. Kaiser).

these quarries were opened, quarrying was manual labour with simple tools. The use of machines and explosives substances started before the First World War and made work easier (Bartolosch et al., 2006; Ludwig, 2006).

Impact on the landscape

Like other mining sectors, the quarry and pit industry can transform landscapes deeply. Prior to industrialization, most quarries were relatively small. But in some areas an intense mining activity led to a great number of quarries. Initiated by the process of industrialization the demand for many kinds of stone increased and the exploitation became easier and faster. That is why the dimension of the quarries grew. Thus, the pit and quarry industry created large-scale mining landscapes.

In comparison to other kinds of mining, this branch also characterizes the appearance of the settlements. People in these regions used 'their' stone wherever possible (Grimm, 2013:42). Such a region developed near Bad Bentheim and Gildehaus. Baptismal fonts of 12th century are the oldest evidence of use of the "Bentheimer Sandstone". It was sold to the surroundings and to the Netherlands. Alongside a walk in Bad Bentheim and Gildehaus, sandstone is exposed in multiple uses: as building stone, paving stone, gravestones or monuments. This material was also used for millstones and grinding stones. Until present the stone is mined and used (Voort, 2000; Sarrazin, 1999).

Protection of environment

Quarrying can deeply change a landscape. Landmarks become destroyed and craters and dumps are left behind. Roads become damaged by huge transports and land gets spoiled by heaps of waste. We do not know a lot about the reactions of people in the past. But new forms of conflicts developed in the 19th century. At that time quarries were seen as lesions and scars in a landscape. It is not only the time of industrialization, but also the beginning of the protection of historical heritage and environment. At first this was influenced by both romanticism and nationalism. Later on, the modern form of nature protection developed. Conflicts because of quarrying gained an important role in developing ideas and practice of nature protection.

A good example of such a conflict offers the Siebengebirge. In this region, quarrying developed since Roman times. Basalt, tuff and trachyte are to be found here. After the 'wars of liberation' at the end of the Napoleonic area the Siebengebirge, and especially the Drachenfels hill with the ruin of a castle and a monument on top, became a German national symbol and an attraction for tourists. Therefore the quarries became a problem. When a part of the old ruins collapsed in 1828 because of the quarrying, an open conflict developed. King Friedrich Wilhelm III. of Prussia initiated the purchase of the hill and monument to protect the site. In person he stopped quarrying at the Drachenfels, (but not in the whole Siebengebirge area). In 1869 a private society for the touristic development of the region was founded. At this time the demand for basalt grew, and the quarries in the Siebengebirge expanded rapidly. A new conflict started. A second society

Fig. 3: The abandoned basalt-quarry „Ostbruch" in the Siebengebirge (M. Kaiser).

Fig. 4: The artificial hermitage on the Rochlitz Mountain was built in 1817 (M. Kaiser).

was founded, and the older society, too, developed into a society for the protection of nature and natural monuments. With political support, and because of new quarries in the Westerwald hills, the movement was successful in the end. In 1909 the last basalt quarry was shut down in that region, and in 1923 the Siebengebirge became a nature conservation area (Plehwe-Leisen et al., 2004; Ludwig, 2006).

The significance of this conflict, however, was relativized by modern research. It was neither the first conflict because of environmental changes, nor the first protected area in Germany. But it was an important and a nationwide perceived conflict. J. Ludwig also showed how many participants and different interests were involved (Ludwig, 2006).

The pit and quarry industry and cultural landscapes

Environmental history often focuses on conflicts. According to calculations by W.-D. Grimm more than 10.000 quarries were run in Germany during the 19th century (Grimm, 2013:56). In comparison to this figure just a few conflicts are known. Either there is a large research-gap or this indicates a relationship between industry and people that was only rarely affected by conflicts. The problem of the perception of quarries is closely connected to this subject. W. Konold identifies impact-factors in this perception, e.g. spatial and temporal contexts, dimension and spatial distribution of quarries, duration of mining operations, (emotive) connections between viewer and landscape, aesthetic impression of a quarry and spatial position of viewers (Konold, 2013:24-26).

Today preservationists underline the influence of pit and quarry industry on cultural landscapes, and they identify quarries as part of its structures. But only 30 years ago every quarry supposed to be backfilled and renatured. For this important change it became decisive, that biologists discovered the importance of quarries as a special habitat for animals and plants. Therefore abandoned quarries can be under nature and monument protection nowadays (BHU, 2013; Siegesmund & Snethlage, 2013).

The relationship of pit and quarry industry and tourism makes up another interesting aspect. On the one hand, there were different interests and conflicts like in the Siebengebirge. In other cases connections between both aspects did develop early. A good example is Rochlitz, Saxony. There is a deposit of a red tuff stone situated near the city, which had been popular as building stone since medieval times. After 1800 the stonemasons and quarry-owners intentionally made their hill and workplaces into a destination for tourism with attractions for every kind of visitor: a monument for the Saxon king for patriots, a hermitage for romanticists, a tower and a restaurant. Of course it was also a kind of advertising for the stone, but the coexistence works still today (Bode, 1865; Kreisstadt Rochlitz, 2008).

Conclusion

The influence of the pit and quarry industry on landscapes and the perception of this influence is an interesting topic for future research. So far, only a few regions have been intensively studied.

In these cases a variety of factors and stakeholders were important. Such studies may help to understand current discussions. Actually some projects are developed in Germany, which try to connect pit and quarry industry and tourism with the protection of cultural and environmental heritage (BHU, 2013; Siegesmund & Snethlage, 2013).

Bibliography

Bartels, C. & Klappauf, L. (2012): Das Mittelalter. In: Bartels, C. & Slotta, R.: Geschichte des deutschen Bergbaus, Bd. 1. Münster, pp. 111-248.

Bartolosch, T. A.; Funk, S.; Gesper, E.; Kessler, K. & Klein, E. (2006): Basaltabbau im Bad Marienberger Raum. Strukturwandel vom Kleinbetrieb zum heutigen Großunternehmen mit besonderer Berücksichtigung der geologischen Verhältnisse. Bad Marienberg.

BHU (ed.) (2013): Werksteinabbau und Kulturlandschaft, Chancen und Konflikte für das Natur- und Kulturerbe. Dokumentation der Tagung am 22. und 23. März 2012 in Maulbronn. Bonn.

Bode, F. (ed.) (1865): Chronik der Stadt Rochlitz und Umgebung. Rochlitz.

Grimm, W.-D. (2013): Die Natursteinprovinzen Deutschland als Identifikationsmerkmale in der Kulturlandschaft. In: Siegesmund, S.; Snethlage, R. (ed.) (2013): Naturstein in der Kulturlandschaft. Halle, pp. 41-58.

Konold, W. (2013): Rohstoffabbau und Kulturlandschaft: ein Widerspruch? In: BHU (ed.): Werksteinabbau und Kulturlandschaft, Chancen und Konflikte für das Natur- und Kulturerbe. Dokumentation der Tagung am 22. und 23. März 2012 in Maulbronn. Bonn, pp. 16-28.

Kreisstadt Rochlitz (ed.) (2008): Auf den Spuren des Rochlitzer Porphyrs. Lehrpfad. Rochlitz.

Ludwig, J. (2006): Basaltabbau im Siebengebirge. Konflikte zwischen Basaltgewinnung und Naturschutz (1871-1914). Königswinter.

Plehwe-Leisen, E. v.; Scheuren, E.; Schumacher, T. & Wolff, A. (2004): Steine für den Kölner Dom. Köln.

Sarrazin, J. (ed.) (1999): Spuren in Sandstein. Baumberger und Bentheimer Sandstein im Gebiet zwischen IJssel und Berkel / Sporen in Zandsteen. Baumberger en Bentheimer zandsteen in het gebied tussen IJssel en Berkel. Coesfeld.

Schaaff, H. (2008): The Origin and Formation of an Industrial Landscape – the Ancient Quarry and Mining District between the Eifel and the Rhine. In: Bartels, C.; Küpper-Eichas, C. (ed.): Cultural heritage and landscapes in Europe / Landschaften: Kulturelles Erbe in Europa. Bochum, pp. 499-508.

Siegesmund, S. & Snethlage, R. (ed.) (2013): Naturstein in der Kulturlandschaft. Halle.

Voort, H. (2000): Abbau, Absatz und Verwendung von Bentheimer Sandstein in acht Jahrhunderten. In: Schriftenreihe des Sandsteinmuseums Bad Bentheim, No. 1. Bad Bentheim.

Living with Lignite. A Glimpse on Lignite-linked Problems in the Rhenish Lignite-Mining Region

Valeska Flor[1]

[1] Institute of History and European Ethnology, University of Innsbruck

Living with lignite: in the triangle bounded by the cities of Aachen, Mönchengladbach, and Bonn this is part of every-day life. Known as the Rhenish lignite-mining region, it covers an area of 2500km². Here we find the largest deposit of lignite in Europe. Lignite is usually quite close to the surface; therefore the deposit is extracted by open pit mines. Compared to underground mining effects of open-cast mining are visible at first glance: but not only the landscape is devastated, there are deep cuts in the social and cultural environment of the people living in the area as well; for the overburden of the mineable lignite must be stripped, including roads, farmland, and complete villages. Since the end of World War II about 90 communities with almost 40,000 people have already been removed in the Rhenish lignite region. The resettlement of entire villages affected in the operations' progress brings drastic change to the lives of their inhabitants; above all it means a change of their social environment and a jolting of their regional identity. But not only are those affected by the process, whose homes will be destructed during lignite mining: in the near future various villages will be bordering lignite mines. In fact, most of them won't lose their property, but they will be affected in several other ways by i.e. noise, light, CO^2, particulate matter, lowering of groundwater, etc. And even more profoundly some of these villages will lose most of their neighbours. In this context it is important to ask some questions to get a more specific overview about what problems occur when a region is affected by lignite mines: What happens to the people during resettlement, how do they cope with losing their home and how do they deal with the imminent loss of their familiar structures? What happens when familiar surroundings change or become non-existent, when a big hole is the next neighbour instead of villages? Are there any codes or narrative strategies acquired by the villagers to cope with the experiences?

Before answering these questions by presenting three case studies of the fieldwork, the reader should have a glimpse of the mining region. The Rhenish Lignite mining region, situated in the west of Germany, is the biggest lignite-mining region in Europe. Therefore, the decicion is to concentrate on just one of the mines: Garzweiler II. Excavation started in 2006. Due to the excavation period of almost 40 years and due to the vast dimension of the mining area, not only sections of two highways will vanish and have to be rebuilt along the pit, but 13 villages with approximately 7600 villagers have to be relocated as well. In my case studies I will introduce seven villages: six relocations and one village that will be close to the mine.

Abb. 1: Open-cast Mine Garzweiler II (Valeska Flor, 2010).

Abb. 2: Umsiedlungsort Keyenberg (Valeska Flor, 2012).

During resettlement

The first case study is the resettlement process and five villages and their lignite-linked problems during this process (Keyenberg, Kuckum, Ober- und Unterwestrich, and Berverath). Officially, all of them are districts of the town of Erkelenz. However, all are more or less independent villages with their own infrastructure, i.e. they have their own churches, schools, kindergartens, banking facilities, smaller shops, etc. Only local affairs, secondary schools, and the bigger shops are centralized in the town centre of Erkelenz. In 2010 the lignite committee authorized the town of Erkelenz to start the resettlement process. The collaboration between the involved parties (the town, citizens' board, RWE, and the district council) is not always easy. Some of the villagers are still enraged about the fact that they have to leave their home behind. In this context it is to say that most of the villagers do not leave voluntarily. But they must. All because of Section 79, subsection 1, of the federal mining law which says that "The assignment of property is permitted in individual cases if it serves the public good, especially to secure the market supply of raw materials, the preservation of jobs in the mining industry, the existence or improvement of the economic structure, or the meaningful and systematic exploitation of the deposit, and if due to the site-dependency of the mining operation the enterprise cannot be carried out by any other reasonable means." (BbergG Section 79(1)). To put it bluntly: energy generation for the public good is more important than the interests of the inhabitants in the recoverable lignite area.

Now what kind of lignite-linked problems can be found during the resettlement process? First of all it is to say that the resettlement process itself is the biggest problem for the villagers as they do not leave voluntarily, but most of them understand and accept that they cannot change the facts and the resettlement process. At the beginning of the process there are the big decisions the resettlers have to make. Do I want to contribute actively to the process? Do I want to resettle with the whole village or not? Where do I want to settle and when? Those questions are just some that have to be answered in the first two to four years of the process.

During the "Suchraumfindung" (the process of finding suitable resettlement locations) some resettlers feel like second class citizens. "We are being displaced, expelled and now we are supposed to decide on a location close to the edge of the [future] mine. For us the edge of the mine is a no-go area." ("Suchraumfindung", March 2012). To understand that it is important to know that the resettlers had to choose between several locations, but four of them were (or will be) close to the mine. Hence, a heated debate followed in the public presentations and discussions of the particular search areas. Furthermore the villagers complained that the protection of species is more important than their interests: "Conservation of landscape, the protection of nature and species are not of interest when our world is excavated and demolished. But now in this discussion it is suddenly most important. All according to the motto: 'No, you cannot go there. The protection of species must be guaranteed.' I'm asking: 'Who is deserving protection? The common hamster or we?" ("Suchraumfindung", March 2012). With every resettlement process there has to be an environmental assessment, and, just as an example, the common hamster is an endangered species in Germany, so development areas are not allowed in places where there are colonies of common hamsters. Of course, the villagers have different opinions. "If we are talking about preservation of species, resettlements should not be allowed to happen." ("Suchraumfindung", March 2012).

After Resettlement

The second case study outlines lignite-linked problems after or close to the end of the resettlement process in the new village of Immerath (Immerath neu). The Resettlement process started in 2000 and most of the villagers have already left their old homes and built houses in the new village. By now Immerath (neu) is recognizable as a village, but there are still many free building sites which makes life in the village not easier. As there is still too much space between houses, forming a new community is even more difficult than thought before.

"So many times 'for the last time'. For the last time a parish festival, a birthday in the old community, I plant flowers in my garden... all for the last time. And those first times [in the new community], they do not exist yet." (RP online, 10.08.2009). This statement is typical for most of those who are part of the resettlement process. The arrival in the new village, after all the strains of resettlement, is often even harder than expected. All the new things – the "first times" – are still lacking. One important new "thing" they have to get used to is the new house they live in. Usually it is completely different to the old one. First of all, the houses in the old villages were often up to 30 or even 100 or more years old. Therefore, the basic structure of the buildings and especially the energy supply was not up-to-date. In contrast, the new houses are more than that. Especially the energy supply is very important to the resettlers. "To be independent from RWE [Rheinisch-Westfälisches Elektrizitätswerk AG] that is the goal. I do not want to use their energy, especially no lignite-based energy." (Interview Gisela Berger, 22.09.2012). After resettlement some resettlers are firmly against using anything which RWE is providing. At least in this context it is possible for them to gain the upper hand. Hence, they build as energy-efficient as possible so that in the end they have a so-called zero energy house and are self-sufficient.

Living close to the mine

The third case study is the village of Wanlo and the problems that occur when villages are close to an open pit mine. Wanlo was supposed to be excavated as well, but in the end they got around that fate. What was considered a blessing in the 1990s is now more like a curse, at least, for those who are directly affected. In recent years it became increasingly obvious that this "blessing" has its negative sides as well. One negative side effect is that Wanlo will lose all of its close neighbour villages and most of its familiar roads. In the near future the mine will border Wanlo in the East and West and in the North there will still be the highway A46. So it can be seen that these aspects will influence Wanlo's quality of life. "Quality of life" is a keyword which is mentioned quite often, always in the context that it is not going to be easy for the villagers as there are (or will be) a lot of different negative impacts for the villages close by the pit. Some of these impacts are the aforementioned light, noise, traffic, CO^2, particulate matter, lowering of groundwater, landslides, etc. In the following paragraphs some of these impacts will be explained in more detail.

Light & Noise: Due to the continuous three shifts system floodlight is necessary in the field of lignite mining. But especially when the lignite excavators get closer to the village, quality of life declines. "There is no genuine night anymore – no real day and night rhythm – which is quite hard to stand." (Interview Dorfinteressengemeinschaft Wanlo e.V., 12.04.2012). The same applies to noise. Inside the mines and close to the mines there is always noise: on the one hand because of all the working machines (lignite excavators, spreaders, conveyor belts, cars, etc.), and on the other hand because of the wells for the draining of groundwater. In lignite mining, a continuous lowering of groundwater level is necessary in order to protect the mining area from flooding.

Particulate Matter & Dirt: According to representatives of BUND NRW [Bund für Umwelt und Naturschutz Deutschland Landesverband Nordrhein Westfalen] open pit mines are the cause for at least 90% of the local particulate matter emissions (Interview Dirk Jansen, 13.03.2012). By now it is scientifically proved that particulate matter is harmful to health and can be the cause for allergies, cardiovascular diseases, lung diseases, and strokes. Besides particular matter there is another problem with dust and/or dirt particles which are affecting all those in the vicinity of the mine. Everyday there is a film of black greasy dust on every surface in the villages: windows, roofs, house walls, cars. Therefore, the villagers, for example, cannot dry their clothes outside anymore. But more important, because of the greasy dust on the houses their current market value is declining.

Landslides: Besides the aforementioned strains which mostly have influences on the health of the villagers, lignite mining has a devastating impact on the landscape. Therefore RWE is required to restore the exploited lands. But this recultivation can be problematic as well. In 2009 a 350m long part of the embankment of the Concordia Lake – an artificial lake created out of the lignite mine in an area of Saxony-Anhalt, Germany – slid into the lake. Two houses of the village of Nachterstedt ended up in the lake and three people died. A more local and recent example for landslides are the landslides at Inden in 2010 and landslides that presumably happened at the Sophienhöhe close to Hambach in 2012 (The Sophienhöhe is the largest artificial hill worldwide created by surface mining at the open cast and lignite mine Tagebau Hambach). One reason for potential landslides is that all open-cast mines in the Rhenish Lignite-Mining district are in a seismic area. Another one is the systematic pumping off of groundwater. RWE has to do this in order to keep the open-cast mines dry.

To conclude: Above all lignite mining means a change of familiar structures of the resettlers. Those fearing their uprooting may react differently: some accept their fate and some even understand its necessity, others are quite vocal to the loss of their homes, and some simply resign to resettlement. The same can be said of those remaining behind: some are quite vocal and try to point out what is happening to them; others are more cautious and wait for what is going to happen in the near future. The resettlers and their neighbours must deal with these impacts on their living environment. Sometimes they develop coping strategies which help them deal with all the socio-cultural changes during resettlement and lignite mining. These coping strategies will be the topic of the PhD thesis which will be finished in 2014.

Bibliography

German Federal Mining Act (BbergG) Section 19(1). http://www.gesetze-im-internet.de/bundesrecht/bbergg/gesamt.pdf, Date 31.01.2013.

Erkelenz, Umsiedlung, ein verdammt langer Prozess. Interview mit Gisela Berger. In: Rheinische Post online, 10.08.2009.

Interview with Gisela Berger, Immerath (neu), 22.09.2012.

Interview with members of the citizens' group Dorfinteressengemeinschaft Wanlo e.V., Wanlo, 12.04.2012.

Interview with Dirk Jansen, Düsseldorf, 13.03.2012.

The "Pfennwerthandel" in the Mining Region of Kitzbühel

Anita Feichter-Haid[1]

[1] Institute of History and European Ethnology, University of Innsbruck, Austria

The focus of this essay is on the Pfennwerthandel of an early modern mining district around the small city of Kitzbühel which is located in the east of northern Tyrol (Austria) close to the border to Germany. Pfennwerthandel means trading with certain goods. Originally Pfennwert denoted goods which were quite cheap – worth only a penny (Pfennig). In early modern times Pfennwert identified very different products, e.g. tallow, iron, cereals, hutches etc.

In this article there will be shed some light on the ‚Tallow and Iron Trade' first and second on the circumstances of the trade with cereals. As an example the trade with comestibles will be explored that was vital to keep the miners at work.

Iron and tallow were both essential for mining activities. Iron was required to produce tools for the miners whereas tallow was needed for lighting in the mines. One miner is considered to have worked eight hours a day and for the whole time he needed tallow to bring light into the dark, hence a huge amount was needed to meet this demand. There were other substances used, like certain oils, but the use of oil was not widespread; at least not in the mines of the Tyrol during the early modern time. The reason might be that tallow was the cheapest and therefore the most profitable substance (vgl. Schmelzer, 1972).

With the boom of silver-mining in the district of Kitzbühel, mainly on the Röhrerbichl, in the second half of the 16th century, the demand for tallow and iron increased dramatically. We know of 1200-1500 workers in the mines of the Röhrerbichl alone (Mutschlechner, 1968). In addition there existed several other smaller mines located closer to the city of Kitzbühel, e.g. on the Jufen or in the region of Sinwell. If the reader keeps in mind that about 2/3 of the miners worked underground for eight hours a day and needed tallow for their pit lamps during all their working hours it becomes apparent how crucial the tallow-trade for a successful enterprise were.

Similar to other mining areas in Tyrol as Schwaz (vgl. Palme, 1997) some companies which owned mines in this district tried to supply their workers sufficiently to guarantee smooth mining operations. They formed several trading companies, for instance the „Gesellschaft und Verwandte des Kössentalerischen Schmelzhandels", short „Kössentaler"[1], which dominated the trade with iron and tallow for a few years in the 1540s (Rupert, 1976).

In 1549 different companies (Kössentaler, Fugger, Kirchberger, Rosenberger and Ligsalzer) signed a five-year-contract to enter a joint venture with the designated aim to supply their mines with tallow, iron, hutches, ropes and other things:

> „die perckhwerch, im gericht Küzpüchl und Prixental gelegen, mit ynnslith, eisen, troegen, saylern, liechtern und annderm, was zu beleichtung und arbait des pergs gehoert, mit guettem zeug und waarn"

It must have been a successful enterprise, since after five years the contract was extended. This contract provides some insight into the shareholding. There was a total of 36 quarters: exactly half of it was owned by the Kössentaler, 9 quarters by the Kirchberger, 4 quarters were held by the Rosenberg, 3 quarters owned the famous Augsburgian family Fugger and finally, the Ligsalzische company owned 2 quarters. Over time, due to the slow decline of the silver-mines, the ownership structures changed; some companies vanished and other took their shares (Rupert, 1976).

After having given a short summary why such a joint-venture as the Tallow and Iron Trade was started and who took part in it, still the question remains: Where was the tallow bought that was needed to keep the mining activities going?

Certainly, it was bought from the butchers in the region. In the city statute of 1503 in Kitzbühel it was regulated that the butchers had to produce tallow quarterly and offer it to the miners in the following eight days at a certain price (Rupert, 1976; Widmoser, 1971). Moreover it is probable that a good portion was imported, since – considering the amount needed – it seems unlikely that the local production could have been sufficient. We know about Schwaz that only about 30% of the tallow needed could be bought from the local butchers; the bulk of tallow came from the more eastern parts of Austria[2] (Spranger, 2006). Therefore it may be probable that the majority of tallow for the Kitzbühel-Mines had to be imported from these regions as well. This assumption is supported by a letter from 1615, in which an official of the Mining Court in Kitzbühel asks for permission to undertake a journey to Linz in order to supply the miners on the Röhrerbichl with tallow and other goods (TLA, Gemeine Missiven (1615/ II), fol. 1230-1231).

As already mentioned the provision of comestibles to mining communities were inevitabely important all over the southern german-alpine mining region (Ludwig, 1997). Although the territorial sovereign extended the days of the weekly market in Kitzbühel to enable the miners to visit it, the miners couldn't depend on this regional market alone. Since the miners delved into the pits from Monday to Saturday[3] and the mines were located often far away from any city. There were neither much time left nor many possibilities to provide for themselves. Therefore it had to be the interest of the different mining companies to supply their workers.

During the entire 16th century Tyrol was never self-sufficient in the production of cereals and other comestibles, maybe also due to the large population within the mining districts of Schwaz, Kitzbühel, Sterzing etc. Wheat and rye were mostly imported from Bavaria and other parts of Germany, Salzburg, Bohemia, Upper Austria and occasionally from Italy (Spranger, 2006). Although favourably located, in the Inn-Valley prices for viands were much higher than in other Austrian regions – e.g. in the first half of the 16th century the cost of wheat was 200% higher than in Vienna or Klosterneuburg (Fischer, 2001).

The situation worsened in the second half of the 16th century when Tyrol was haunted by crop failures. Especially bad was the situation in years from 1550 to 1552, in the turn of the year 1566 to 1567 and in the years from 1569 to 1572 (Fischer, 1919). During the whole 16th century neither in Schwaz, nor in Kitzbühel a joint venture comparable to the Tallow-and-Iron-Trade was organized (Rupert, 1976; Palme, 1997). That means all the different (trading) companies within and of the several mining districts competed for the so desperately needed cereals.

In years of poor harvests free trade was replaced by a system of allowances. Therefore the trading companies and even the Tyrolean prince Ferdinand II. had to ask the respective lord for an allowance to buy a certain amount of cereals within his territory (Spranger, 2006). Even if it was intended only to transport the cereals through the respective territory, the landlord had to give his permission. To add to the already complicated situation, logistic problems had to be tackled. In any case there were customs and excise dues to be paid. Another obstacle was the fact, that the river Inn was more or less unnavigable from May on. In the years of crisis the situation even worsened. Due to the lack of cereals there was a lack of fodder (oats). Therefore it was harder to find pack animals, like horses and higher transport prices had to be paid. In several regions which were not as much affected by the bad harvests there were other reasons for the rise of transportation costs, in parts of Italy, for instance, the transport system was already overloaded by the dispositions for the war with the Turks etc. (Fischer, 1919).

To give a better understanding of the complex and difficult situation a specific correspondence between the archbishop of Salzburg, Johann Jakob von Kuen-Belasy, the "Kössenthaler"-company and the duke Albrecht V. of Bavaria will be now examined.

The whole correspondence deals with the trade in grain of Mühldorf, a small city (today in Germany, about 70km north from Salzburg), where from 1571 on the archbishop resided, since Salzburg was haunted by the pest. This city seems to have been a regional centre of the trade in cereals.

In November 1570 the „Verwanndten des Cössenthalerischen Schmölzhanndls zu Kizpühl" wrote to the Archbishop of Salzburg. They appealed to Johann Jakob to intervene on their behalf, since although they possessed allowances to buy grain in Mühldorf they were not allowed to transport it.

From June on they had ordered and in most cases already paid certain amounts of cereal, but due to some difficulties they had not been able to ship it in time. Now some sellers denied to deliver with the argument: "das abermallen ain furstlich bevelch solle an euch ausgeganngen sein, welcher mit bringt, das ir nichts verkauffen oder wegkh fiern lassen soldet" (Geheimes Archiv, XXVIIII, 12; 16. November 1570).

We do not know the reaction of the archbishop in that case, but we do know his actions in another: One month later the same company appealed to the archbishop again. This time they had bought cereals and intended to buy even more in the Duchy of Bavaria and planned to ship the grain on the Inn to Tyrol. Now their request was to make sure that they were allowed to bring the cereals through Mühldorf without being pressed to unload and offer it. Again there seemed to be no reaction of the archbishop.

A few days later the duke of Bavaria (who owned a certain amount of shares of the "Kössentaler"-company) intervened on their behalf. He wrote a letter to Johann Jakob to ask for permission to transport the rest (!) of the grain that the company had bought and paid for. His letter allows us an even deeper insight into the whole situation. It seems that the company had not only bought cereals in Bavaria but also around the city of Mühldorf and even from the townsmen with an allowance granted by the duke. But Johann Jakob did not seem to take offence in that. The archbishops reaction this time was swift. On the next day he wrote a letter to the "Statgerichts-verwallter, burgermaister und rath zu muldorf" explaining that he had received the request in question from the duke of Bavaria and ordered them to release the cereals. His main argument was that it was neither wise nor an option at all to stop this freight, since otherwise it might be possible that no cereals form Bavaria would reach Mühldorf anymore (Geheimes Archiv, XXV-VIIII, 12; 20. Dezember 1570).

Finally the question is picked up how the territorial prince Ferdinand II. dealt with these supply crises, since he must have had a twofold interest in keeping the situation stable. On the one hand, to prevent hunger meant preventing riots[4]; on the other hand he made enormous profit out of the mines and therefore it must have been his utmost concern to keep the workers in the mines (and working) and that meant to guarantee them a living without hunger.

So what did the Tyrolean sovereign do? First, in order to keep the cereals in the country in the years of crisis he passed a ban on exports and established a system of allowances as did the other lords in the adjacent areas. Second, he allowed a free price formation in order to motivate the traders to come into the country, which lead to sudden price explosion (vgl. Schmelzer, 1972).

Moreover, he tried to get allowances to buy cereals and transport them to Tyrol. A huge correspondence with the sovereigns of Bavaria, Salzburg, Bohemia etc. testifies his efforts (Fischer, 1919). Often also the different mining companies appealed to the sovereign to act in their interest, which he obviously tried to do. A letter (sent to the archbishop of Salzburg) in October 1570 shows that Ferdinand (or his chamber) had been successful in obtaining allowances to buy and ship cereals for several companies, such as the "yenpacherischen hanndlsverwandten" and Hans Dreyling, both providing the mining region of Schwaz, to buy and transport grain. But – as the letter goes on – although Heinrich Ruedl who was the purchasing agent of the "yenpacher"-company held an allowance, the amount cereals he had bought in Mühldorf and which was already being shipped was stopped by the officials of the city. Now the sovereign intervened in the interest of this company and asked to give the cereals free (Geheimes Archiv, XXVIIII, 12; 22. Oktober 1570). So even though allowances were granted they did not always guarantee a successful and in-time supply.

The examples given were intended to shed some light on the sometimes wearisome and risky venture of trade in wheat during that time. Although mainly the difficulties which trading (mining) companies had to face while importing material and supplying the mines in Tyrol were highlighted above, it should be kept in mind, that the "pfennwerthandel" could be an exceedingly lucrative business, e.g. in the 2nd half of the 17th century the Fugger did not succeed in getting a tangible income out of their mines in Kitzbühel but made a substantial profit from their trade to provide comestibles for their workers (vgl. Mutschlechner, 1968).

Endnotes

[1] The „Gesellschaft und Verwandte des Kössentalerischen Schmelzhandels" were also know as the "Fröschlmoserische Gesellschaft" (vgl. Rupert, 1975).

[2] "Österreich ob und unter der Enns und Niederösterreich".

[3] The weekly shift ended with Saturday noon. On Saturday the miners worked only 4 hours.

[4] In the great upheavels of 1525 the miners complained about the expensive prices for comestibles as cereals, wine, butter, oil, and cheese (vgl. Fischer, 2001).

Bibliography

Tiroler Landesarchiv, Kammerkopialbuchreihe der oberösterreichischen Kammer: Gemeine Missiven 1615.

Salzburger Landesarchiv, Geheimes Archiv, XXVIIII, 12.

Fischer, J. (1919): Tirols Getreidepolitik von 1527 bis 1601. Innsbruck.

Fischer, P. (2001): Die gemeine Gesellschaft der Bergwerke. Bergbau und Bergleute im Tiroler Montanrevier Schwaz zur Zeit des Bauernkrieges. St. Katharinen.

Ludwig, K. (1997): Unternehmenserfolge im süddeutsch-alpenländischen Montanwesen in der ersten Hälfte des 16. Jahrhunderts in Abhängigkeit von Lösungen der Versorgungs- und Ressourcenprobleme. In: Westermann, E.: Bergbaureviere als Verbrauchszentren im vorindustriellen Europa. Stuttgart.

Mutschlechner, G. (1968): Kitzbühler Bergbau. In: Widmoser, E.: Statdbuch Kitzbühel 2. Kitzbühel.

Palme, R. (1997): Die Unschlittversorgung von Schwaz Mitte der zwanziger Jahre des 16. Jahrhunderts. In: Westermann, E.: Bergbaureviere als Verbrauchszentren im vorindustriellen Europa. Stuttgart.

Rupert, M. (1976): Vom Aufkommen des Rerobichl-Bergbaus (1540) bis zum Ende der bei der Stadt Kitzbühel gelegenen Schmelzhütten im 17. Jahrhundert. Archaelogia Austriaca 59/60, pp. 273-437.

Schmelzer, M. (1972): Geschichte der Preise und Löhne in Rattenberg. Innsbruck.

Spranger, C. (2006): Der Metall und Versorgungshandel der Fugger in Schwaz in Tirol 1560-1575 zwischen Krisen und Konflikten. Augsburg.

Widmoser, E. (1971): Blick in das Leben der Stadt. In: Widmoser, E.: Stadtbuch Kitzbühel 2. Kitzbühel.

The development of social stratification in the Montafon – transformation of a former mining area in the 17th century

Michael Kasper[1]

[1] Montafoner Museen, Schruns, Austria

In the following here will be presented some results of a socio-historical research in the Montafon, the southernmost valley of the Austrian state Vorarlberg. Silver-bearing copper ore and iron ore were mined in this mountainous, rural region of western Austria at least since the Middle Ages. Several evidence indicates that the exploitation of iron had already begun in this former mining area in the ninth century AD. The activities were then changed into copper and silver mining in the 11th and 12th centuries AD. Although the ore deposits were only of regional importance, the Tyrolean government set up the "Berggericht Montafon" in the 15th century. (Neuhauser, 2012:82) Maybe there was a considerable influx of miners around 1500 (Burmeister, 2009:199), but most of them were born in the Montafon as their surnames indicate (Neuhauser, 2011:26). The main mining-district was situated around the villages Bartholomäberg and Silbertal. In the mid-16th century, however, a rapid decrease of ore mining began and at the beginning of the 17th century, the mining in the Montafon ended. Johann Georg Schleh stated in his Embser chronicle about the Montafon in 1616:

"Ist ein Volckreich Thal, darneben Vieh und Molckreich / tragt auch Obs vnd Korn / hat erwan vil Berckwerck gehabt / von Silber vnd Eysen / der zeit aber er loschen / hat auch Wasserbäder darinen von Schwebel vnd ander Mineral / die Berg seind alles hohe / wilde Gebirg / darinnen treffenliche Alppen." (Schleh, 1616:61)

Here should be presented a brief overview of the development of the complex socio-historical microcosm Montafon in the 17th century. Conclusions about social structures and social transformation processes can be drawn for example by analysing data from tax records (Kasper, 2011:7). The focus of this research is especially on tax records about the mining-communities of the Montafon that date from the 17th century.

Tax registers can provide an insight into population structures and socio-historical developments in early modern regions. They are an important basis for demographical calculations because they list all taxable residents of a community and, thus, they mention a large part of the population at that time. Tax registers are not only an important source of information for historical demography, but they also represent a snapshot of the rural population. Therefore, they can represent a solid basis for socio-historical research about early modern societies. In this context it is important to consider that the quality of tax lists was not consistently good. Furthermore, it has to be emphasized that, often, only taxpayers were registered and that the parts of the population which were exempt from taxes for various reasons remained anonymous. Nevertheless, in most of the tax registers of the Montafon also tax-exempt persons were mentioned, so that a full coverage of the regional population can be assumed.

Based on the analysis of the tax rolls, in which an average household size of 3.5 persons was assumed for each taxable unit (Klein, 1969:68), the following rounded population figures were revealed. By taking recourse to census results of the 18th century, a comparison of the calculated figures with assured population numbers is possible (Klein, 2012).

village	taxpayers	population (rounded)	population in 1754
Bartholomäberg	1610: 278	970	1208
	1645: 333	1165	
	1660: 383	1340	
	1697: 355	1240	
Gaschurn	1638: 234	820	1010
	1668: 300	1050	
Lorüns	1697: 21	70	68 (1762)
St. Anton	1610: 31	110	71
	1645: 46	160	
	1660: 29	100	
	1697: 21	70	
St. Gallenkirch	1638: 417	1460	1351
	1672: 402	1410	
Schruns	1610: 174	610	1236
	1645: 344	1410	
Silbertal	1656: 185	650	578
Stallehr	1697: 20	70	55 (1756)
Tschagguns	1631: 318	1.110	1155
Vandans	1631: 174	610	704

Schruns, which had been part of the mining municipality Bartholomäberg until the end of the 16th century, became independent then and grew extremely fast from the beginning to the middle of the 17th century. In the meantime, the population growth in the other villages developed rather moderately. In the second half of the 17th century it seems to have stagnated or even decreased in some places. The most populous communities were St. Gallenkirch and Bartholomäberg. Gaschurn and Schruns reached a level of more than 1,000 inhabitants during the 17th century. Due to massive changes concerning clusters of family names in some villages within short periods, a considerable mobility of the population can be assumed. (Tschaikner, 2010: 82)

The differences in the accumulation of surnames as well as their diversity indicate, for example, a difference between Bartholomäberg and Schruns in the 17th century: Bartholomäberg was the former mining center but turned then into an agrarian settlement. This village was dominated by a few long-established lineages. There was certainly some migration but the fact that 23% of the population carried one of two last names, either Staimer or Ganal, indicates nevertheless, that these two family names dominated in Bartholomäberg. In the upcoming village of Schruns the situation was diametrically opposite, as there was a great variety of names. There were some slightly more common surnames, most of them appeared only once, twice or three times. This fact indicates that there was immigration to Schruns in the first half of the 17th century. This village was an important settlement of the Montafon and represented a first point of contact for members of poorer classes, for example ex-miners. They hoped to achieve an improvement of their living situation in Schruns, which had the most important economic and political power in the valley. (Kasper, 2008: 56-59)

Some structures and trends concerning social inequality can be identified for the research period. Bartholomäberg and St. Anton, for example, which have a particularly long tradition of tax books, show a decrease in the average taxes paid per household between 1610 and 1697. In Gaschurn, St. Gallenkirch and Schruns a similar but less pronounced trend can be observed from the first to the second half of the century.

Analysing the median of the more populous municipalities, it can be noticed that in the former mining villages Bartholomäberg and Silbertal, but also in Tschagguns and Vandans, higher figures were achieved than in Gaschurn, St. Gallenkirch and Schruns. Therefore, a more prosperous society can be presumed in the "Außer-Montafon" (without Schruns). In the "Inner-Montafon" and in Schruns the majority of the population tended to be poorer and the wealth of the households was lower.

Anyhow, in Gaschurn and Schruns the average of the taxes was relatively high and refers to a higher inequality within their districts. This interpretation can be confirmed by the amount of the total tax revenue that was contributed by the upper class because in Gaschurn and Schruns where the tax-payments of this social class made up about 60% of the tax revenue of the whole population. In other words, the richest 10% of the population owned 60% of the assets. In the rather prosperous village Bartholomäberg, which had a relatively large middle class, the richest tenth reached only an amount between 42 and 45%. In Gaschurn and Schruns, in comparison, the rate of tax-exempt persons reached 20% and was the highest one in the whole valley. Only in Tschagguns, where 28% of the population were tax-exempt, the rate of people living on the poverty line was even higher.

Considering the fact that the sum of all taxes paid per municipality represented the entire possessions of the local population, the average wealth of the inhabitants can be estimated. If one assumes that one tax-stamp represented an amount of 100 guilders, a reduction of the total wealth in the Montafon can be revealed for the research period. Particularly in the mining community Bartholomäberg, the entire village assets of nearly 400,000 guilders in 1610 decreased to an amount of 280,000 guilders in 1697, although, or probably because the population slightly increased during that period. Even in the relatively poor village of St. Gallenkirch with a nearly stagnant population, a sharp decline in assets occurred (from 237,000 guilders to 160,000 guilders). Only in Schruns, which almost doubled its population between 1610 and 1645, the total assets of the residents increased significantly. (Kasper, 2011:212-214)

In the tax lists the professions of the taxpayers were rarely listed so that hardly any connection between profession and economic prosperity can be noticed. The basic trend, however, shows that manual workers, such as millers, blacksmiths, locksmiths and carpenters, almost exclusively belonged to the poorer classes. In Schruns, a particular concentration of craftsmen can be remarked. While in the other municipalities of the Montafon only several millers, locksmiths and carpenters were recorded, in Schruns a "Schüsslendreyer", a locksmith, a tailor, a dyer, a table maker and a hatter were registered in the tax book (Kasper, 2011: 219). During the 17th century, Schruns definitely evolved into the main village of the Montafon. This development was illustrated by the fact that many central functions were transferred to Schruns. Therefore, the village outranked the formerly dominant mining-settlement of Bartholomäberg. It is likely that this development was closely related to the decline of mining around 1600. Many former mining workers from Bartholomäberg and Silbertal settled to Schruns, the new "capital" of the Montafon. The considerable social contrasts in Schruns testify to this movement. While the rural, land-owning population remained in Bartholomäberg, numerous landless people, who mainly worked as manual workers, settled down in Schruns. However, some individuals from the latter group managed to achieve a rapid social advancement, for example the former miners-family Zumkeller.

During peasant unrest around 1525, the miner "Jos zum Keller" lived in the Montafon. Together with the farmer Sebastian Nusch from St. Gallenkirch, he encouraged the regional population to cooperate with the South Tyrolean insurgents and to rise up against the reign (Burmeister, 1996:143). He intended to move to the nearby situated town of Bludenz with his partisans, where he wanted to „hausen, solange die Obrigkeit gehaust habe" (Bilgeri, 1977:38). "Joder zum Keller" was said to be a very influential man (Bilgeri, 1977:28). The family Zumkeller was mentioned again around 1580. In a list of hosts of the Montafon, a certain "Bascha Zum Keller" appeared in Schruns (Pecoraro, 1995:206). The directories on an old Montafon court called "Frevelgericht" show that those trials took place in the taverns of Schruns (in 1583, 1586 and 1591 in the tavern owned by "Bascha Zum Keller") (Welti, 1963: 202). In 1587 a certain Sebastian Zumkeller appeared as an associate of the mining company in the "Aschentobel" and on the "Silberberg" (Welti, 1971:73).

A few years later, in the fall of 1605, Jos Zumkeller held already the office of an assessor in a trial at Christa Durig's tavern in Schruns.[1] Two years later, the abovementioned negotiations of the court called "Frevelgericht" took place at the tavern of Jos Zumkeller (Welti, 1963:202). Jos Zumkeller, first an assessor at the court and then a host, was a very well-known person in the Montafon during the first half of the 17th century. In 1645, he paid 180 marks of taxes, which was the second highest amount in the whole tax-district of Bartholomäberg and Schruns. Jos Zumkeller and the ensign Peter Fitsch were the only ones who were highlighted by the letter "H" in the tax book which expressed high respect. That sign meant something like "Herr" and showed that the two men were superiors of the Montafon (Tschaikner, 1993:12). In 1615, Jos supervised the edition of an inventory for the smelter in Tschagguns (Welti, 1971:83). Six years later, the steward of Bludenz reported on Jos Zumkeller to the Privy Council in Innsbruck. Right at the beginning, it was stated that Zumkeller was said to be "ains schlechten herkhumens" and that his mother was said to be "ain hexen maisterin". Eleven or twelve years earlier, he had possessed nearly nothing, so that "ime nit wol ain [Fässchen] weins verthrawt [wurde]". Afterwards, however, his assets amounted to around 13,000 to 15,000 florins. He had achieved this prosperity thanks to his flourishing tavern and by transporting grain. From time to time, he had bought lard in the Prättigau in Switzerland and had sold it at Innsbruck and Hall. Zumkeller was said to be "höffertig, stolz und ubermietig". He attained that the "gemaine ainfeltige paurs man" did not do anything without his advice. During the unrest of those days Zumkeller – was said to have "das ganze wesen gefierth". All meetings took place at his tavern and nothing was decided without him. According to the steward it was not possible to guarantee peace and to obtain the obedience of the subjects as long as Zumkeller's influence was not ended by special means, for example a ban. Nevertheless, he was allowed to stay (Tschaikner, 1997:54f). The miners-descendant Jos Zumkeller had quickly managed to become one of the wealthiest men in the valley and he had been an active merchant and innkeeper.

One can conclude that only a few former miners succeeded in their economic ascent. Most of them migrated to Schruns, the new centre of the valley, and worked there as manual workers. Only some of them managed to become landowners and farmers. The formerly privileged miners had become the poor class of the population which was a significant change in the regional history. Schruns had not always been the centre of the Montafon. The end of the mining industry was one of the main reasons for its rise.

Endnotes

[1] Vorarlberger Landesarchiv (VLA), Hds. u. Cod. Stand und Gericht Montafon 8, fol. 178.

Bibliography

Bilgeri, B. (1977): Geschichte Vorarlbergs Bd. III. Ständemacht, Gemeiner Mann – Emser und Habsburger. Wien-Köln-Graz.

Burmeister, K. (1996): Bludenz 1420 – 1550. In: Tschaikner, M.: Geschichte der Stadt Bludenz. Von der Urzeit bis zum Beginn des 20. Jahrhunderts. Sigmaringen, pp. 101-160.

Burmeister, K. (2009): "Montafonium Nostrum" – Das Montafon in der Zeit um und nach 1500. Vom Schweizerkrieg bis zum Dreißigjährigen Krieg. In: Rollinger, R.: Montafon 2. Besiedlung – Bergbau – Relikte. Von der Steinzeit bis zum Ende des Mittelalters. Schruns, pp. 178-227.

Kasper, M. (2008): Ein Montafoner Steuerbuch aus dem Jahr 1645. Bemerkungen zur regionalen Wirtschafts- und Sozialgeschichte in der frühen Neuzeit – Edition und sozialstatistische Auswertung. Saarbrücken.

Kasper, M. (2011): Montafoner Steuerbücher. Quellen zur Sozialgeschichte des Montafons im 17. Jahrhundert (Quellen zur Geschichte Vorarlbergs 13). Regensburg.

Klein, K. (1969): Die Bevölkerung Vorarlbergs vom Beginn des 16. bis zur Mitte des 18. Jahrhunderts. Montfort 21, pp. 59-90.

Klein, K. (2012): Historisches Ortslexikon. Statistische Dokumentation zur Bevölkerungs- und Siedlungsgeschichte. Vorarlberg. http://www.oeaw.ac.at/vid/download/histortslexikon/Ortslexikon_Vorarlberg.pdf (23.01.2013).

Neuhauser, G. (2011): Die Geschichte des Berggerichts Montafon in der frühen Neuzeit. Masch. phil. Diss. Innsbruck.

Neuhauser, G. (2012): Die "perckhrichter" im Berggericht Montafon in der frühen Neuzeit. In: Kasper, M.: Jahresbericht 2011. Montafoner Museen. Heimatschutzverein Montafon. Montafon Archiv. Schruns, pp. 82-91.

Pecoraro, D. (1995): Wirte, Bäcker und Kornführer im Montafon um 1580. Bludenzer Geschichtsblätter 24-26, pp. 204-206.

Schleh, J. G. (1616): Emser Chronik. Hystorische Relation oder Eygendtliche Beschribung der Landschaft unterhalb St. Luzis Stayg und dem Schallberg bayderseits Rheins bis an den Bodensee. Hohenems.

Tschaikner, M. (1993): Lukas Tschofen von Gaschurn – Zur Geschichte einer Montafoner Oberschichtfamilie im 16. und 17. Jahrhundert. Bludenzer Geschichtsblätter 14+15, pp. 9-86.

Tschaikner, M. (1997): Magie und Hexerei im südlichen Vorarlberg zu Beginn der Neuzeit. Konstanz.

Tschaikner, M. (2010): Das St. Gallenkircher Beichtregister von 1613. Bludenzer Geschichtsblätter 95+96, pp. 82-97.

Welti, L. (1963): Siedlungs- und Sozialgeschichte von Vorarlberg. Studien zur Rechts-, Wirtschafts- und Kulturgeschichte I, Innsbruck.

Welti, L. (1971): Bludenz als österreichischer Vogteisitz 1418-1806. Eine regionale Verwaltungsgeschichte. Zürich.

Medieval mining in Dippoldiswalde (Saxony). New approaches on research of mining impact

Ivonne Burghardt[1], Christiane Hemker[1] & Yves Hoffmann[1]

[1] Archaeological Heritage Office Saxony, Dresden, Germany

To illustrate what might have happened in Freiberg (Saxony) in the 1170s, the time right after the rich ore deposits had been discovered, Peter Spufford compared this event to what happened in the time of the gold-rush in California in 1848 (Spufford, 1988, 112). Unfortunately we are not able to tell what exactly happened in the area of later Freiberg, since written records from these times are rare and reports of impacts of mining on nature and people are literally nonexistent. But one can learn from indirect sources, as we will demonstrate in the following paper.

State of Research

Due to the excavations and archival researches by Wolfgang Schwabenicky on medieval mining sites of the 12th and 13th century in Saxony since the 1970s, mining research has played an important role in European mining archaeology. Saxon towns and villages, like Freiberg and Scharfenberg (near Meißen), which by written sources were known to hold productive silver mining in that period, were investigated in detail by historians. But since mining in the following centuries and urban sprawl in the 20th centuries destroyed most of the medieval mining relicts and landscape, archeologists were not able to undertake systematical or large-scale excavations, especially in the mines. Also a lot of questions concerning the development, structure and influence on the immediate environment of these mining towns remained open. The situation changed with the discoveries of medieval mining sites in Dippoldiswalde and Niederpöbel. Because of its actual political and economic status medieval Dippoldiswalde always was considered as a small village of minor economic importance, founded as a part of the colonization in the 12th century. So far this was confirmed by written documents. In 2008 medieval mining sites in the underground of Dippoldiswalde, which extend over large parts of the town area (*Fig. 1*), were discovered and meticulous archeological investigations and documentation followed (Hemker & Scholz, 2010; Smolnik, 2011). The detailed research and comparison to other important mining districts in the lower and upper Ore Mountains, like Freiberg and Treppenhauer (Sachsenburg) already answered some questions about the extension of medieval mining areas and their influence on economy, population and landscape.

First Impact – Colonization

In the middle of the 12th century the colonization of the Ore Mountains (Erzgebirge) began. In the following 100 years "the main parts of the Erzgebirge mountains (sic!), especially along the river banks, were colonized and a great part of the wild forest was changed into farming land."

Fig. 1: Site map of Dippoldiswalde and the so far documented mines in the city area. © Archaeological Heritage Office of Saxony, adapted by Heide Hönig.

Fig. 2: The coloured ink-drawing by Johann Carl Goldberg shows the extensive and numerous smelting areas in and around Freiberg in 1727. © Sächsisches Staatsarchiv, Bergarchiv Freiberg (Repro Waltraud Rabich, Dresden).

(Billig/Geupel, 1992). This process could be observed on the medieval Waldhufenfluren, which are still apparent in some villages. Waldhufen are oblongness farmsteads with one end on a river, which proved to be the optimal way, to use the land for agriculture.

Second Impact – Mining

It is quite probable that the above mentioned wave of immigration happened in part and among other reasons as a reaction to a major regulation in the Freiberger Bergrecht (mining law) that reads as follows: "Wo eyn man ercz suchen wil, das mag her thun mit rechte" (Ermisch, 1886:268). It said that everyone was free to dig for silver, wherever he wants and whether one was the owner of the land or not. Although the law had not been codified until the 14th century the name Freiberg („free mountain"), which was first mentioned in 1218 (Ermisch, 1886:1) indicates that the above mentioned regulation was much older, maybe right from the beginning of the mining in Freiberg. The reason to declare this freedom of mining was with some certainty to attract professional miners to come to Freiberg. What this meant to the environment is evident. Former farmland, cultivated just a few decades earlier as part of the colonization, became completely destroyed by miners digging for treasures of the soil, the silver. From a charter drafted in 1185 (Ermisch, 1883:1) we know the names of the small villages, Berthelsdorf, Christiansdorf and Tuttendorf, located in the area of today's Freiberg. Significantly the last one must have provided a lot of ore deposits, because the land was so heavily destroyed, that nowadays it is almost impossible to tell, where it was located exactly (Hoffmann & Richter, 2012:103). Nevertheless from the 18th century the coloured ink drawing by Johann Carl Goldberg (*Fig. 2*) suggest how heavy the destruction might have been in the middle ages, due to numerous mining and smelting activities. The mining town Freiberg was founded soon after. Another example from the lowland of the Ore Mountains demonstrating the massive destruction is the medieval mining area Treppenhauer (Schwabenicky, 2009). (Field)surveys and airborne-laser-scans (*Fig. 3*) revealed that quite clear. Numerous sinkholes covering the whole surface imply the vast numbers of mines underground. In summary it can be said, that with first mining activities farming villages became deserted due to massive destruction of former agricultural areas or the formation of mining towns. The destruction of these agricultural areas entails to an increasing demand for food supplies from other regions, and, as in the case of Freiberg, encouraged trade for commodities like cloths and other luxury goods.

When intensive mining activities ceased …

The silver-mining in Freiberg, like all important European mining districts, suffered a recession in late medieval times. But mining never stopped here completely like in the north-western area of the Harz Mountains. The current state of research assumes, that the reason for Freiberg surviving the recession was, that its economy not only relied on mining, but had also developed a brisk trade-system. Another essential clue might be the location of a town. The medieval mining town Bleiberg, near the Treppenhauer was also abandoned and became deserted in the 14th century, probably earlier. As stated before intensive mining came along with an irreversible

Fig. 3: Airborne Laserscan of the medieval mining area Treppenhauer (Sachsenburg). © GeoSn <2008>.

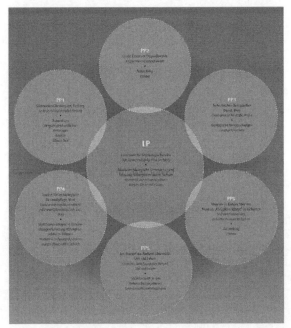

Fig. 4: The Partner of the "Archaeo-Montan"-project, with the Archaeological Heritage Office of Saxony as lead partner in the centre. © Rainer Mietsch – cuadrilla.

destruction of farm land that meant the loss of the towns food supply. So with the absence of nearby trade routes, which Dippoldiswalde and Freiberg had, but the mining town Bleiberg lacks, the latter had lost its economic basis with the decline of mining.

Remaining Questions

Nevertheless a lot of questions remain open. The exact impact of smelting areas on the environment is still unknown, because neither are we able to tell how far these areas extended nor do we have a detailed understanding of the techniques the workers applied. Also the proposed explanation why Bleiberg on the Treppenhauer was deserted while other villages like Dippoldiswalde continued after the crisis of mining at the end of the Middle Ages needs to be further investigated.

New Approaches – Dippoldiswalde, ArchaeoMontan and the Upper Ore Mountains

Becoming aware of the unique chance to get new insights in medieval mining and the impact of the latter on the environment, the archeological heritage office started to intensify its research work on the mines of Dippoldiswalde. As one of the more important steps the Ziel 3-project ArchaeoMontan was initiated in 2012 to investigate and record the results of the excavations in Dippoldiswalde and Niederpöbel and to explore other medieval mining sites in the Ore Mountains in Saxony and Bohemia. The project is financed by the European Regional Development Fund (ERDF). The Lead Partner of the project is the Landesamt für Archäologie (Archaeological Heritage Office of Saxony), the other partners are the Sächsisches Oberbergamt (Saxon Mining Office), the Kreisstadt Dippoldiswalde (major district town Dippoldiswalde), the Ústav archeologické památkové péče in Most (Archeological Heritage Management in Most), Univerzita Jana Evangelisty Purkyně, Česká geologická služba, Praha (Czech Geological Service Office in Prag) and the museum Karlovy Vary with its local exhibition royal mint in Jáchymov (*Fig. 4*). In a cross-border cooperation archaeologists, historians, geologists, site technologists, survey engineers and museologists work closely together to the explore, document and investigate archeological mining relics in the Czech and the Saxon Ore Mountains.

So far, as part of the project, archeological surveys on the Czech and the German side, systematical examination of maps, registers, and similar archival material and the applications of scientific analyses, like dendrochronological analyses and geophysical surveys, are in progress. In October 2012 Dippoldiswalde hosted the first of three scheduled symposiums. 200 experts from all over Europe presented their latest results of research on the topic and discussed new methods. The next symposium is going to be hold in Kadaň from 26th-28th of September 2013. Another main goal is the public presentation of the findings of Dippoldiswalde and Niederpöbel in an exhibition that is in progress right now. It is going to be presented in Jachymov from 22th of June 2014 and from 23rd of October 2014 in Dippoldiswalde.

Acknowledgements

The Project ArchaeoMontan is being funded by the European Regional Development Fund within the Ziel 3/Cíl 3 Programme for promoting cross-border cooperation between the Free State of Saxony and the Czech Republic.

Bibliography

Ermisch, H., (1883): Urkundenbuch der Stadt Freiberg in Sachsen. I. Band. In: Ermisch, H. (Ed).: Codex diplomaticus Saxoniae regiae I, 12. Leipzig.

Ermisch, H., (1886): Urkundenbuch der Stadt Freiberg in Sachsen. II. Band. Bergbau, Bergrecht, Münze. In: Ermisch, H. (Ed).: Codex diplomaticus Saxoniae regiae II, 13. Leipzig.

Billig G.; Geupel V. (1992): Entwicklung, Formen und Datierungen der Siedlungen in der Kammregion des Erzgebirges. In: Siedlungsforschung. Archäologie-Geschichte-Geographie 10. Bonn, pp. 173-194.

Hemker, C.; Scholz, V. (2010): Archaeological Finds and Results regarding high-medieval Mining at Dippoldiswalde (D). In: Silvertant, J. (Ed.): Mining archaeological Research Interdisciplinary Methodology. 5th International Symposium on archeological Mining History, Freiberg 2010. Valkenburg aan de Geul, pp. 108-119.

Hoffmann, Y.; Richter, U. (2012): Entstehung und Blüte der Stadt Freiberg. Die bauliche Entwicklung der Bergstadt vom 12. bis zum Ende des 17. Jahrhunderts. Halle/Saale.

Schwabenicky, W. (2009): Der mittelalterliche Silberbergbau im Erzgebirgsvorland und im westlichen Erzgebirge unter besonderer Berücksichtigung der Ausgrabungen in der wüsten Bergstadt Bleiberg bei Frankenberg. Chemnitz.

Smolnik, R. (Ed.) (2011): Aufbruch unter Tage. Stand und Aufgaben der montanarchäologischen Forschung in Sachsen. Dresden.

Spufford, P. (1988): Money and its use in medieval Europe. Cambridge.

The Role of Italian Businessmen and Entrepreneur in the Beginnings of Central Slovakian Metal Mining with special regard to the Productivity of Gold in Kremnica in the 1st Half of 14th century

Martin Štefánik[1]

[1] Odd. najstarších dejín HÚ SAV, Department of Medieval History of the Slovak Academy of Science, Bratislava, Slovakia

During the reign of the Angevin dynasty, Italian merchants, bankers, and entrepreneurs came to play an important role in the Kingdom of Hungary including its nord-western part, which is the area of present-day Slovakia. They were particularly active in the trading in precious metals and also became prime agents in the administration of state functions connected with the mining of metals and the coining of money.

In every important mining city there was a Mining Chamber presided over by a state-appointed official, the Chamber Count (comes camerae). His function was to collect on the king's behalf the tax on minerals (so called urbura), consisting of a proportion of the mined metals. In the case of the mining chambers, the job was often combined with those of the mint master, the comes monetae, who is very often also called simply "chamber count". The principal task of the comes monetae was coining new money and exchanging it for old (Štefánik, 2009:51-59).

While the Arpád period (until 1301) was prevalently characterized by Venetian influence, at the end of the thirteenth century new era of the rise of the Florentines began. A certain Balduinus from Florence held the office of chamber count, and was related by marriage to the Florentine Cipriani family.[1] In the early fourteenth century the Florentine banks participated directly in the financing of arrival of the new Angevin king Charles Robert in Hungary.[2]

Over the following decades Florentines established themselves firmly in Hungarian business. A certain Ciccus of Florence and a Guidotto are mentioned in 1310 as agents operating in Bratislava and Buda respectively.[3] At the same time Florentine gold coins are described as minted from high-quality Hungarian gold - demonstrating that the city of Florence must already have been a significant trading outlet. However, Venetians still played an important role in Hungarian trade: the king Charles I invited them to the country repeatedly between 1316 and 1319. The relevant document specifically refers to gold and silver exported by Hungarian merchants to Venice, and it mentions Carinthia as a territory of transit. Charles I carried out several financial and economic reforms in the field of mining and minting. Before 1326 florins were introduced as the national coinage. Hungarian golden florins were a specific imitation of Florentine gold coins ("ad modum florenorum Florencie"), the most prestigious currency of that time. On 13th February 1327 Charles I met with John of Luxembourg, King of Bohemia. It is supposed that on that occasion they discussed sending some coiners and experts from the Czech mining town of Kutná Hora to Hungary (Štefánik, 2011:60-61). The pinnacle of his reforms and decrees in the field of mining was the elevation of mining settlements in the area of Kremnica to the status of a town by a privilege conferred on 17th November 1328. Town privileges were granted along similar lines to those of Kutná Hora in Bohemia, where coins had been minted under guidance from Florentine contractors since the early fourteenth century. Since "Kutná Hora" is specifically referred to in the text of the foundation privilege for Kremnica, Italian merchants must also have been present at the foundation of that mining town. The development of Kremnica in following years confirms their activity.[4]

Together with the mint in Kremnica a coin chamber was established, it was headed by the chamber count, who leased the office from the king for a term of one year. The rental contracts for Kremnica chamber from 1335, 1338, and 1342 are still preserved.[5] In the surviving contracts we find mention of individuals associable with Italian mercantile and banking circles. The Kremnica chamber count mentioned in the first and third contracts was Hyppolitus-Leopold. He is referred as a technical specialist – "magister machinarum per Ungariam." He was one of the most influential people in Hungarian minting and mining, holding the office of chamber count in Kremnica more years between 1331-48. Leopold may have been linked to the Florentine company of the Bardi. He owned a smelt house in Nová Baňa as well. Another known Kremnica chamber count in its beginnings was certain Frithko. In 1330 he held office in the Smolník chamber, while in 1336 and 1339 he was the count, together with Nicolaus Szatmary, in the Buda-Esztergom chamber, and in 1338 simultaneously in Kremnica and Smolník. Nicolaus Szatmary, called "the first Hungarian banker," took part through the Venetian affiliate branch of the Bardi company in papal tithe transfers amounting to 8000 florins. Frithko himself, in the name of the king, handled a transaction with Jacopo Berengario, papal collector in Hungary. He was thus, like Leopold, linked to Italian banks. In 1350-52 Frithko (variously called Frithko, Friczko, Cratherius) was chamber count in Nová Baňa. He is documented once again as a chamber count in Kremnica in 1361 and 1371 (Štefánik & Lukačka, 2010:219-222, 230; Horváth & Huszár, 1955-56:23-25).

Individuals of Italian origin could be found not only among the leaseholders of the Kremnica chamber, but also among the mining entrepreneurs themselves in the early years of the mint and the town. Stephanus Marsigli (Marsilii), who financed the ore-processing by local miners, came from a family of Florentine merchants (Štefánik & Lukačka, 2010:297).

Under the terms of the contract signed in 1331 owed the local miner Jeclin of Saxon origin to Italian Marsilii total of 150 common marks (= 525 gold florins = 8400 grossi), most of which was financial debt of 129 marks, the rest were the debts for supplies of Flemish cloth and wine. The charter settles method of debt repayment, and that were the weekly installments of one 12-carat gold mark (50% precious metal content). As a guarantee of repayment, Jeclinus mortgaged his entire fortune worth 135 common marks (= 472.5 gold florins = 7560 grossi), which consisted of 3 mining mills (worth 30-50 common marks, ie 105-75 gold florins), one smelt house worth 40 marks (= 140 gold florins), one stamping-mill worth 5 common marks (= 17.5 gold florins) and a house with land worth 10 common marks (= 35 gold florins).

As virtually all Jeclin's property except the house were the devices for ore processing (125 of 135 marks), it can be assumed that he got into debt for building them, as it is shown by the method of repayment: weekly installments were made by the products of these facilities (12-carat gold). On above mentioned installment, Jeclin's mining company was therefore able to pay off debt in less than a half year and almost to triple its value within a year, what was really high rentability.[6]

Marsilii was most likely a representative of some Italian bank, which did not run mining directly, but only provided necessary resources and international connections. He also supplied foreign goods (Flemish cloth is mentioned) to local miners, thus he dealt with foreign trade.

As a result of recent research we also know of other individuals presumably from the same family resident in other mining cities in Slovakia, for example "Henricus Marsilii de Sceniz" (probably Banská Štiavnica), who in 1319 paid, in the name of the parish priest of Gelnica (a mining city in the east of Slovakia), nine marks of silver to Rufino, collector of the papal tiths in the Kingdom of Hungary. These tax revenues were subsequently sent to Rome through the Florentine Bardi company. Another individual presumably of Italian descent was Hanlin Rezzinghi, recorded as a civis iuratus (one of the twelve council members) at Kremnica in 1342 (Štefánik & Lukačka, 2010:60, 223).

In the following period the presence of many Florentine merchants continued. The most important was the activity of the Medici family in copper mining and processing in the second Half of the fourteenth Century in Banská Bystrica, mining town situated about 18 km east of Kremnica. But this is another chapter of the metals mining from Slovakia, which I have analyzed in other works.

Acknowledgement

This research was supported by the Slovak Research and Development Agency under contract no. APVV-0166-07, VEGA 2/0064/11 (Hospodárske privilégiá a obchodné aktivity vybraných slovenských miest v stredoveku, Economic privileges and commercial activities of selected Slovak cities in the Middle Ages) and CE SDDE. The author is an employee of the Institute of Historical Studies of SAS in Bratislava.

Endnotes

[1] Fejér, 1839-44, vol. 6/2:249 AD 1300, vol. 6/1:222-223 AD 1292.

[2] Wenzel, 1874:150 no. 185 AD 1300, p. 174 no. 224 AD 1305; Fejér, 1839-44:156-157 vol. 8/1 no. LXVII AD 1303.

[3] Sedlák, 1980:348 no. 809, p. 444 no. 1040; Davidsohn, 1901:109-110 no. 551 AD 1308; p. 112 no. 568 AD 28 June 1309.

[4] "In ceteris autem omnibus eisdem libertatibus, quibus hospites de Kutunbana regni Bohemie existunt, iidem hospites nostri perpetuo perfruantur": Juck, 1984:115-116 no. 136 AD 1328.

[5] Dedek, 1924:255-258 no. 379 AD. 1335, pp. 306-312 no. 445 AD 1338; Dezsö et al., 1899:150-163, § 13, AD 1342.

[6] State Archive in Banská Bystrica, branch Kremnica, collection Municipality of town Kremnica (abbreviated MMKr) I.37.1.1: 14.VII.1331. The exchange rate of coins corresponding to the rental contract from 1335: 1 common mark (marca communis sev pagamenti) was worth 56 grossi or 3.5 Hungarian gold florin. Mark of fine silver (marca fini argenti), ie with higher content of precious metal, was worth 64 grossi or 4 florins. Dedek, 1924:255-258 no. 379 AD. 1335.

Bibliography

Davidsohn, R. (1901): Forschungen zur Geschichte von Florenz. Vol. 3. Regesten unedirter Urkunden zur Geschichte von Handel, Gewerbe und Zunftwesen. Berlin.

Dedek, L. C. (1924): Monumenta Ecclesiae Strigoniensis. Vol. 3: 1321-1349. Strigonii.

Dezsö, M.; Nagy, Gy.; Kolosvári, S.; Óvári, K. (1899): Corpus iuris hungarici 1000-1526. Budapest.

Fejér, G. (1839-1844): Codex Diplomaticus Hungariae Ecclesiasticus et Civilis. 41 vols. Buda.

Horváth, T., Huszár, L. (1955-56): Kamaragrófok a középkorban. Numizmatikai Közlöny 54-55. pp. 21-35.

Juck, Ľ. (1984): Výsady miest a mestečiek na Slovensku (1238-1350), Bratislava.

Sedlák, V. (1980): Regesta Diplomatica nec non Epistolaria Slovaciae. Vol. 1. Bratislava.

Štefánik, M. (2009): Entstehung und Entwicklung der Berg- und Münzkammern und ihrer leitenden Beamten in den mittelslowakischen Bergstädten im Mittelalter. In: Westermann, E.; Westermann, A.: Wirtschaftslenkende Montanverwaltung – Fürstlicher Unternehmer – Merkantilismus. Husum, pp. 29-78.

Štefánik, M. (2011): Úloha kremnického zlata v európskej finančno-hospodárskej kríze 14.storočia. Slovenská numizmatika XIX, pp. 57-78.

Štefánik, M.; Lukačka, J. (2010): Lexikon stredovekých miest na Slovensku. Bratislava.

Wenzel, G. (1874): Magyar diplomacziai emlékek az Anjou-korból. vol. 1. Budapest.

Names as Indicators of Mining Activities in the Area of Klausen/Villanders (South Tyrol/Italy)

Elisabeth Gruber[1] & Irina Windhaber[1]

[1] University of Innsbruck, Institute of Languages and Literature, Department of Linguistics

Introduction

This paper deals with the toponomastic environment of the mining area in Klausen and Villanders, both in South Tyrol, Italy, and focuses on those names, whose etymologies are related to mining activities in this region. The analysed place names have their origins in different linguistic layers and consequently reflect the historical, cultural and living environment of this region.

The following paragraphs examine the theoretical groundwork of Yvonne Kathrein and Peter Anreiter, who have analysed the onomastic environment of the mining area at Mitterberg in Salzburg, Austria. During their exploration of the names surrounding Mitterberg, they were able to identify four semantic fields, which directly refer to or indicate mining. These are: a) *names referring directly to mining activities*, b) *names in connection with clearance and the timber industry*, c) *stock farming* and d) *vegetation* (Anreiter & Kathrein, 2011). As a result, the further investigation of place names around Klausen and Villanders concentrates on these four semantic fields.

Linguistic Layers

In general, to achieve an appropriate evaluation of place names, it is necessary to be aware of the linguistic layers which are present in the area of investigation. In the case of Klausen and Villanders, we come across three different linguistic layers, including the Pre-Roman, the Alpine-Romanic and the Germanic/Bavarian layer (Anreiter, 1997:98).

The Pre-Roman layer is the oldest linguistic substrate and comprises names originating from Proto-Indo-European, the Indo-European idioms of the eastern Alps, Rhaetic and Celtic. An example for names of this layer is the name **Villanders** (1018: *Filanders*, 1039: *Filanders*, 1085: *Filanders*, 1142: *Vilanders*). The suffix *-andr* indicates that the root of the name can be found in Indo-European, but the exact meaning of the root is not yet known. In fact, there are many Pre-Roman names around Klausen and Villanders like **Verdings** (1193: *Fridines*, 1211: *Fridinnes*, 1226: *Virdinnes*, 1253: *Verding*), **Latzfons** (1050 - c 1165: *Lazevvnes*, 1070 - c 1080: *Lazeuunes*, 1142 - c 1147: *Lazeuons*) and the river **Eisack** (Finsterwalder, 1995:1029f.).

After the Roman conquest, the local inhabitants gradually assimilated the Roman way of life and the Latin language, which further developed into the Alpine-Romanic (Rom.) or Proto-Ladin languages. The names **Tschafaun** and **Patschid** have their roots in this language. *Tschafaun* means "large cave" and is composed of the basic word **cavu*, in combination with the augmentative suffix *-ōne. *Patschid* originally meant "pine forest" and contains the basic word ***picea*** "pine" and the collective suffix *-ētu*.

In the sixth century, the Bavarians settled in the area of investigation and local inhabitants began to adopt the German, or more specifically, Bavarian language. Often, it is fairly easy to find the original meaning of these names, because they are often transparent compositions of words still known today. An example for such a name is the **Schönbergalm** near the Villanderer Alm. The element *schön* (< Middle High German [=MHG] *schœn[e]* < Old High German [=OHG] *scôni* "beautiful") in this name does however not indicate the beautiful landscape there, but rather focuses on the economic value of the pasture (Kühebacher, 1991:422f).

Semantic field: Mining

The etyma of names with an obvious connection to mining give information about the natural resources in the mining district, environmental changes because of mining activities and the technical terminology, which was commonly used by the miners.

One of the names in this group is **Puchen**, which is the name of a farm in the Thinne Valley. The name comes from the nearby stamp mill (*Pochwerk*), where stones containing ore were crushed by stamp blocks. The stamp mill was built in 1836 near Garnstein, as historical evidence indicates (1854: *seit der Erbauung des Pochwerkes zu Garnstein im Jahre 1836* [HS 6636/16]). Due to convincing evidence of this stamp mill and the local pronunciation [pu:χən], an etymology like "place where beech trees (*Fagus sylvatica*) grow" can be excluded. In fact, the name incorporates the technical term *pochen* (< MHG *bochen, puchen* "thump, defy, loot"), which describes the working procedure of a stamp mill. Furthermore, the geographical position of the farm *Puchen* and the stamp mill in the Thinne Valley supports the etymology, as both are very close to the silver mine in Villanders.

The **Eisenstecken** farm in Sauders (municipality of Villanders) and the alpine pasture **Eisteck Alm**, near the Villanderer Alm, contain direct information about mining activities (1753: *von dem Eissensteckh Hof* [Villanders Nr. 1, 10v]; 1783: *Besitzt den Eysenstecken* [Villanders Nr. 2, 6v]; Kompass Wanderkarte Blatt 059). Both names can be traced back to the family name *Eisenstecken* and are composed of the two German words *Eisen* (OHG *îsan*, MHG *îsen* "iron") and *Stecken* (OHG *stecko*, MHG *stecke* "stick"). The word *Eisen* is one of the most frequent constituents of late medieval smith names, beside the word *Nagel* (< MHG *nagel* < OHG *nagal* "nail") (Finsterwalder, 1990b:259).

Even tools could be used to name different places. An example is **Hammerwald** which refers to a forest close to a mine in Tanzbach Valley. The name is a compound consisting of the German words, *Hammer* "hammer" and *Wald* "forest". The *Hammerwald* received its name either directly from the tool (hammer) or from the stamp (*Pochhämmer/Pochstempel*) of a stamp mill, which is located in its vicinity.

Another example could be **Schlegl** (1753: *Aber ain Stuckh Weingarten genant d(er) Schlegl*

[Villanders Nr. 1, 323v]), a vineyard. *Schlegl* can be interpreted in many different ways and it is unfortunately impossible to determine which meaning is correct. The first interpretation refers to the sledgehammer (*Schlägel* < MHG *slegel* < OHG *slegil*), which has an octagonal profile, resembles a hammer, and was used by miners and barrel-makers alike (Grimm, 1984). It is possible that the vineyard's shape was octagonal, therefore named after the tool. In addition, *Schlegl* can be interpreted as a *nomen agentis* of MHG *slahen* "thump, beat, crack". Thus, the original meaning might be "man who thumps" and refer to a miner.

Semantic field: Clearance/Timber Industry

The methodic clearance fulfilled two important aspects of the mining activities. On the one hand, clearance was absolutely necessary for the production of timber and charcoal. On the other hand, meadows could be created in the course of the clearing processes. These meadows were used for cattle destined to supply the hard working miners with meat (Anreiter & Kathrein, 2011).

Klausen and Villanders feature place names whose origins can be found in the Romanic language. These names are derivations from rom. **runcu/*runca* "clearance". Apparently, these nouns are a back-formation from *runcāre* in Latin with the meaning "picking weeds" (first at Varro). The names **Runggen** (1302: *Ain Hof ze Runke* [Mikrof. 2045, 5r], 1640: *Rothof aüf Rungg* [Cod. 174, 39r], 1652: *Der ganz Runckh Hof* [Cod. 217, 97v], 1753: *Jnhaberin des Rungger hofs auf Runggen* [Cod. 176, 23v]) and **Runggerer Alm** are directly related to this explanation. Furthermore, different suffixes were added to the basic lexeme, like in the case of **Ratschein** (1371: *Runtschein* [Finsterwalder 1995:950], 1640: *Ratscheiner Hof* [Cod. 174, 35r], 1753: *Jnhaber Zu Rotschein* [Cod. 176, 52r], 1753: *Von der Herrschafft wisen Ratschein* [Cod. 176, 23v]). The diminutive suffix *-īno/-īna* was attached to the primary word and provokes a transformation in rom. **runčīnu/*runčīna* „small clearance". **Rungallen** incorporates another connection with the suffix *-āle*. The result is rom. **runcāle* „appendent to the clearance".

Semantic field: Stock Farming

The semantic field of stock farming deals with toponyms comprising of animal names. It is necessary to investigate this group of names because they provide information about the food supply of the miners.

Due to its geographic vicinity to the galleries at Pfunderer Berg, it is very likely that the **Jausenstation Rinderplatz** (1819: *Rinder-Platz* [KP 2691]) was formerly used for cattle breeding, in order to provide the miners with meat. Further examples for place names containing names of animals include **Rossboden**, **Saueben** and **Schafwald**, which incorporate the horse, pig and sheep, respectively.

Semantic field: Vegetation

As already mentioned, timber is a quite significant resource for the mining industry. Thus, toponyms including names of utile trees emerge quite often in the surroundings of mining areas. In the analyzed historical material the oikonyms **Eichnerhof** (1640: *Aichner Hof* [Cod. 174, 14v], 1753: *des ganzen Aichner Hofs* [Cod. 176, 11v]) und **Feichthof** (1753: *die Paurecht des Feichthofs* [Villanders Nr. 1, 356r]) appeared, which refer to oak (*Eiche, Quercus*) and common spruce (*Fichte, Picea abies*). Another example is **Lärchhof**, which includes the German word *Lärche* (*Larix*). It refers to a farm, which is closer to the mining region in the Tanzbach Valley than to the mines in Klausen.

Toponomastic Environment

When taking the geographic distribution of place names into consideration, initial conclusions can be made. In the area of investigation, animal names accumulate above Klausen (Fraktion Latzfons) and are fairly distant relative to the production facilities which leads to the assumption that animals were purposely bred there. In contrast, clearance names exist near the galleries and place names with direct reference to mining activity. Reasons for this distribution could be that timber was an essential component of the mining industry, therefore having a short route to the mines was advantageous.

Bibliography

Historical Records of the South Tyrolian Regional Archive/Bozen

Signature	Year	Description
Cod. 174	1640	Urbar d. Haubtmanschafft Seeben
Cod. 176	1750-01-07, Klausen; 1753	Reitungslibell, so über insteend zu d. Haubtmanschafft Sebnerischen Urbario gehörigen Grundt u. Zinspartheyen vorgangen
Cod 217	1652	Gufidaunisch Plegamtsurbary
Villanders Nr. 1	1753 - 1755	Villanders. Steuer-Peraequotion
Villanders Nr. 2	1783	Steuer Cataster von Villanders u. Babian

Historical Records of the Tyrolian Regional Archive/Innsbruck

Signature	Year	Description
HS 6636/16	1854	Über die Herstellung, respektive Verstärkung der Radwelle des Garnsteiner Pochwerkes der kk: Berg u. Hütten Verwaltung in KLAUSEN
KP 2691	1891	Tagreviersplan Copia d. Pfundererberger Bergbaues naechst Klaussen samt den angraenzenden Gegenden

Anreiter, P. (1997): Die Besiedlung Nordtirols im Spiegel der Namen. In: Onoma 33, pp. 98-113. Leuven: International Centre of Onomastics.

Anreiter, P.; Kathrein, Y. (2011): Der Mitterberg und sein toponymisches Umfeld (im Vergleich mit anderen Bergbauarealen). In: Oeggl, K.; Goldenberg, G.; Stöllner, T.; Prast, M.; (Hg.): Die Geschichte des Bergbaus in Tirol und seinen angrenzenden Gebieten. Proceedings zum 5. Milestone-Meeting des SFB HiMAT vom 7.-10.10.2010 in Mühlbach. Innsbruck, pp. 161-171.

Anreiter, P.; Gruber, E.; Windhaber, I. (2012): Zu einigen onymischen Bergbauindikatoren im Raum Klausen/Villanders. Oeggl, Klaus/Schaffer, Veronika (Hg.): Die Geschichte des Bergbaus in Tirol und seinen angrenzenden Gebieten. Proceedings zum 6. Milestone-Meeting des SFB HiMAT vom 3.-5.11.2011 in Klausen/Südtirol. Innsbruck: Innsbruck University Press, pp. 155-161.

Finsterwalder, K. (1990a-1995): Tiroler Ortsnamenkunde. Gesammelte Aufsätze und Arbeiten. Bände 1-3, Schlern-Schriften, pp. 285-287.

Finsterwalder, K. (1990b): Tiroler Familiennamenkunde. Sprach- und Kulturgeschichte von Personen-, Familien- und Hofnamen, Schlern-Schriften 284.

Grimm, J.; Grimm, W. (1984): Deutsches Wörterbuch. Nachdruck der Erstausgabe. 33 Bände. München. Onlineversion: http://dwb.uni-trier.de/Projekte/DWB/ [09. 01. 2012].

Kompass (2009): Kompass-Wanderkarte 1:25 000 WK 059, Klausen und Umgebung – Chiusa e dintorni. Rum/Innsbruck: Kompass-Karten GmbH.

Kühebacher, E. (1991-2000): Die Ortsnamen Südtirols und ihre Geschichte. Bände 1-3, Bozen.

Scheuchenstuel, C. v. (1856): Idioticon der österreichischen Berg- und Hüttensprache zum besseren Verständnisse des österr. Berg-Gesetzes und dessen Motive für Nicht-Montanisten. Wien.

Characterising vegetation changes in former mining and metalworking areas during prehistoric and Roman times: Perspectives from Britain and Ireland

Tim Mighall[1], Antonio Martínez Cortizas[2], Noemí Silva Sánchez[2], Simon Timberlake[3], Frank M. Chambers[4] & William O'Brien[5]

[1] School of Geosciences, University of Aberdeen, Aberdeen, UK
[2] Departamento de Edafología y Química Agrícola, Facultad de Biología, Santiago de Compostela, Spain
[3] Cambridge Archaeological Unit, Department of Archaeology, University of Cambridge, Cambridge, UK
[4] Centre for Environmental Change and Quaternary Research, School of Natural & Social Sciences, University of Gloucestershire, Cheltenham, UK
[5] Department of Archaeology, National University of Ireland, Cork, Ireland

Introduction

A multi-proxy methodology has now been developed to investigate the environmental impact of early mining and metallurgy. Mighall et al. (2006) suggested that vegetation changes associated with mining or metallurgy can only be discerned from pollen records alongside archaeological evidence with a firmly established chronology and/or other evidence from peat bog proxies such as geochemistry. A combination of geochemistry (preferably total concentrations, fluxes and/or isotope ratios) and radiocarbon dating has been used successfully to identify evidence for, and constrain periods of, non-ferrous mining and metallurgical activity recorded in peat bogs (e.g. Mighall et al., 2002a,b; Monna et al., 2004; Jouffroy-Bapicot et al. 2007; Breitenlechner et al., 2010). Such data can be used to examine pollen records of vegetation change (e.g. Mighall & Chambers, 1993; Mighall et al. 2006; Mighall et al. 2010).

This paper will review vegetation changes that have occurred as a result of prehistoric and Roman mining and/or metallurgy based on pollen-analytical and geochemical research undertaken in Britain and Ireland. The paper considers evidence primarily from four sites: three in Wales (Copa Hill, Borth Bog, Llancynfelin) and one in Ireland (Mount Gabriel).

Pollen data from Copa Hill and Mount Gabriel has been published elsewhere (Mighall & Chambers, 1993; Mighall et al., 2000) and selected geochemical data has been published for Copa Hill and Borth Bog (Mighall et al., 2002a,b; 2009). Each of these sites have been discussed in detail, and Mighall et al. (2006, 2010, 2012) also undertook a review of the main impacts that were common more than one of the sites. However, given the increased number of sites that now exist, the availabilty of comparative data elsewhere in Europe and the development of new approaches to examine the data, a new review is timely.

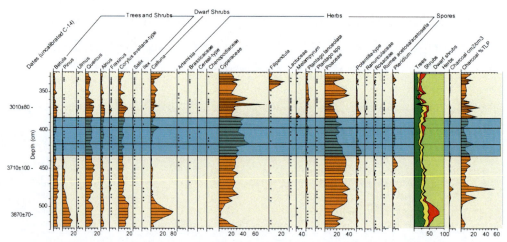

Fig. 1: Selected percentage pollen data from Mount Gabriel, SW Ireland. Based on an age-depth model produced by Clam (Blaauw, 2010), the mining activity corresponds to a best estimate peat depth of approximately between 418 and 396cm at site MG1 but when accounting for the uncertainty associated with the radiocarbon dates, the depth range could stretch to between 434 and 384cm (shaded areas). Adapted from Mighall et al. (2000; 2012).

Vegetation change associated with early mining and metallurgy

The pollen evidence shows a commonality in the nature of the impact on woodland across several British and Irish sites. Woodland impact was negligible during prehistory: a pattern shown at Mount Gabriel (MG) (*Fig. 1*). Prehistoric copper mining occurred on the southern and eastern slopes of MG between approximately 1700 and 1500 BC (O'Brien, 1994). Mining corresponds to a best estimate peat depth between ca. 418 and 396cm but when accounting for the uncertainty associated with the radiocarbon dates, the depth range could stretch to between 434 and 384cm. During this period, small-scale and short-lived declines in arboreal pollen taxa (*Betula*, *Alnus* and *Corylus avellana*-type) occurred. Herbaceous taxa indicative of pasture and/or disturbance are also recorded, (e.g. *Plantago lanceolata*, *Artemisia*-type, Chenopodiaceae) while microscopic charcoal values remain relatively high (but dip around 425cm) and they could be indicative of firesetting. By the end of the archaeologically-inferred period of prehistoric mining on MG, total arboreal pollen percentages are of a similar value to those found before mining commenced, suggesting that there was no long-term impact on woodland. Similar patterns occur at Borth Bog, Copa Hill and Llancynfelin (Mighall et al., 2012). Even though the overall impact on woodlands appears to have been limited, it does not mean that woodland was not exploited during prehistory. Clear impacts are recorded on individual taxa but they vary from site to site. There are several factors influencing the nature of vegetation change associated with mining: the natural density of local woodland and the intensity and duration of mining. Major tree and shrub taxa are mainly exploited at each site and the evidence for selectivity of wood fuel is not consistently observed. Firm evidence for firesetting in microscopic charcoal records is less forthcoming.

More sizeable but ultimately non-permanent impacts are recorded during the Iron Age and Roman period at Copa Hill and Borth Bog (Mighall et al., 2012). Elevated lead (Pb) concentrations coincide with larger-scale changes in vegetation that appear to have been strongly influenced by mining. Total arboreal percentages reach their lowest recorded level with the major trees and shrubs (*Quercus, Alnus, Betula* and *Corylus avellana*-type) all affected. A transformation of a well-wooded landscape into one dominated by heather-rich blanket peat and acidic grasslands coincides with a rise in Pb concentrations attributed to Roman mining and smelting (Mighall et al., 2002b). However, a period of recovery follows the demise of Roman activity at Copa Hill and Borth Bog. Tree and shrub pollen increased simultaneously with a fall in Pb concentrations. For example, total arboreal pollen percentages reached pre-Roman values by AD 605, suggesting that woodland has regenerated within approximately 200 years at Copa Hill.

Mighall et al. (2012:126) drew a number of conclusions from this pollen-analytical research: prehistoric mining and/or metallurgical activities had a limited impact on woodlands. Disturbances are generally characterised by being small-scale, non-permanent and spatially constrained. More significant woodland clearance associated with mining and/or metalworking occurred during the late Iron Age and Roman period, with the most sizeable impacts recorded during Roman times. However, woodland recovery occurred after activities cease. Are such patterns also evident in other European-based mining areas? If so, we can start to consider developing a conceptual model of early mining impact on the environment.

Deciphering impacts from mining and metallurgy in the palaeoenvironmental record

A useful approach to identify more specifically past impacts of mining and metallurgy on the environment is to employ principal components analysis (PCA). Successful separation of chemical and biological signals in environmental archives has been achieved using PCA (e.g. Muller et al., 2008; López-Merino et al., 2011; Martínez-Cortizas et al., 2013). We also used such an approach to separate the possible contribution of lithogenic (i.e. soil dust) and pollution sources of Pb and other metals in the Borth Bog record (see Mighall et al., 2009, for site details etc.). This was accomplished in two stages. First the concentrations of major, minor and trace lithogenic elements and trace metals and metalloids of the peat were obtained by X-ray fluorescence dispersive EMMA-XRF analysis. Second, a factor analysis by PCA was performed using the lithogenic and metal elements (Zn, Pb, Fe, As, Cu, Ga, Ni, Si, Zr, Ti, Rb, Al, Y, P, K, Sr, Ca, S, Br, Cl, Se, Mn, Cr, Nb). Before analysis, the data were transformed to Z-scores to avoid the scaling effect and obtain average-centered distributions (see Martínez-Cortizas et al., 2013). PCA analysis was done using SPSS 15.0. A varimax rotation solution was applied to maximize the loadings of the variables on the components and by doing so, allocate the component variables (the elements) that are highly correlated. Thus each main factor score shows the profile distribution of elements that show very similar records (*Fig. 2*).

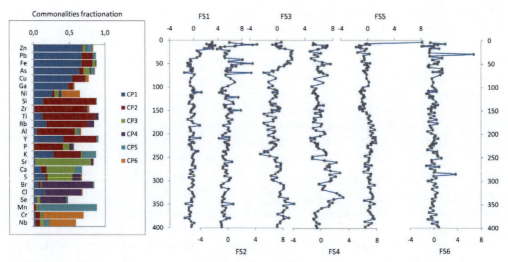

Fig. 2: Factor scores for the 6 principal components for the Borth Bog geochemical data (CP – Principal component; FS – factor scores for each principal component).

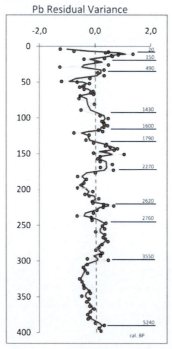

Fig. 3: Pb residual variance scores from PCA analysis of the Borth Bog peat record. Depth in centimetres (vertical axis); residual variance factor score (horizontal axis).

Six principal components accounted for 76.3% of the total variance (*Fig. 2*). PC1 explains 23.9% of the variance: high positive factor loadings were found for Zn, Pb, Fe, As, Cu, Ga, Y, K and Ni suggesting that PC1 could be related with atmospheric metal pollution; Ga, Y and K possibly reflect deposition in particulate form (dust) as a result of mining. Factor scores show a high increase in the upper 40cm, so this PC is related to recent poly-metallic pollution. PC2 explains 23% of the variance: high positive factor loadings occur for lithogenic elements (e.g. Si, Zr, Ti, Rb, Al & Y). PC2 appears to be explained by land use changes and increased dust deposition (excluding mining). The results of the PCA suggest that most pollution in the Borth Bog area occurred in the last 500 years and may have been related to mining but proportions (15-20%) of the deposited Fe, Cu and Pb seem to have also had a lithogenic origin. In this instance the extracted components do not reveal the history of pre-industrial metal contamination: this signal is not so strong.

To check if the Pb record contains information on other pollution sources we analysed the residual variance from a second PCA analysis that only used the metallic elements. This revealed that 80% of the total Pb variance is explained by recent mining and other land use changes but 20% remains unexplained. A downcore plot of the residual 20% (*Fig. 3*) shows relatively elevated values were detected for several phases: >5240 cal. BP, 3550-2760 cal. BP, at 2620 cal. BP, between 2270-1790 cal. BP, 1600-1430 cal. BP, by 490 cal. BP. In the last 150 years there was an increase in Pb followed by large decrease in the last two decades. These variations seem to reconstruct both pre-industrial and industrial Pb pollution. Therefore the analysis confirms origins of mining and metallurgy possibly extend back to the Bronze Age in central Wales as reported by Mighall et al. (2009). The results also suggest that periods of deforestation (data not shown) occur during each phase of early mining/metallurgy but other activities (as identified by the pattern of lithogenic elements recorded in the PCA) such as land use changes associated with agriculture, also may have been influential. The use of PCA in this way appears to be a valuable tool to separate changes related to metallurgical activities from other sources.

References

Breitenlechner, E.; Hilber, M.; Lutz, J.; Kathrein, Y.; Unterkircher, A. & Oeggl, K. (2010). The impact of mining activities on the environment reflected by pollen, charcoal and geochemical analyses. Journal of Archaeological Science 37, pp. 1458-1467.

Jouffroy-Bapicot, I.; Pulido, M.; Baron, S.; Galop, D.; Monna, F.; Lavoie, M.; Ploquin, A.; Petit, C.; de Beaulieu, J-L. & Richard, H. (2007): Environmental impact of early palaeometallurgy: pollen and geochemical analysis. Vegetation History and Archaeobotany, 16, 251-258.

López-Merino, L.; Martínez Cortizas, A. & López-Sáez, A. (2011): Human-induced changes on wetlands: a study case from NW Iberia. Quaternary Science Reviews 30, pp. 2745-2754.

Martínez Cortizas, A. M.; López Merino, L.; Bindler, R.; Mighall, T. M. & Kylander, M. (2013): Atmospheric pollution in Northern Spain in late Iron Age/Roman times reconstructed using the high-resolution record of La Molinia (Asturias). Journal of Palaeolimnology, 50(1), pp. 71-86.

Mighall, T. M. & Chambers, F. M. (1993): The environmental impact of prehistoric copper mining at Copa Hill, Cwmystwyth, Wales. The Holocene 3, pp. 260-264.

Mighall, T. M.; Chambers, F. M.; Lanting, J. & O'Brien, W. F. (2000): Prehistoric copper mining and its impact on vegetation: palaeoecological evidence from Mount Gabriel, Co. Cork, southwest Ireland. In: Nicholson, R. A. & O'Connor, T. P. (eds): Prehistoric People as Agents of Environmental Change. Oxford: Oxbow, pp. 19-29.

Mighall, T. M.; Abrahams, PW.; Grattan, J. P.; Hayes, D.; Timberlake, S. & Forsyth, S. (2002a): Geochemical evidence for atmospheric pollution derived from prehistoric copper mining at Copa Hill, Cwmystwyth, mid-Wales UK. Science of the Total Environment 292, pp. 69-80.

Mighall, T. M.; Grattan, J. P.; Timberlake, S.; Lees, JA. & Forsyth, S. (2002b): An atmospheric pollution history for lead-zinc mining from Ystwyth Valey, Dyfed, mid-Wales, UK as recorded by an upland blanket peat. Geochemistry: Exploration, Environment, Analysis 2, pp. 175-184.

Mighall, T. M.; Timberlake, S.; Jenkins D. A. & Grattan, J. P. (2006): Using bog archives to reconstruct paleo-pollution and vegetation change during the late Holocene. In: Martini P.; Martínez Cortizas A. & Chesworth W. (Eds): Peatlands: Evolution and records of Environmental and Climatic changes, Amsterdam: Elsevier, pp. 413-432.

Mighall, T. M.; Timberlake, S.; Foster, I. D. L.; Krupp, E. & Singh, S. (2009): Ancient copper and lead pollution records from a raised bog complex in central Wales, UK. Journal of Archaeological Science 36, pp. 1504-1515.

Mighall, T. M.; Timberlake, S. & Crew, P. (2010): Vegetation changes in former mining and metalworking areas of Wales and Ireland during prehistoric and medieval times. In: Belford, P.; Palmer, M. & White, R.: Footprints of Industry. BAR British Series 523, pp. 19-26.

Mighall, T. M.; Chambers, F. M.; Timberlake, S. & O'Brien, W.F. (2012): Characterising vegetation changes in former mining and metalworking areas during prehistoric and Roman times. Notizie Archeologiche Bergomensi 20, pp.117-130.

Monna, F.; Galop, D.; Carozza, L.; Tual, M.; Beyrie, A.; Marembert, F.; Chateau, C.; Dominik, J. & Grousset, F. E. (2004): Environmental impact of early Basque mining and smelting recorded in a high ash minerogenic peat deposit. Science of the Total Environment 327, 197-214.

Muller, J.; Kylander, M.; Martínez Cortizas, A.; Wüst, RAJ.; Weiss, D.; Blake, K.; Coles, B. & García-Sánchez, R. (2008): The use of principle component analyses in characterising trace and major elemental distribution in a 55 kyr peat deposit in tropical Australia: implciations to paleoclimate. Geoch Cosmoch Acta 72, pp. 449-463.

O'Brien W. F. (1994): Mount Gabriel. Galway, National University of Ireland.

Reconstruction of the vegetation in the region of Kitzbühel (Tyrol) and the impact of different mining phases since the Neolithic

Barbara Viehweider[1] & Klaus Oeggl[1]

[1] University of Innsbruck, Institute of Botany

Introduction

The development of todays cultural landscape in the Eastern Alps was affected by human activities since millennia. Among other settlement activities all operations around mining and metalworking had an impact on both the vegetation and the surrounding environment on a local and a regional scale. The trees from the surrounding woodlands were used for constructions, tools and for building material of settlements in the vicinity of the mines. Additionally, wood and charcoal were the main energy sources for several metallurgical activities (fire-setting, smelting, metal working) in ancient times (Stöllner, 2003). By this means the production of raw materials has always been accompanied by the reclamation and the cultivation of agricultural land.

This paper deals with the vegetation history of the former prominent mining area of Kitzbühel. The aim of this study is to evaluate the paleoecological effects of prehistoric and historic mining on the vegetation in the region of Kitzbühel. On a regional scale the impact of mining on the vegetation in terms of deforestation for settlement and agricultural activities to subsist the mining activities will be investigated.

Study area

The mining district Kitzbühel is located in the northern Greywacke zone of Northern Tyrol (Geologische Bundesanstalt, 2003) between the mining areas Schwaz and Mitterberg in Salzburg, both key study areas of the research centre HiMAT. The study area extends from St. Johann to Pass Thurn and was a prominent copper and silver ore deposit in the Eastern Alps during the Bronze Age and the Mediaeval or rather Early Modern Times. Main focus is laid on the area between the communities of Kitzbühel and Jochberg. The study area is bordered by mountains of the Kitzbüheler Alps in the west, east and south, and to north by the Kaiser Mountains. The Kelchalm as a prominent prehistoric mining district is part of the township Aurach and the current area of investigation. The investigated site is located on the Laubkogel, a 5km long mountain ridge of the Kitzbüheler Alps. 1.5km south of the Kelchalm, in the immediate vicinity of the mine, a 1ha sized peat bog – called 'Rauber' – is located on 1762m a.s.l. From this bog a 1.6m thick core was extracted for pollen and heavy metal analyses.

The dominant vegetation on the Kelchalm is a high-mountain and subalpine spruce forest, which is thinned out by wood pasture activities. Today alpine pastures and meadows dominate the landscape. There are mostly extensive grazing fields which neither are fertilized nor irrigated (Meisel et al., 1984).

Methods

The peat core was extracted with a sample tube of 2m length from the central parts of the fen Rauber on the Kelchalm (1762m a.s.l.) in the immediate vicinity of a mine to evaluate the impact on the environment by mining activities. The chemical treatment of the samples for the palynological analysis follows the usual standardized methods (Erdtman 1960; Seiwald 1980). The identification and quantification of the pollen occurs by a light microscope with 400x magnification (in critical situations also with 1000x magnification and with supporting phase-contrast). For generating a high data quality every sample is counted standardized until 1000 arboreal pollen grains (AP). The pollen and spore types are determined with standard identification keys of the central European pollen flora (Beug 1961; Punt 1976; Punt and Clarke 1980; 1981; 1984; Punt et al. 1988; Moore et al. 1991; Reille 1992; 1995; Faegri and Iversen 1993) and the reference collection of the Botanical Institute of the University of Innsbruck. Additional to pollen and spores also Non-Pollen Palynomorphs (NPPs) like spores of coprophilic fungi and zoological micro fossils as well as micro charcoals (*Particulae carbonae* of size classes < 50μm, > 50μm, > 100μm) were identified and quantified.

The radiocarbon dating of ten samples (*Tab. 1*) from the peat core has been conducted at the VERA-Laboratorium of the Isotope Research on the Faculty of Physics, University of Vienna. The sidereal age was generated with the INTCAL09 calibration curve (Reimer et al., 2009) and the calibration programme OxCal (Bronk Remsey, 1995). The calibrated age values given in *Table 1* correspond to a 2σ-confidential interval.

Tab. 1: Radiocarbon dating's from the bog 'Rauber' at the Kelchalm.

lab-no.	depth [cm]	material	^{14}C age [BP] (1σ-range)	cal. age [AD/BC] (2σ-range)	cal. age [BP, 1950]	calendar year [AD/BC]
VERA-5673HS	41	peat	695 ± 50 BP	1220-1330 AD	675 BP	1275 AD
VERA-5674HS	59	peat	1160 ± 35 BP	770-980 AD	1075 BP	875 AD
VERA-5812HS	70	peat	1835 ± 35 BP	80-260 AD	1780 BP	170 AD
VERA-5675HS	80	peat	2800 ± 40 BP	1050-830 BC	2890 BP	940 BC
VERA-5813HS	90	peat	2940 ± 40 BP	1270-1010 BC	3090 BP	1140 BC
VERA-5814HS	100	peat	3215 ± 35 BP	1540-1410 BC	3425 BP	1475 BC
VERA-5815HS	110	peat	3495 ± 40 BP	1930-1730 BC	3780 BP	1830 BC
VERA-5676HS	118	peat	3840 ± 35 BP	2460-2200 BC	4280 BP	2330 BC
VERA-5677HS	134	peat	4160 ± 45 BP	2890-2580 BC	4685 BP	2735 BC
VERA-5673HS	153	mud	5790 ± 35 BP	4720-4540 BC	6580 BP	4630 BC

The weight percentage determination of organic and minerogenic (silicate, carbonate) matter in the sediment core is based on the standard loss of ignition analysis (LOI) specified in Heiri et al. (2001).

Results and Discussion

The pollen diagram from the bog Rauber shows six local pollen assemblage zones (lpaz) with different distributions of the dominant pollen and spores. The oldest pollen strata in the pollen profile were deposited in Mesolithic Times, more than 7500 years ago. In 153-160cm depth the minerogenic components (silicate and carbonate) of the sediment add up to 80%. Between 140 and 135cm (c. 3000 BC) peat accumulation begins and the organic components of the sediment gain values over 80%.

The development of the vegetation begins with a sparse spruce forest (lpaz R1, *Picea-Alnus-*Poaceae-zone, 163-138cm) with a lot of herbs taxa as true grasses (Poaceae), pink family (Caryophyllaceae), bellflower family (Campanulaceae), yarrow (*Achillea*), mugwort (*Artemisia*) or spikemoss (*Selaginella*) in the two lowermost samples. Fir (*Abies*) and beech (*Fagus*) have already immigrated in lower altitudes of the investigation area.

With the onset of peat accumulation in lpaz R2 (*Picea-Abies*-zone, 138-110cm) fir (*Abies*) expands and a spruce-fir forest (Piceeto-Abietetum) evolves in the surroundings of the bog which persists until Medieval Times (750 AD). In the Late Neolithic (2500 BC, 126cm) there are first indications of human impact, by decreasing values of spruce (*Picea*) and fir (*Abies*) and increasing values of grasses (Poaceae) and herbs (Asteraceae, Cichoriaceae, Ranunculaceae, *Artemisia*, *Senecio* type) as well as charcoals (*Particulae carbonae* 50-100µm), in the wider vicinity of the mire. However, this early human interference has to be verified by a second peat core from the valley floor. At the end of the lpaz R2 (2000 BC, 113cm) a first clearance of the forests is reflected and takes c. 200 years (*Fig. 1*). Declining values of spruce (*Picea*) and fir (*Abies*) indicate the clear-cutting. Towards the end of this clearing phase the values of charcoals (*Particulae carbonae* 50-100µm) are increasing because of enhanced fire activities, which substantiate a human impact. Additionally a secondary succession with alder (*Alnus*), birch (*Betula*) and hazel (*Corylus*) is starting. In the following 150 years the spruce-fir forest regenerates.

From the Middle Bronze Age until the end of the Late Bronze Age three more forest clearings are recorded in the pollen diagram by decreasing spruce (*Picea*) and fir (*Abies*) values. The first starts at the beginning of lpaz R3 (*Picea-Abies-Fagus*-zone, 110-81cm) around 1700 BC, superseded by the second at 1500 BC and finally the third one at about 1100 BC. Additionally, the settlement indicators curve (dock – *Rumex acetosella*, *R. acetosa* type, goosefoot family – Chenopodiaceae type) and the pasture indicators curve (plantain – *Plantago alpina* type, mugwort – *Artemisia*, bracken – *Pteridium aquilinum*) as well as the charcoal particles (*Particulae carbonae* 50-100µm) reach higher values synchronously.

Since the Late Bronze Age pollen of crop plants – cereals (Cerealia) – occur, which indicate human presence and agricultural activities in the valley bottoms.

The lpaz R4 (Picea-Abies-Alnus-zone, 81-61cm) covers the Late Bronze Age, Iron Age, Roman Times and the Early Medieval Times (*Fig. 1*). At the beginning of this lpaz R4 (80cm) a maximum of grasses (Poaceae) and herbs (Plantago lanceolata) becomes obvious in the pollen diagram. Simultaneously the charcoal particles (Particulae carbonae 50-100µm) and the

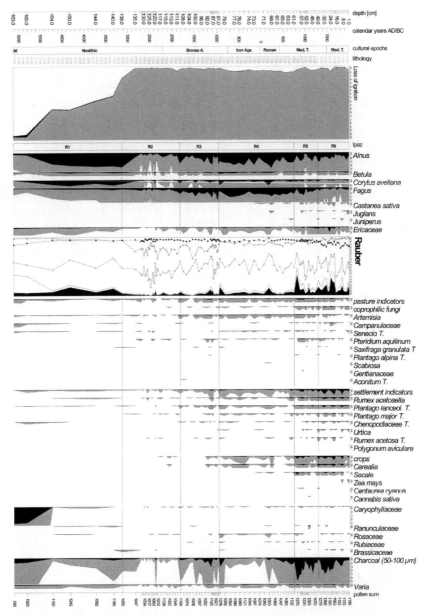

Fig. 1: Relative pollen diagram (selected species) of the bog 'Rauber' at the Kelchalm. Taxa curves with black background correspond to percentage values %, those with grey background reflect a 10x exaggeration; symbols in the main diagram: cross = fir (Abies), triangle = spruce (Picea), dot = pine (Pinus), solid line = border of fraction of tree- and non-tree species, black area = values of grasses (Poaceae).

non-arboreal-pollen (NAP) are increasing. These effects can be explained by fire events. Since the beginning of this lpaz R4 settlement and pasture indicators as well as coprophilic fungi (*Podospora, Cercophora, Sporomiella*, Sordariaceae) are more frequent and corroborate local pasture activities. Also crop plants (Cerealia) show increasing pollen values. During the Late Iron Age (0-100 BC; 70-72cm) the pollen diagram shows a decline of spruce (*Picea*) in combination with a rise of grasses (Poaceae) again. This decline is also visible in the pollen accumulation rates (PAR), which corroborates a clearing. This short phase marks the beginning of intense human impact, indicated also in increasing values of settlement indicators and crops. Between 150 and 500 AD (70-65cm) in Roman and Early Medieval Times a regeneration of the spruce forest (*Picea*) is recorded and also fir (*Abies*) reclaim suggesting declining anthropogenic influence.

An increase of pasture and settlement indicators (e.g. *Rumex acetosella, Plantago lanceolata-type, Urtica*) as well as crop plants reflects an intensification of human impact due to forest clearances during Medieval and Modern Times (lpaz R5 *Picea*-Poaceae-zone, 61-41cm; lpaz R6: *Picea*-Poaceae-Cyperaceae-zone, 41-1cm). The grasses expand drastically since Early Middle Ages (700 AD; 60cm), like the curves of pasture and settlement indicators, crop plants and charcoals. This pattern suggests slashing and burning. During the High Middle Ages (1050-1250 AD; 52-42cm) the pollen diagram shows a slightly reduction of human impact which is increasing again in the Late Middle Ages (1250-1492 AD; 42-28cm).

In lpaz R5 (*Picea*-Poaceae-zone, 61-41cm) pasture activities are increasing, reflected in higher values of grasses (Poaceae), herbs and pasture indicators as well as coprophilic fungi. At the lower limit of lpaz R6 a decreasing of fir (*Abies*) values occurs. It may be a selective removal of the species or a reaction on fire (Tinner, 1999), which is documented by increasing charcoal values.

Conclusions

The pollen analysis from the sequential peat samples near the mining area reflects human activities since 2500 BC suggesting mining activities. This is reflected by a series of clearings in the spruce-fir forest combined with the occurrence of anthropogenic indicator plants, which are interrupted by secondary successions and forest regeneration.

The clearences correspond with mining activities which are dated by dendrochronology (Pichler et al. 2009, 2010) as well as archaeological results (Preuschen & Pittioni 1954, Klaunzer 2010).

Acknowledgements

These studies are supported by the Austrian Academy of Science (ÖAW) in the course of a DOC-team fellowship (grant-nr. 70208). We acknowledge Dr. Eva Maria Wild, University of Vienna, for AMS-dating.

Literature

Beug, H.-J. (1961): Leitfaden der Pollenbestimmung für Mitteleuropa und angrenzende Gebiete, Stuttgart.

Bronk Ramsey, C. (1995): Radiocarbon Calibration and Analysis of Stratigraphy: The OxCal Program. Radiocarbon 37(2), pp. 425-430.

Erdtman, G. (1960): The acetolysis method. A revised description. Svensk Botanisk Tidskrift 54, pp. 561-569.

Faegri, K.; Iversen, J. (1993): Bestimmungsschlüssel für die nordwesteuropäische Pollenflora. Gustav Fischer Verlag, Jena.

Geologische Bundesanstalt (Hrsg.) (2003): Geologische Karte der Republik Österreich, 1:50.000. Wien.

Heiri, O.; Lotter, A. F.; Lemcke, G. (2001): Loss on ignition as a method for estimating organic and carbonate content in sediments: reproducibility and comparability of results. Journal of Paleolimnology 25, pp. 101-110.

Klaunzer, M.; Goldenberg G.; Staudt, M (2010): Tirol, KG Aurach, OG Aurach, VB Kitzbühel. Fundberichte aus Österreich 48, pp. 389-390.

Meisel, K.; Schiechtl, H. M.; Stern, R. (1984): Karte der aktuellen Vegetation von Tirol 1/100.000. 10. Teil: Blatt 3, Karwendelgebirge – Unterinntal. Documents de cartographie ecologique, XXVII, pp. 65-84.

Moore, P. D.; Webb, J. A.; Collison, M. E. (1991): Pollen Analysis, second ed. Oxford.

Pichler, T.; Nicolussi, K.; Goldenberg, G.; Klaunzer, M. (2009): Die Hölzer des bronzezeitlichen Bergbaus auf der Kelchalm bei Kitzbühel. Dokumentation und erste Ergebnisse dendrochronologischer Analysen. In: Archäologisches Korrespondenzblatt 39, pp. 59-75.

Pichler, T.; Nicolussi, K.; Klaunzer, M.; Goldenberg, G. (2010): Dendrochronological Analysis and Dating of Wooden Artefacts from the Prehistoric Copper Mine Kelchalm/Kitzbühel (Austria). In: Anreiter, P.; Goldenberg, G.; Hanke, K.; Krause, R.; Leitner, W.; Mathis, F.; Nicolussi, K.; Oeggl, K.; Pernicka, E.; Prast, M.; Schibler, J.; Schneider, I.; Stadler, H.; Stöllner, T.; Tomedi, G.; Tropper, P.: Mining in European History and its Impact on Environment and Human Societies – Proceedings for the 1st Mining in European History-Conference of the SFB HiMAT, 12.-15. November 2009, Innsbruck University Press, Innsbruck, pp. 227-231.

Preuschen, E.; Pittioni, R. (1954): Untersuchungen im Bergbaugebiet Kelchalm bei Kitzbühel, Tirol. 3. Bericht über die Arbeiten 1946-53 zur Urgeschichte des Kupferbergwesens in Tirol. Arch. Austriaca 15, pp. 3-97.

Punt, W. (1976): The Northwest European Pollenflora, vol. I. Elsevier, Amsterdam.

Punt, W.; Blackmore, S.; Clarke, G. C. S. (1988): The Northwest European Pollenflora, vol. V. Elsevier, Amsterdam.

Punt, W.; Clarke, G. C. S. (1980): The Northwest European Pollenflora, vol. II. Elsevier, Amsterdam.

Punt, W.; Clarke, G. C. S. (1981): The Northwest European Pollenflora, vol. III. Elsevier, Amsterdam.

Punt, W.; Clarke, G. C. S. (1984): The Northwest European Pollenflora, vol. IV. Elsevier, Amsterdam.

Reille, M. (1992): Pollen et spores d'Europe et d'Afrique du nord, Marseille.

Reille, M. (1995): Pollen et spores d'Europe et d'Afrique du nord, Suppl. 1, Marseille.

Reimer, P. J.; Baillie, M. G. L.; Bard, E.; Bayliss, A.; Beck, J. W.; Blackwell, P. G.; Bronk Ramsey, C.; Buck, C. E.; Burr, G. S.; Edwards, R. L.; Friedrich, M.; Grootes, P. M.; Guilderson, T. P.; Hajdas, I.; Heaton, T. J.; Hogg, A. G.; Hughen, K. A.; Kaiser, K. F.; Kromer, B.; McCormac, F. G.; Manning, S. W.; Reimer, R. W.; Richards, D. A.; Southon, J. R.; Talamo, S.; Turney, C. S. M.; van der Plicht, J.; Weyhenmeyer, C. E. (2009): IntCal09 and Marine09 radiocarbon age calibration curves, 0-50,000 years cal BP. Radiocarbon 51(4), pp. 1111-50.

Seiwald, A. (1980): Beiträge zur Vegetationsgeschichte Tirols IV: Natzer Plateau, vol. 67. Villanderer Alm. Berichte Naturwissenschaftlich-medizinischer Verein, Innsbruck, pp. 31-72.

Stöllner, T. (2003): Mining and Economy – A Discussion of Spatial Organisations and Structures of Early Raw Material Exploitation. Der Anschnitt, Beiheft 16, pp. 415-446.

Tinner, W.; Hubschmid, P.; Wehrli, M.; Ammann, B.; Conedera, M. (1999): Long-term forest fire ecology and dynamics in southern Switzerland. Journal of Ecology 87, pp. 273-289.

Neubulach and Freudenstadt: Foundation, development and impact of medieval and early modern mining towns in the Northern Black Forest (SW-Germany)

Uwe Meyerdirks[1]

[1] Eberhard-Karls-Universität Tübingen, Germany

The establishment of mining settlements and especially mining towns may be regarded as one of the most significant and longest-lasting impacts of medieval and early modern mining on both, the natural environment and the social and economic structures. This paper investigates this claim by presenting two concrete examples from south-western Germany: Neubulach and Freudenstadt, the centres of the two principal districts of silver and copper mining in the Northern Black Forest. Both towns are fine examples for small medieval and early modern Renaissance mining towns, respectively. Even though the two districts are only 30km apart, they underwent very different and distinct developments with a wide range of effects on the natural, social and economic landscape.

The Northern Black Forest

Neubulach and Freudenstadt are both situated on the eastern fringe of the Northern Black Forest, one of the many wood-covered mountainous ranges of Central Europe. Further to the east, the landscapes known as Gäu are highly fertile and have been settled since the Early Neolithic Period (mid 6th century BC). Westwards, i.e. towards and into the Black Forest, the landscape slowly rises and the climate becomes less favourable as temperatures are lower and precipitation ranges between 900 and 1900mm. The inner parts of the Northern Black Forest are largely dominated by triassic sandstones. Here, the soils are thus sandy and rather poor.

Prehistoric colonisation and other human activities in the Northern Black Forest seem to have been limited to certain places, such as the Iron Age iron mining district around Neuenbürg in the northeasternmost part which has been investigated in recent years (Rösch et al., 2009). Nevertheless, it is generally assumed that large parts of the Northern Black Forest remained uninhabited woodland until the High Middle Ages, when wide areas were cleared and colonised, especially in the north-east. Recent pollen analyses hint at earlier periods of considerable human activity (Rösch, 2009; Rösch & Tserendorj, 2011), but these data are hindered by a lack of historical and archaeological evidence.

In the north-eastern part of the Northern Black Forest, the landscape can be characterised as an upland plain which is segmented by deeply cut valleys and rises from 500m to 800m a.s.l. During the High Middle Ages, larger areas were cleared on the plateaus and villages founded in their centres. As a result, the settlement pattern may be described as inhabited islands within a sea of wood.

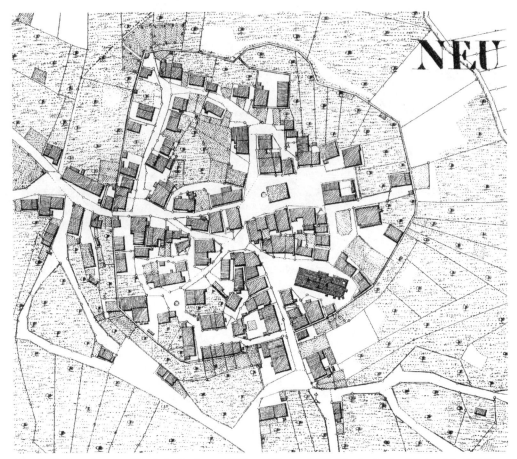

Fig. 1: Cadastral map of Neubulach, drawn 1836, rectified c. 1840 (Flurkarte des Königreichs Württemberg 1:2500, NW XIV-23).

Neubulach – the medieval mining town

On one of these plateaus, which is almost entirely encircled by deep valleys, an area of about 10km² has been cleared of wood and turned into farmland. This clearing comprises the three villages of Altbulach, Oberhaugstett and Liebelsberg, and, at its centre, the medieval town of Neubulach, first mentionend in AD 1275, probably one or two generations after its foundation (Matzke, 2003).

Looking on the settlement pattern, the town seems to be somewhat squeezed in between the older villages, and the town's boundary and lands were rather restricted and probably insufficient for agricultural subsistence. The town's younger age is also indicated by the place names: Altbulach (also called Altenbulach) means "Old-Bulach", while the town used to be called Bulach well into

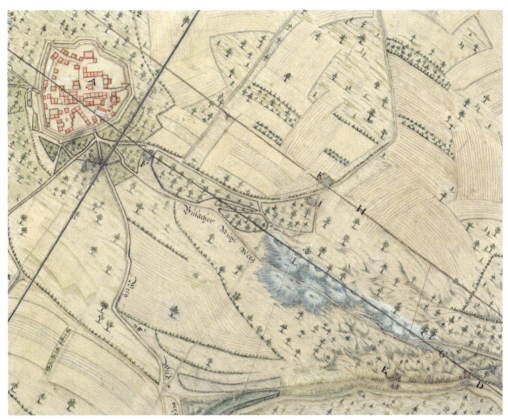

Fig. 2: Detail from the elaborate mine map of Neubulach from 1719 showing some of the extensive tailings and collapsed shafts from elder mining periods (L) along the outcrop of the principal vein (diagonal line G); HStA Stuttgart, N 1, Nr. 83.

the 17th and 18th century, when the name changed to Neubulach ("New-Bulach").

The location of Neubulach is somewhat unusual and inconvenient: water supply is insufficient and the town lies on a gentle slope directly below the highest part of the clearing. On the other hand, the town is placed in the centre and directly upon the outcrops of several silver and copper bearing veins which strike across the upland plateau. Therefore, the town most likely emerged as a mining settlement, where the miners lived next to their workplaces and as the mines flourished, the settlement developed and was granted the legal rights of a town most probably in the 1270s.

Mining faded in the later Middle Ages and the town stagnated or even declined until the 18th century. But in contrast to other small mining towns, such as Prinzbach in the Central Black Forest or Bleiberg on the Treppenhauer in Saxony, Neubulach survived and is now a fine example of a small medieval mining town. The oldest structure is the well-preserved fortification wall. One of the gates still exists and most probably originates from the later 13th century. At least three of the preserved residential houses in the town date from to the 14th and 15th centuries, and the elaborate church was most probably built in the 1430s (Breyvogel, 2003).

The first cadastral map from 1836/40 shows a rather heterogeneous town inside the town wall comprising 77 residential houses and various annexed or separate commercial buildings such as barns or workshops (*Fig. 1*). The market square with the town hall at its centre as well as the square in front of the church are surrounded by more or less regular rows of houses, while the houses in the western half seem to be scattered unsystematically. In the town's northern parts, larger areas are only gardens. The map shows only two gates in the south and west, and the main street bends between them by-passing the market square. However, the Merian engraving published in 1643, a very elaborate mine map from 1719, and other documents from the 17th and 18th centuries indicate a certain decline of the town, which is most apparent within the fortification (Meyerdirks, in print; in prep.): the 1719 map still shows an outer town wall in the south-west, the ruins of a possible third gate in the eastern wall and a rectangular block of eight houses instead of the main street (*Fig. 2*). This indicates that the original structure of the town may have been based on two orthogonal axes running from the western to the eastern gate and from quarters (Meyerdirks, 2011; in print; in prep.).

Direct evidence of medieval mining at Neubulach is rather limited. Nevertheless, some information about the extent of medieval mining can be gained by the simultaneous analysis of 16th century mining records, 18th century mine maps and the partly accessible underground workings (Meyerdirks, 2003a; 2003b; in prep.): With a total length of at least 3.5km, several parallel veins were exhausted down to a depth of about 100m. Mining reports from the 1550s onwards repeatedly describe extensive surface relics from older and forgotten mining periods. Even then, nobody could recall when and how these had been worked. These surface remains, which were destroyed during the 19th and 20th centuries, are clearly depicted on 18th century mine maps (Fig. 2): the relics consisted of tailings and collapsed shafts stretching all along the outcrops of the principal veins. When the map was drawn, the tailings were at least 200 years, most likely 400 or 500 years old. Nevertheless, the area was still largely barren land and those parts that were used were simply orchards.

These old tailings were an important monument of medieval mining and at the same time, they represented an important and obvious impact on the environment, but also on the medieval economy as they were dumped on cultivated land which remained infertile for centuries. In total, about half a square kilometre of arable land was consumed by the mining and the mining town. In addition, the former agrarian economy became more diversified: Mining, smelting and metal trade constituted new and very different components by themselves, and there were collateral effects, as the increase in population and the specific needs of the mining let to a wider range and a higher number of craftsmen such as smiths, bakers or butchers, who also provided tallow for the miners' lamps. Most certainly, the population was altered by the immigration of miners from other districts. Furthermore, the town of Neubulach became the new local centre. This is even reflected in the ecclesiastical structure being a fundamental and rather conservative framework of medieval society: De facto, the parish priests settled in Neubulach and its church became more important than the older parish church in the close-by village Effringen which lost its primacy although legally, it remained the parish church (Janssen, 2003).

Freudenstadt: the early Renaissance mining town

The silver and copper-bearing veins around Freudenstadt are linked to the Freudenstädter Graben, a tectonic rift structure which is about 8km wide. The most important veins cluster around the western fault on both sides of the Forbach valley (*Fig. 3*). The rift structure also creates a sharper boundary between the sandstones of the Northern Black Forest in the west and the limestones of the fertile Gäu landscapes to the east. Therefore, the district spans across the natural frontier between the Black Forest and the Gäu.

In consequence, the eastern half of the district has been cleared of wood and settled from at least the 8th century AD onwards (Lorenz & Kuhn, 1992), while the western half remained dense and more or less pristine forest well into the 16th century AD. In the eastern half, some small villages and the town of Dornstetten were established. A significant feature of the medieval and early modern landscape was an important interregional highway, which ran from the town of Strasbourg (Straßburg) on the Rhine across the heights of the Northern Black Forest, passed through the mining district and continued towards the inner parts of Württemberg. In addition to its rôle as the local centre, Dornstetten was an important station on this highway.

The 16th century mining records show quite clearly that medieval mining in the district was limited and that most of the deposits remained unexploited or even unscraped into the 16th century

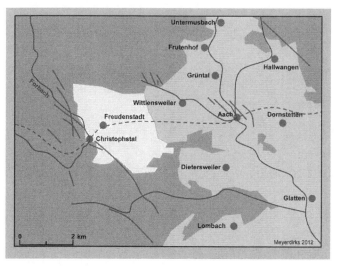

Fig. 3: Mining district of Freudenstadt, showing the elder villages, the town of Dornstetten and the new mining settlements Christophstal and Freudenstadt, the principal ore-bearing veins, the interregional highway (dashed line) and the clearance for the foundation of Freudenstadt; (Meyerdirks, in print).

AD. This corresponds with the archaeological evidence, as there are only few surface remains of possible medieval origin. In the second half of the 16th century, the Dukes of Württemberg took a strong personal interest in the mines and developed a new mining district in the Forbach valley which was now given a new name: Christophstal. A smelter was built close to the highway's river-crossing in 1572, and in the following years, a small mining settlement sprouted next to the smelter. However, the mines declined in the later 1570s and were closed in 1580/81. Nevertheless, the new settlement persisted (Meyerdirks 2011; in prep.).

A new impetus came, when Frederick I became Duke of Württemberg in 1593. He was strongly influenced by early mercantilist and absolutist ideas and took a strong interest in mining as well as other enterprises. The mines were re-opened in 1594, the smelter was rebuilt, new pumping machinery was installed underground, and most prominently, in 1599 a new town was founded in the woods on the highland plateau above Christophstal directly upon of the highway. Two years later, in 1601, the town got its name: Freudenstadt. Settlers were granted a building lot, construction wood and some land for agriculture, which they still had to clear (Meyerdirks 2011; in prep.).

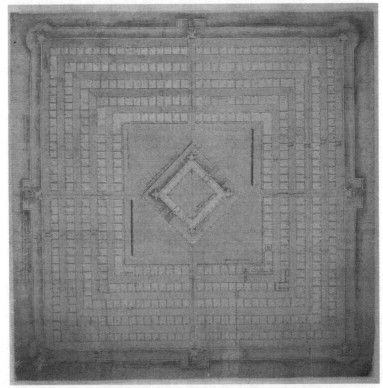

Fig. 4: Plan of Freudenstadt, showing the regular street plan with the four built rows of houses as well as the projected palace, fortification and fifth row. The three inner rows of houses represent the original town plan of the foundation in 1599. Heinrich Schickhardt, 1602/07; HStA Stuttgart, N 220, B 14.

The physical parameters of the town-site are not too favourable: It is situated 720m a.s.l., the average temperature is just above 7°C and there is a substantial annual precipitation of about 1500mm.

The town was entirely planned on the drawing board of the architect Heinrich Schickhardt. The State archives in Stuttgart still hold some of the original town plans showing the successive stages of the urban planning (HStA Stuttgart, N 220). At first, Schickhardt arranged the houses in blocks around a central market square and placed the ducal palace in one of the four corners. Duke Frederick preferred the houses to be lined up in rows and his palace to be placed in the centre. The resulting and final plan resembles a nine men's morris board with the ducal palace in the centre and still characterises Freudenstadt today (*Fig. 4*). The central square was surrounded by three rows comprising 222 standard houses, 16 larger houses, the church and three representative buildings, offering sufficient space for about 250 families and thus about 1200 to 1300 inhabitants (Meyerdirks 2011; in print; in prep.).

The new town prospered and only four years after foundation, a register from February 1603 already lists 244 male citizens. Obviously, the town had reached its intended size and at that time, it was enlarged by a forth row. A very elaborate and representative plan (*Fig. 4*), drawn between 1602 and 1607 or 1612, even shows a fifth row, which obviously had been projected, but was not built at that time. The same is true for the fortification and the never-built ducal palace (Meyerdirks, in print).

In addition to the mines, iron, steel, copper and brass workings were established along the Forbach creek in Christophstal during the first decade of the 17th century. They processed the copper from the mines and made use of the water-power and the immense quantities of wood in the surrounding forests. In the long run, these works were more successful than the mines and Christophstal developed into an early industrialised valley (Thier, 1965; Meyerdirks, in prep.).

Both, the mines and – more importantly – the metal works brought new elements into the formerly rural economy. Although the mines proved less profitable than expected and the ducal palace was never built, the foundation of Freudenstadt became a success and within a few years the new town became a regional centre and overran the older town of Dornstetten. It also took over its function as a station on the highway.

Generally, the miners in the district came from the most important mining regions and towns in the German-speaking parts of Central Europe, such as Schwaz in Tyrol, the Salzburg region, the Harz Mountains, Buchholz, Schneeberg and Joachimsthal in the Saxon and Bohemian Ore Mountains or Ste-Marie-aux-Mines (Markirch) and Giromagny in the partly French-speaking Vosges (Meyerdirks, in prep).

However, the rapid growth of Freudenstadt was only partly due to the mining. Another important impetus came with Protestant refugees from so-called Inner-Austria, i.e. Styria, Carinthia and Carniola, where they fled the Catholic Counter-Reformation. Some of these refugees came to

Württemberg, which was the southernmost stronghold of Protestantism in Germany.

Significant parts of the population obviously did not stay for long in Freudenstadt. The register from 1603 lists 244 male citizens and 9 grown-up sons. 13 years later, a second register from 1616 lists 275 male citizens and widows including 14 households from Christophstal. So population numbers remained constant, but surprisingly, only 41 of the citizens from 1603 or their widows can be found in 1616. For another 44 citizens, at least their family names are listed in 1616, but the remaining 168 citizens (66%), either died or left Freudenstadt between 1603 and 1616, and their places were taken by new settlers. Thus, in the first one or two decades, Freudenstadt experienced an immense migration to and from the new town, exchanging two thirds of its population (Meyerdirks, in print; in prep.).

Looking at the effects of mining on the ecosystems around Freudenstadt, the most obvious and most important impact stems from the foundation of the new town: an area of around 7km^2 of more or less pristine forest was cleared for the town and its surrounding fields and grasslands. This clearing probably represents one of the latest and largest single advances of colonisation into woodland in south-western Germany. At the same time, it constitutes the strongest and ongoing impact on the environment in the mining district. A second long-lasting effect on a specific ecosystem resulted from the metal-works: the Forbach creek was thoroughly regulated and its water was diverted into various canals leading to the numerous water wheels. The more immediate effects of mining had a much shorter life-time, as the woods have regenerated even on the tailings and other mining remains, although due to modern forestry, they differ significantly from the primeval forest.

Conclusion

Due to their very different history, the two examples of Neubulach und Freudenstadt show a wide range of the various effects medieval and early modern mining had on the natural and cultural landscape. These may be categorised in two groups.

At first, there are the immediate effects on the environment, such as the accumulation of tailings, alterations to the natural water system or the more or less intense cutting of wood for mining and especially smelting. However, in the moderate and humid climate of Central Europe, the woods will usually recover and start to regenerate even on the tailings once the mining has ended, whereas arable land is more likely to be permanently ruined by tailings. Generally, mining led to a more diversified economy, society and population, especially as a result of the immigration of miners, metallurgists and craftsmen.

However, more indirect effects may be more significant and last on for longer periods, especially if they stem from changes in the settlement system, most prominently the foundation of mining towns. Concerning the environment, clearings, i.e. the transformation of woodland into farmland, have an even stronger impact than simple wood-cutting, especially because they tend to become permanent. The new towns usually became local or even regional centres thereby replacing elder central places and changing the existing or establishing new settlement systems. The privileges and legal status of the towns and their citizens intensified and solidified the social and economic diversification.

So in general, mining towns may be seen as catalysers or amplifiers, intensifying the effects of mining on environment, economy and society and enabling them to outlast the mining activities.

Bibliography

Breyvogel, B. (2003): Bau- und Kunstdenkmäler. In: Lorenz, S. & Schmauder, A. (2003): Neubulach – Eine Stadt im Silberglanz, pp. 293-315.

Janssen, R. (2003): „Aefferingen sive Bulach" – ein Sonderfall der Kirchengeschichte im Nordschwarzwald. In: Lorenz, S. & Schmauder, A. (2003): Neubulach – Eine Stadt im Silberglanz, pp. 76-108.

Lorenz, S. & Kuhn, A. (1992): Baiersbronn – Vom Königsforst zum Luftkurort.

Matzke, M. (2003): Die Stadt und der Bergbau bis 1440. In: Lorenz, S. & Schmauder, A. (2003): Neubulach – Eine Stadt im Silberglanz, pp. 119-146.

Meyerdirks, U. (2003a): Pingen, Halden, Schächte und Stollen – Spuren des Bulacher Bergbaus über und unter Tage. In: Lorenz, S. & Schmauder, A. (2003): Neubulach – Eine Stadt im Silberglanz, pp. 176-200.

Meyerdirks, U. (2003b): Bergbau in Neubulach (1534-1700). In: Lorenz, S. & Schmauder, A. (2003): Neubulach – Eine Stadt im Silberglanz, pp. 257-292.

Meyerdirks, U. (2011): Der Bergbau auf Silber und Kupfer in Württemberg von den Anfängen bis um 1700: Grundzüge seiner Entwicklung und Möglichkeiten seiner Erforschung. In: Zeitschrift für Württembergische Landesgeschichte 70, pp. 193-227.

Meyerdirks, U. (in print): Bergbau und Stadtentwicklung im Nordschwarzwald. In: Rohstoffgewinnung und Stadtentwicklung, Siedlungsforschung 30.

Meyerdirks, U. (in prep.): Der Silber- und Kupferbergbau in Württemberg von den Anfängen bis um 1700. Doctoral thesis, Universität Tübingen.

Rösch, M.; Gassmann, G. & Wieland, G. (2009): Keltische Montanindustrie im Schwarzwald: eine Spurensuche. In: Die Kelten am Rhein, Vol. 1, pp. 263-278.

Rösch, M. (2009): Botanical evidence for prehistoric and medieval land use in the Black Forest. In: Medieval Rural Settlement in Marginal Landscapes, Ruralia VII, Turnhout (Belgium), pp. 335-343.

Rösch, M. & Tserendorj, G. (2011): Florengeschichtliche Beobachtungen im Nordschwarzwald (Südwestdeutschland). In: Herzynia, N.F., 44, pp. 53-71.

Thier, M. (1965): Geschichte der Schwäbischen Hüttenwerke 1365-1802. Ein Beitrag zur württembergischen Wirtschaftsgeschichte.

Copper Mining in Ireland during the Later Bronze Age

William O'Brien[1]

[1] Department of Archaeology, University College Cork

By 1400 BC primary copper production involving organized mining was coming to an end in both Britain and Ireland. This included those parts of south-west Ireland, mid and north Wales and the English midlands where copper mining was well established earlier in the Bronze Age. The decline of copper mining was a wider phenomenon across Atlantic Europe, which is all the more interesting as it coincided with a growing demand for metal in societies with extensive trade connections.

Several theories can be advanced to explain these developments in copper supply during the later Bronze Age. One possibility is that mines existed, but have not survived or cannot be easily recognised today. The former might relate to a change in the type of ores mined, possibly involving deep extraction in deposits that were intensively worked in later periods. The destruction of evidence is certainly possible, but is unlikely to be the entire explanation. Archaeological visibility may be a problem, particularly if there were significant changes in mining technology. The replacement of fire-setting would remove distinctive wallrock patterns, while reducing the sample material available for radiocarbon dating. The occurrence of stone hammers in large numbers in earlier Bronze Age copper mines is relevant, as their replacement by specialised bronze tools would remove an important surface indicator of this activity. However, with no evidence that the latter were used to any extent during the Late Bronze Age, depending on the geological setting there may have been few options but to continue with the older technology.

A more likely explanation is that copper mining did in fact decline after 1400 BC, finally ending by 1000 BC, in both Britain and Ireland. This is the picture presented by radiocarbon data from some twenty sampled copper mines. The rise and fall of different mining regions could be understood in terms of boom/bust cycles that would be familiar from historic times. The abandonment of established mines in the Bronze Age was not driven by economic forces alone, but must be considered with reference to technological constraints and alternative means of metal supply, such as recycling and long-distance trade, but particularly to the socio-political context of these ventures.

The Irish situation

Following the introduction of primary copper production to Ireland in the mid third millennium BC, and the rapid adoption of tin bronze from 2000 BC, there was a growing dependency on bronze by the Middle Bronze Age. This is reflected in the output of flanged axeheads and palstaves, dirks, rapiers and looped spearheads during the Killymaddy phase of the Middle Bronze Age (ca. 1550-1350 BC). Metal production intensified during the Bishopsland phase (ca. 1350-1100 BC), when influences from Continental Europe coming through southern Britain led to

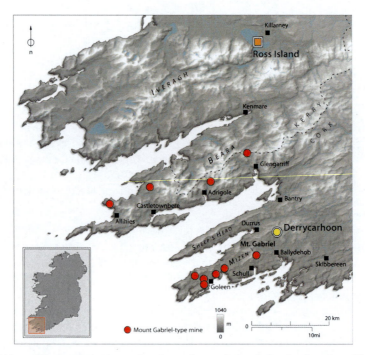

Fig. 1: Chalcolithic and Bronze Age copper mines in south-west Ireland, showing location of Derrycarhoon mine in the Mizen Peninsula of West Cork.

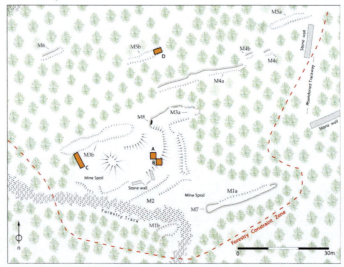

Fig. 2: Plan of early mine workings at Derrycarhoon (trenches M1 to M6), as well as location of archaeological excavations (cuttings A-D).

the new metalworking techniques and a novel range of bronze artifacts (Waddell, 2010:87-213). Advances in bronze casting are reflected in the use of clay moulds, to make new object types such as the first bronze swords (Ballintober type).

The growth of metal hoarding from 1400-1000 BC testifies to a marked increase in the amount of metal in circulation across Ireland. Much of this bronze was sourced through recycling and foreign trade, and the discovery of scrap hoards suggests that this was a well-organized activity. Some primary metal may have been imported from Wales, where probably only the Great Orme mine was still in operation after 1400 BC, declining by 1000 BC with only limited mining after this date. Trade links with the Continent led to new sources of copper (Northover, 1982), with the most important supply possibly from the east Alpine mines in Austria.

The consumption of bronze in Ireland increased further during the Dowris phase of the Late Bronze Age, ca. 1000-600 BC. Metalworking reached new heights in terms of the scale of production, the great variety of metal products, and the technical accomplishment of the craft workers. The amount of metal in circulation is attested by a great increase in hoarding, with some 130 deposits (80% of the Bronze Age total) recorded from this period. The proliferation of new tool, weapon and ornament types shows influences from southern and western Britain, northern and central Europe, and different parts of Atlantic Europe. Irish metalwork was exchanged widely in Britain and the Continent in this period, contacts that resulted in the supply of raw metal from primary or secondary sources.

Derrycarhoon mine

The south-west region of Cork and Kerry was the most important source of copper during the Chalcolithic and Bronze Age in Ireland (*Fig. 1*). Copper mining began ca. 2400 BC at Ross Island in Killarney, Co. Kerry and continued there to ca. 1800 BC (O'Brien, 2004). The abandonment of that mine coincided with the commencement of copper extraction on Mount Gabriel and at nine other locations in the peninsulas of West Cork (O'Brien, 1994; 2003). This is a region of late Devonian geology, where beds of green sandstone can contain low-grade disseminations of oxidised copper minerals. These 'copper-beds' were first mined in surface drift mines of the Mount Gabriel type using fire-setting and stone hammers. Until recently it was believed that copper mining had ceased in the region after 1400 BC, however a new discovery in Cork points to continued extraction of copper into later centuries.

This site is located in a forest clearing at Derrycarhoon, on a low ridge on the north-east side of the Mizen Peninsula (*Fig. 1*). The mine was first recorded in 1846 when it was re-opened for a brief period, leading to the much-publicized discovery of old workings and mining tools, attributed at that time to the 'Danes'. The finds included stone hammers and wooden equipment, including a notched tree trunk ladder and a curved wooden tube believed to be part of a suction pump. The latter is radiocarbon dated 1044-1284 AD, suggesting there was more than one phase of mining or prospection prior to the discoveries of 1846.

A recent survey at Derrycarhoon identified a number of surface mine workings across the site

Fig. 3: Mine 5b-1 after excavation.

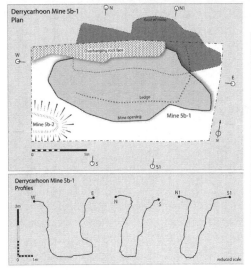

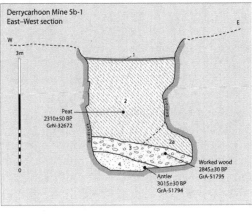

Fig. 4: Plan and profiles of Mine 5b-1, Derrycarhoon.

Fig. 5: Infill sequence of Mine 5b-1, Derrycarhoon.

(*Fig. 2*). These include two vertical mine shafts that were sunk in the nineteenth century and are now infilled. The underground workings of that period are inaccessible. There is evidence of earlier copper mining in the form of six parallel trenches (M1-6), up to 30m in length and 2-3m in width, which cross the site in a north-east/south-west direction. One of these, Mine 5, is a row of closely spaced vertical pits, now mostly infilled with peat. An exposed section on the western side (Mine 5b) measures 11.5m long by 2.15m wide. A 3.35m long section of this trench was excavated in summer 2011 (cutting D). This exposed a near-vertical, rock-cut pit (Mine 5b-1) measuring 2.75m long by 1m wide by 4m deep (*Figs 3 and 4*). The shape and size of this mine was determined by its stratabound position along a steeply dipping 'copper-bed'.

The upper part of this working was filled to a depth of 2.4m by compact peat (Layer 2), which formed over some 3000 years as dead vegetation blew into the flooded mine (*Fig. 5*). This is confirmed by a radiocarbon date of 516-206 BC for a sample of peat taken at a depth of 1.5m in the mine. This peat overlay a deposit of stony sediment (Layer 3), which comprised slabs of sandstone up to 0.6m in size and smaller rock fragments. A large number of broken stone hammers were recovered from this layer, as well as fragments of waterlogged wood. The latter included some lengths of roundwood with chop marks, one of which is radiocarbon dated to 1114-921 BC.

Further excavation exposed a deposit of finely broken stone (Layer 4) at the base of the mine. The deposit contained broken stone hammers, as well as occasional fragments of roundwood. Some items of worked wood were found, including part of a stone hammer handle, a wedge and two large branches used as crude ladders. Part of a red deer antler pick was recovered, the first such find from an early copper mine in Ireland. A radiocarbon date of 1386-1132 BC for this antler, together with a result of 1378-1119 BC for a hammerstone withy, indicate the working period of this mine.

This working was part of an alignment of closely-spaced pits (Mines 5a joining with 5b) along the east-west direction of the copper-bed (*Fig. 2*). As mining progressed the individual pits were partially backfilled with discarded rock from adjacent pits, with subsequent build-up of 2-3m of peat in the flooded interiors. Elsewehere in the site there is evidence of continuous trenches (e.g. Mines 1 and 4), with nineteenth-century sources referring to arches of rock left in those narrow workings, presumably for support, access and/or haulage purposes.

This trench mining produced surface deposits of broken rock spoil in the central mine area, which were added to by later mining. Test-pit excavation was undertaken in 2010 (cuttings A and B) in the central mine area (*Fig. 2*). This uncovered a thin deposit of Bronze Age spoil containing broken stone hammers and fragments of waterlogged wood. A fragment of rowan roundwood with chop marks is radiocarbon dated 1370-1021 BC, while a piece of young oak is dated 1369-1059 BC, and a twisted hazel withy 1410-1114 BC. These results confirm that this spoil came from a mine contemporary with the Mine 5b-1 working, including the adjacent Mine 3 trench that was emptied in the 1846 operations.

Mining strategy and techniques

The recent investigations provide much detail on the approach to copper mining at Derrycarhoon, ca. 1300-1000 BC. Unlike other prehistoric copper mines in south-west Ireland there is no evidence for the use of fire-setting. The wallrock profile in Mine 5b-1 does not have the smooth concavities produced by fire-setting, nor were fuel residues in the form of charcoal or burnt roundwood identified in Mine 5b-1 or in the excavated surface spoil. Fire-setting is not particularly suited to the sinking of vertical workings such as the Derrycarhoon mine trenches.

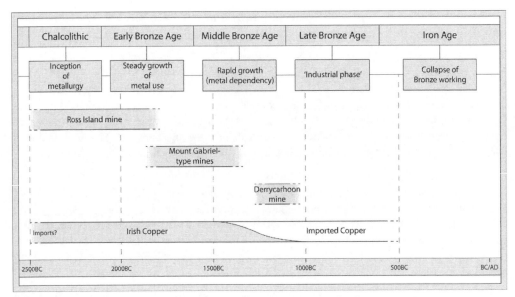

Fig. 6: The chronology of prehistoric copper mining in south-west Ireland.

To extract rock the miners instead exploited natural weaknesses in the sandstone geology. These copper-beds are steeply dipping with a penetrative rock cleavage on a near-vertical axis. This allowed the miners to drive down into the lamination of the hard siliceous rock using wedges and pick-like tools. In this way, rock could be prised apart along a 2-5cm wide cleavage, which partly determined the size of the rock extract.

Stone hammers were an important tool in the extraction and beneficiation of copper ore in this mine. There are numerous broken examples on the exposed spoil heaps, while 63 examples were recovered in the excavation of Mine 5b-1 and 273 from spoil trenches A and B. These are mostly well-rounded natural cobbles, 130-213mm in length and 500-3500g in weight, generally broken through heavy use. These cobbles came from local glacial drift or from beach deposits along the coastline of the Mizen Peninsula. Some were used hand-held, while shallow abrasion marks on some examples were made to grip a twisted withy handle, an example of which was found in Mine 5b-1. Minimal effort was spent on modifying these sandstone cobbles for hafting, mainly because they were used to strike bedrock of similar lithology and so broke after a short time.

These hammerstones were used to strike the mine face to remove rock, and were also employed in combination with other implements, several of which were found in the mine. These include a short wooden wedge and a number of pointed hazel rods used as prise-sticks. The use of antler picks is also significant, as these implements are known from Neolithic flint mines in Europe and are recorded in some Bronze Age copper mines, including the recently excavated site at Ecton in England (Timberlake this volume).

The excavation of Mine 5b-1 at Derrycarhoon provides information on the practical operation of this mine. Though only 4m in depth, access to this working would have been awkward due to its near-vertical profile and smooth walls. The miners may have used ropes and some form of basket to haul broken rock extract to the surface. Excavation did uncover two lengths of round-wood, both with short projecting branches, placed in an inclined position against the west wall to allow miners to climb in and out of the working. Though undated and now lost, the monoxlyous wooden ladder found at Derrycarhoon in 1846 may be from this period.

Natural lighting may not have been a problem in these mine trenches, at least down to depths of around 4m. Pine lighting chips, similar to those used at Mount Gabriel (O'Brien, 1994), may have been required for deeper workings. The extent of any drainage problems depended on rainfall during the mining season, which may have been confined to drier months. The excavation of Mine 5b-1 did encounter water seepage at a depth of 4m. This might explain why the working was abandoned or it may have been when the mineralization ran out, with the miners moving to an adjacent portion of the 'copper-bed'.

The end of an era

The investigations at Derrycarhoon continue the story of copper mining in south-west Ireland into the later Bronze Age (*Fig. 6*). This is the first early copper mine in that region not connected to the use of fire-setting. Radiocarbon dating of worked wood and antler confirms Derrycarhoon was worked in the 13th century BC, with mining continuing to possibly as late as the 11th century BC. This was a period when the use of bronze greatly expanded in Ireland. While this was once attributed to imported metal, there is now evidence of some native production.

Derrycarhoon mine is a development from the earlier Mount Gabriel-type extraction of oxidized mineralization in this region. The continued reliance on surface occurrences of low-grade, but accessible, malachite relates to an inability to process copper-iron sulphidic ore at this site, or indeed elsewhere in Ireland or Britain during the prehistoric period. This technological constraint, combined with the exhaustion of easily worked deposits of oxidized ore, explains the decline and eventual cessation of copper mining during the later Bronze Age in this part of Europe.

References

Northover, J.P. (1982): The exploration and long distance movement of bronze in Bronze Age and Early Iron Age Europe. Bulletin of the Institute of Archaeology 19, 45-72.

O'Brien, W. (1994): Mount Gabriel: Bronze Age Mining in Ireland. Galway University Press, Galway.

O'Brien, W. (2003): The Bronze Age copper mines of the Goleen area, Co. Cork. Proceedings of the Royal Irish Academy 103C, 13-59.

O'Brien, W. (2004): Ross Island: Mining, Metal and Society in Early Ireland. Bronze Age Studies, Galway.

Waddell, J. (2010): The Prehistoric Archaeology of Ireland. Wordwell, Dublin.

Session V
Data Base, Modelling & Geoinformation supporting Mining Research

Medieval mining sites, trade routes, and least-cost paths in the Bergisches Land, Germany

Irmela Herzog[1]

[1] LVR – The Rhineland Regional Council, The Rhineland Commission for Archaeological Monuments and Sites, Bonn, Germany

Many mining sites have been recorded in the hilly region known as the Bergisches Land, east of Cologne (Nehls, 1993). According to archaeological evidence, mining in this area dates back to roman times, and Gechter (2012) refers to several intensive mining phases in the late medieval and modern periods. Iron, copper, lead, and sphalerite were mined in this region, and a silver mine was close to Wildberg (*Fig. 1*). A silver mine near Wildberg is not only depicted on the Mercator map (1575 AD; Weirich, 1999) and the Waye map (1607 AD; Weirich, 2004), but also on modern maps. According to historical sources, since about 1250 AD silver coins were manufactured in Wildberg (Nehls, 1993). In 1275 King Rudolf allowed Count Adolf of Berg to move the mint to Wipperfürth. So the silver had to be transported for at least 33 km, if the shortest path – as the crow flies – was taken.

The old routes in the study region were derived from historical maps (*Fig. 1*): the Mercator map, the Waye map, the Ploennies maps (1715 AD; Dietz, 1988) and the oldest map of the territory of Gimborn-Neustadt (Nehls, 1996). In total these maps cover roughly the study area, and some parts overlap. The accuracy of the historical maps is far from perfect, and it is well-known that the routes depicted are generalized, i.e. more direct than in reality. The routes were crudely digitised on the basis of the place names shown on the maps. These routes coincide quite well in areas covered by two or more maps. On these maps only the main trade routes are shown, and many settlements are located at some distance to these roads. So additional minor road connections must have existed. It is assumed that silver was transported from Wildberg to Wipperfürth on an efficient route, but not necessarily on the main trade routes.

Least-cost path (LCP) modelling can be applied to identify probable routes (Herzog, 2013b). But the LCP approach requires a cost model. Quite a few cost models have been used in archaeological LCP studies (Herzog, 2013a), and ground-truthing is required to validate a cost model. In this case study, the historical routes in the study region are the basis for calibrating the cost model. Figure 2 shows the result of the efforts to derive a cost model: In the southern part of the map some of the most successful attempts to reconstruct the old trade route known as Brüderstraße between Heckhaus and Erdingen are displayed. Several slope-dependent cost functions were applied, and it was found that the quadratic cost function with a critical slope of 13% performed well. If the gradient exceeds the critical slope it is more efficient to use switchbacks than to ascend (or descend) the steep slope directly. A critical slope in the range of 8 to 16% is expected for wheeled vehicles, whereas the critical slope of walkers is higher (Herzog, 2013a). Avoiding

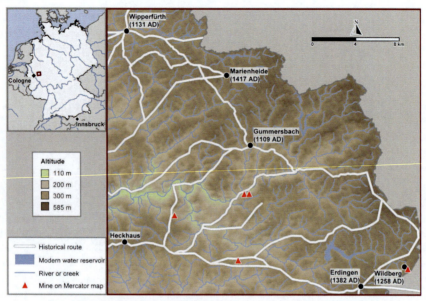

Fig. 1: Study area, digital elevation model on the basis of the ASTER GDEM (ASTER GDEM is a product of METI and NASA).

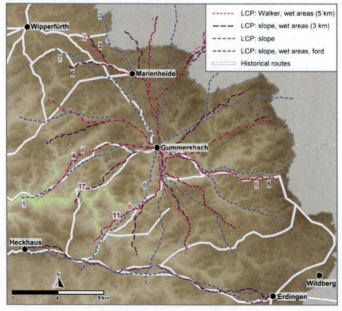

Fig. 2: Reconstruction of historical routes by LCPs (in the south) and by a least-cost central point network (origin: Gummersbach).

wet areas is also important. Figure 1 shows that many creeks and small rivers can be found in the study area. Most, but not all historical routes shun the wet valleys surrounding these streams.

So in addition to a slope cost model (blue LCPs in *Fig. 2*) a cost model combining slope and avoiding wet areas (derived from the digital soil map) was applied (dark violet LCPs in *Fig. 2*). The Mercator map depicts two alternative routes for a section of the Brüderstraße, and the LCPs resulting from the two cost models each choose a different alternative. The fit of the LCP to the route on the Mercator map can be improved by including known ford (or bridge) locations in the model (light violet LCP in *Fig. 2*).

However, many other slope-dependent cost models resulted in LCPs which fitted the Brüderstraße between Heckhaus and Erdingen nearly as well. For this reason, the cost models were checked by an alternative approach: Central point networks were generated assuming that Gummersbach was a central place where many important routes meet. Gummersbach is not only in the centre of the study area but was already an important central place when first mentioned in a deed of 1109 AD (Pampus, 1998). The deed refers to a church in Gummersbach, and according to Pampus, the parish belonging to this church covered a large area. The historical map of Gimborn-Neustadt shows the church and three roads that meet in Gummersbach. The road to the west forks after covering about 1.7 km. The aim was to reconstruct this road layout by a central point network and to identify appropriate cost models for this purpose. The upper part of Figure 2 shows some results of these attempts. The method for generating such central point networks was proposed by Fábrega Álvarez and Parcero Oubiña (2007). They determine all non-self-intersecting paths from the origin that stop after expending a predefined cost limit. Those paths which cover the largest distance from the origin are considered probable route reconstructions because progress is most effective on these paths. To ensure that distinct paths are selected for the network, the target locations of the selected paths should keep a user-defined minimum straight-line distance. In Figure 2 three different central point networks for Gummersbach are depicted, for each network the paths stop at an effort corresponding to covering 15 km on level ground without wet areas.

The central point network that does not take wet areas into account consists of 12 paths, and the distance between any pair of target locations exceeds 5 km (blue paths in *Fig. 2*). The path covering the longest distance is labelled by the blue number 1: This path coincides quite well with the historical road from Gummersbach in the west direction. The path that comes second (labelled by 2) coincides for about 3.5 km with the historical route to the north but leaves this route to pass through Marienheide. A corresponding road is depicted on the map of Gimborn-Neustadt by a thin line. Path number 5 first runs the wet valley of a creek but later agrees fairly well with a historical route. In general, the progression on those network paths with the lowest numbers is most effective, and for this reason it seems more likely that these paths correspond to ancient routes than the other paths in the reconstructed network.

When penalties for wet areas are included but the cost limit is not changed, a central point network with shorter routes results. Two networks taking wet areas into account are depicted in Figure 2: A network consisting of 17 paths where the minimum distance between any pair of target locations is 3 km (dark violet); the second network uses a slope-dependent cost function

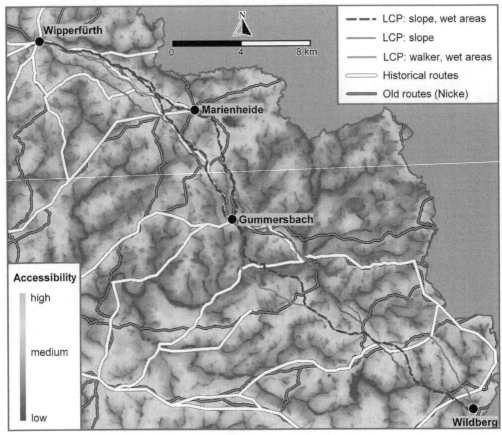

Fig. 3: LCPs connecting Wildberg and Wipperfürth.

for walkers based on physiological data (Herzog, 2013a) and includes only 10 paths with a target location distance greater than 5 km (pink).

The second best paths in both networks traverse Marienheide, but not on any of the old routes depicted on the historical maps considered. However, Nicke (2001) describes an old road that coincides quite well with these paths. In all networks depicted in Figure 2, at least one path passes through Marienheide. According to Nicke (2001), Marienheide is a central place where several long-distance routes meet (*Fig. 3*). But Marienheide was first mentioned about 300 years later than Gummersbach or Wipperfürth. Marienheide may have been neglected by the historical sources because it was located near the border of two territories: The settlement belonged to Gimborn-Neustadt but its location is also indicated on the map by Ploennies covering the Berg territory.

In both central point networks with penalties for wet areas, paths number 4 and 5 coincide quite well with the historical routes. Moreover, path number 6 of the 17 paths network reconstructs a route to the west after leaving Marienheide. All networks in Figure 2 include a path from Gummersbach to the south for about 3 km, and again a corresponding road is depicted on the map of Gimborn-Neustadt by a thin line.

The three cost models (1: critical slope of 13% only; 2: slope-dependent cost function as in the first model combined with penalties for wet areas; 3: slope-dependent walker function with taking the wet areas into account) were applied to construct the most efficient route from Wildberg to Wipperfürth (*Fig. 3*). Two LCPs were calculated for each cost model, the direct route and a route with an intermediate stop at Gummersbach. All LCPs with the exception of a walker LCP seem to converge in Gummersbach, and in fact the distance of these LCPs to the intermediate location is less than 200 m. But north of Gummersbach the LCPs diverge again. The walker cost model is anisotropic, i.e. different costs are assigned for ascending or descending a slope. Implementing this model sometimes results in two different LCPs for each direction of the connection. For this reason, Figure 3 actually shows four walker LCPs, two of these coincide most of the time.

In the background of Figure 3 an accessibility map is displayed (Herzog, submitted). This map is based on the cost model that combines penalties for wet areas with a slope-dependent cost function (critical slope: 13%). Figure 3 shows that most historical routes prefer areas of high accessibility. This applies also to the ancient routes described by Nicke (2001). These routes coincide with the routes derived from the historical maps in many parts, but there are also some differences. If the reconstructed routes and the historical routes show similar differences, the reconstructions are probably not too bad. Moreover the accessibility map can help to identify plausible routes: For example, starting from Wildberg, the pedestrian route proceeds on areas of high accessibility and probably is a better choice than the two other calculated routes for the first section of the journey. A corresponding road can be found on the historical map of 1840.

Substantial parts of the LCPs between Wildberg and Wipperfürth coincide with the old trade route Bergische Eisenstraße. According to Nicke (2001) this old route dates back to the late middle ages, i.e. the time when silver was transported from Wildberg to the mint in Wipperfürth.

References

Dietz, B. (1988): Erich Philipp Ploennies, Topographia Ducatus Montani (1715), (1988), Bergische Forschungen XX.

Fábrega Álvarez, P. & Parcero Oubiña, C. (2007): Proposals for an archaeological analysis of pathways and movement. Archeologia e Calcolatori 18, pp. 121-140.

Gechter, M. (2012): Bergbau in Mittelalter und Neuzeit. In: Kunow, J.: 25 Jahre Archäologie im Rheinland 1987-2011, pp. 418-420.

Herzog, I. (2013a): Theory and Practice of Cost Functions. In: Contreras, F.; Farjas, M. & Melero, F. J.:

Fusion of Cultures. Proceedings of the 38th Annual Conference on Computer Applications and Quantitative Methods in Archaeology, Granada, Spain, April 2010. BAR International Series 2494, pp. 375-382.

Herzog, I. (2013b): The Potential and Limits of Optimal Path Analysis. In: Bevan, A. & Lake, M.: Computational Approaches to Archaeological Spaces. Walnut Creek, pp. 179-211.

Herzog, I. (submitted): Calculating accessibility. Proceedings of the 40th Conference on Computer Applications and Quantitative Methods in Archaeology, CAA 2012 in Southampton.

Nehls, A. (1993): Aller Reichtum lag in der Erde. Die Geschichte des Bergbaus im Oberbergischen Kreis. Gummersbach.

Nehls, A. (1996): Als in den Tälern die Hämmer dröhnten. Wiehl.

Nicke, H. (2001): Vergessene Wege. Das historische Fernwegenetz zwischen Rhein, Weser, Hellweg und Westerwald, seine Schutzanlagen und Knotenpunkte. Nümbrecht 2001.

Pampus, K. (1998): Urkundliche Erstnennungen oberbergischer Orte. Beiträge zur Oberbergischen Geschichte. Gummersbach.

Weirich, H. (1999): Grenzen des Bergischen Amtes Windeck und der Herrschaft Homburg (1575) von Arnold Mercator. Nümbrecht.

Weirich, H. (2004): Die Wayekarte von 1607. Ein Kartendokument zum Siegburger Vergleich. Nümbrecht.

Underground surveying with 3D-laserscanning of the "Galeria dos Alargamentos" in the Roman gold mining district of Três Minas and Campo De Jales (Northern Portugal)[1]

Markus Helfert[1], Britta Ramminger[2] & Regula Wahl-Clerici[2]

[1] Goethe-Universität Frankfurt/M., Institut für Archäologische Wissenschaften, Frankfurt/M., Germany
[2] Universität Hamburg, Archäologisches Institut, Vor- und Frühgeschichtliche Archäologie, Hamburg, Germany

Introduction

In the past decade the 3D laser scanning is increasingly used as a new method of surveying in various fields of archaeological and cultural heritage preservation applications. The survey method is used in the historical building research with great success for the documentation and reconstruction of monuments (e. g. Wiedemann, 2004). Particularly, the use of laser scanning from an airplane (airborne laser scanning) helps in archeology to create detailed terrain models and especially to identify so far undiscovered findings in forest areas (Bofinger et al., 2007; Heine, 2011). So this practice becomes more and more a valuable tool in archaeological prospection (Reindl & Wagner, 2008; Hesse, 2010). More recently 3D laser scanning is introduced as a method with its gain in mining archaeology (Grussenmeyer et al., 2010). The benefits and opportunities of such an application in a Roman mine will be presented below using the example of the "Galeria dos Alargamentos".

The mining district of Três Minas (Vila Real, Vila Pouca de Aguiar) is one of the most important primaries gold and silver ore deposits of Portugal and one of the best preserved in the Roman Empire. This almost unique situation includes not only the well preserved monuments of the opencast exploitation but also the monuments of the further metallurgical processes to gain the gold from the ore and all the items which were necessary to make these processes go.

Archaeological prospection and surveying in the mining district of Três Minas has a long tradition. Jürgen Wahl and Regula Wahl-Clerici performed after the excavations in the settlement and mining area (Wahl, 1988; 1993; 1998; 2003; Wahl & Wahl-Clerici, 1993; Wahl-Clerici & Wiechowski, 2013) large surveys in the surrounding region of more than 1km² (*Fig. 1*). In such a wide district the previous excavations could only give a small notion of the large settlement and its inner structures and buildings. At the same time it has to be remarked that scientific knowledge of mining settlements in Roman times is still poor, also the detailed building history of the shafts, galleries and tunnels. Therefore it is of great interest, not only for the scientific community but also for the larger public, to have more information about these structures, to protect the monuments and to present a detailed map of the Três Minas-site. After small excavations

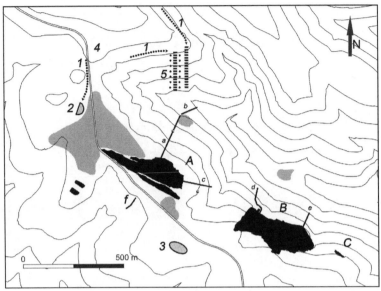

Fig. 1: Thematical map of the mining area of Três Minas. 1 = Aqueducts, 2 = Water collector, 3 = Amphitheatre, 4 = Cemetery, A = Corta de Covas, B = Corta da Ribeirinha, C = Corta dos Laginhos, a = Galeria do Pilar, b = Galeria do Texugo, c = Galeria dos Alargamentos, d = Galeria dos Morcegos, e = Galeria do Buraco seco, f = Galeria Esteves Pinto.

between 2007 and 2010 at this point the Câmara Municipal of Vila Pouca de Aguiar asked the Archaeological Institute of the University of Hamburg to perform the first geomagnetic measurements inside a larger area of the settlement and the surrounds of the opencast mining area and to do also 3D-laserscans of selected galleries and opencasts (Wahl-Clerici et al., 2011; 2012). During a summer campaign in 2010 it was possible to carry out geomagnetic prospections in the Roman settlement area and to have a complete survey of the "Galeria dos Alargamentos".

3D-Laserscanning of the "Galeria dos Alargamentos"

Basically the archaeologist asks 3 questions to a building: How was it constructed, for what purpose did it serve and when was it built? With these questions it is possible to understand an object in its historical context. And it is obvious that these 3 questions can be of remarkably difficulty to be answered. The "Galeria dos Alargamentos" is no exception.

The 3D surveying and mapping of the "Galeria dos Alargamentos" and the terrain in the surrounding of the "Corta de Covas" was carried out by means of a 3D-Laserscanner Ilris 36D-HD (Optech) of the Archaeological Institute of the University Hamburg. For the survey inside the gallery a time span of one week was necessary. The scanner has an accuracy of position of 5mm at 100m distance. From about 60 survey points inside the gallery 80 3D measurements were taken (*Fig. 2*). Each single scan includes in a range of 10m from the instrument to the gallery surface round about 6 million points. The complete registered model was independently proven by reference measurements with a Leica total station. As we have seen, the registration error for the complete gallery is one centimetre over the 140m length. For the virtual models of the gallery different resolutions of the point cloud density were taken. For detailed reconstructions we use one point per $1cm^3$, for overviews and animated models one point per $10cm^3$ and for the geographical information system of the project one point per $50cm^3$.

For a long time the "Galeria dos Alargamentos" (*Fig. 3*) was understood by the scientific community as well as by laity to have been an important part of the exploitation executed by the Romans in the part of the open cast mine called "Corta de Covas". There has to be considered that the actual appearance of the "Corta de Covas" differs remarkably from that in Antiquity. The mine was divided in at least 5 different parts which were exploited to different depths. The opencast was in some parts at least the double of the actually visible depth (over 120m). Furthermore, the present eastern slope of the "Corta de Covas" is not identical with the one in Roman times, because it is the result of various landslips which occurred along a natural gap in a time unknown. What we see today was in fact completely hidden under the surface of the mountain. This means that the two pits (one of them is connected to the gallery), their shapes are easy to identify in the rocks, were not part of the opencast mining activities. Considering this and the fact that the "Galeria dos Alargamentos" shows no proper reference to have ever been enlarged towards the opencast pit, there always remained the question of its aim.

This discussion about the purpose of the "Galeria dos Alargamentos" started long before the possibilities of 3D-Laserscanning were adapted in the archaeological survey. At first sight the "Galeria dos Alargamentos" corresponds largely with the appearance of the large galleries in Três Minas (Galeria Esteves Pinto, Galeria do Pilar, Galeria do Texugo, Galeria dos Morcegos) constructed for the transport of the ore by chars, the circulation of men and – very important – for draining. But there are the following items which prevent this interpretation:

- There is no evidence of any construction or installation for draining.
- There is no evidence for a connection with the opencast.
- The "Galeria dos Alargamentos" is connected by the great pit well visible in the eastern slope of the "Corta de Covas" with the surface of the hill.
- This pit was sinked for the transport of the ore.
- In this area a big cavern was hewed for placing a capstan (*Fig. 4*).
- Former surveys show that the "Galeria dos Alargamentos" was a composition of two branches which were each one in itself approximately straight. The two encounter in the middle of the gallery where there is an enlargement (small cavern).
- The sections of the two branches seemed to be of a different construction.

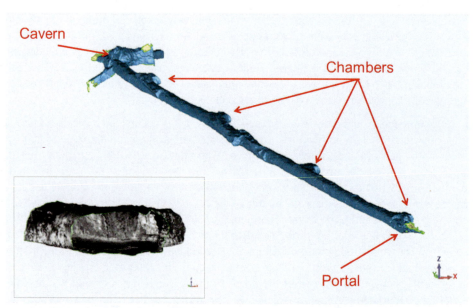

Fig. 2: View from southeast on the 3D model of the "Galeria dos Alargamentos" with the small chambers to the northern side, and a view into the gallery in the area of Chamber 1 (below left).

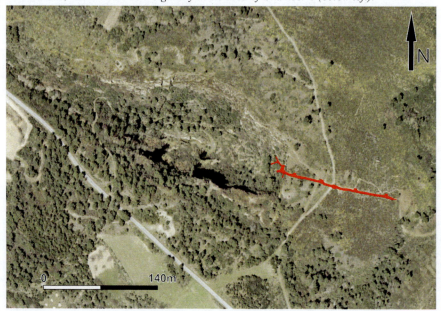

Fig. 3: View into the „Corta de Covas" and the subterranean course of the „Galeria dos Alargamentos" (red).

All these items lead to a different conclusion than to the interpretation of the gallery as a connection between the opencast area and the hillside. Furthermore there were some items that the construction of the gallery was constructed by opening it, beginning at both ends (Gegenortverfahren). One end started at the surface of the hill, today used as entrance and with the dump below. And the other end began in the part that later would be the large cavern. This basically well-known proceeding in tunnelling has its inherent perils, namely the difficulties of precise measurements in ancient times. In Três Minas all the other large galleries (exception: Galeria Esteves Pinto) where constructed with the help of a "Richtungsstollen" (= small gallery – one hewer large – for orientation in direction and level) and enlarged afterwards, mainly to save time. But there are only very few rest of this "Richtungsstollen" visible in the Galeria dos Alargamentos which were even not definite in their interpretation.

It has again to be emphasized that these were reflections which included all the visible items but only after the survey by 3D-Laserscanning these reflections became evidence.

- There are definitely two branches (P1 and P2) which overlap in the middle (*Fig. 4*).
- The two branches show a very different section. In P1 the section is square. In P2 the section is a segment of a circle.
- The P1-branch has a gradient of 2.11m on 55.40m. P2 is almost on one level. This is an important indication for the construction by "Gegenortverfahren" because there was always the problem of the water (Bergwasser). By giving P1 a gradient this problem was easily eliminated, the water flew down and out of the gallery, whereas the situation in P2 is different. There was no place, where the water was not annoying men and their work.
- The survey by 3D-Laserscan shows also the difficulties by the Roman libratores (surveyors) for the indication of the proper line to connect P1 with P2. The 3D-Laserscan makes it visible how difficult this process was. Even we can approve that the result is of the highest quality.
- The position of the cavern in relation to the gallery and the great pit show that there was real planning in connection with the "Galeria dos Alargamentos" before any stone was moved. This planning included the pits visible in "Corta de Covas".
- The interpretation of the results by 3D-Laserscanning in the part of the cavern shows the different steps of work that were executed by the Romans.

It is of great importance to emphasize that the Roman work in connection with the "Galeria dos Alargamentos" was not only executed under the surface of the mountain but there can be proved that they included the surface in this area. There is no doubt that the position of the "Galeria dos Alargamentos" and the pits are strongly connected with the well visible rocks which build a line from the top to the bottom of the hillside. By using this line the perils of the measurements could be kept low. It is of high importance that our team could prove that there is more evidence for the activities of the Roman surveyors.

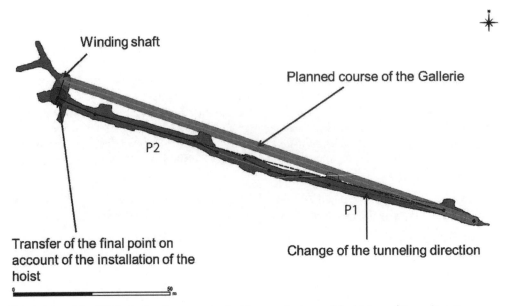

Fig. 4: Map of the "Galeria dos Alargamentos" with some features of the history of its construction.

After the intense discussion about the construction of the "Galeria dos Alargamentos" and its connected pits and smaller galleries, we will discuss now the second item: why did the Romans build them? There is only one possible answer: prospection. The Romans were keen prospectors who did not avoid any trouble to control the possible contents of gold in a place. The position of the pits and the Galeria dos Alargamentos between the two opencast mines was for the Romans indication enough to prospect this part of the mountain. More difficult is the question about the time when it did happen. Any indicator until known hints to the first century AD.

Results and further perspectives of the 3D laser scanning at Três minas

The surveying of the "Galeria dos Alagamentos" has shown that, with 3D laser scanning, historical mining sites can be recorded with great precision and accuracy in addition to a comparatively short time. By this means the "Galeria dos Alagamentos" was able to be documented completely in its 2010 state. It will therefore be easy to demonstrate all future interventions and changes. This survey has produced a document of unique significance for science, one which helps to decode the building history of this site. But this also lays the foundations for the public presentation of the site. In the future it will be possible to present the gallery as a virtual 3D model, enabling the public to understand it and imagine what it was like. The method offers, furthermore, an ideal basis for discovering how the Romans mined the gold. It thus becomes easier to understand and represent the basic approach of the Roman miners when planning the mining operation, the construction of facilities (galleries, shafts), and the rate of advance.

Endnote

[1] This article is related to the paper „Três Minas: A discussion of some aspects of the evidence for the use of water in mining" by Regula Wahl-Clerici, in this volume.

References

Bofinger, J; Kurz, S. & Schmidt, S. (2007): Hightech aus der Luft für Bodendenkmale. Airborne Laserscanning (LIDAR) und Archäologie. Denkmalpflege in Baden-Württemberg: Nachrichtenblatt der Landesdenkmalpflege 36, 3, 2007, pp. 153-158.

Grussenmeyer, P.; Cazalet, B.; Burens, A. & Carozza, L. (2010): Close range terrestrial laser scanning and photogrammetry for the 3D-documentation of the Bronze Age cave „Les Faux" in Perigord (France). In: Anreiter, P.; Goldenberg, G.; Hanke, K.; Krause, R.; Leitner, W.; Mathis, F.; Nicolussi, K.; Oeggle, K.; Pernicka, E.; Prast, M.; Schibler, J.; Schneider, I.; Stadler, H.; Stöllner, Th.; Tomedi, G. & Tropper, P. (Hrsg.): Mining in European History and its impact on environment and human societies – Proceedings for the 1st Mining in European History-Conference of the SFB-HIMAT, 12.-15. November 2009, Innsbruck. Innsbruck, pp. 411-421.

Hesse, R. (2010): LiDAR-derived Local Relief Models – a new tool for archaeological prospection. Archaeological Prospection, 17, 67-72. doi: 10.1002/arp.374

Heine, H.-W. (2011): Vom Orbit auf den Boden. Airborne Laserscanning im Weserbergland. Archäologie in Niedersachsen 14, 2011, pp. 124-128.

Ramminger, B.; Helfert, M. & Wahl-Clerici, R. (2011): Non-invasive archaeological research in the Roman gold mining district of Três Minas and Gralheira (Vila Pouca de Aguiar, northern Portugal). International Conference on Engineering UBI2011, Innovation and Development. Covilhã, pp. 1-9.

Reindel, M. & Wagner, G. (2008): New Technologies for Archaeology. Natural Science in Archaeology (Dordrecht 2008).

Wahl, J. (1988): Três Minas. Vorbericht über die archäologischen Untersuchungen im Bereich des römischen Goldbergwerks 1986/87. Madrider Mitteilungen, 1988, pp. 221-244.

Wahl, J. (1993): Três Minas. Vorbericht über die archäologischen Ausgrabungen im Bereich des römischen Goldbergwerks 1986/87. In: Steuer, H. & Zimmermann, U.: Montanarchäologie in Europa. Berichte zum Internationalen Kolloquium „Frühe Erzgewinnung und Verhüttung in Europa" in Freiburg im Breisgau vom 4.-7. Okt. 1990. Sigmaringen, pp. 123-152.

Wahl, J. (1998): Aspectos tecnológicos da indústria mineira e metalúrgica romana de Três Minas e Campo de Jales (Concelho Vila Pouca de Aguiar). Actas do Seminário Museologia e Arqueologia Mineira. Pub. Do Museu do I.G.M., Lisboa, pp. 57-68.

Wahl, J. (2003): Zur Wasserversorgung des römischen Goldbergbaues von Três Minas und Campo de Jales (Vila Pouca de Aguiar, Trás-os-Montes, Portugal). In: Stöllner, Th; Körlin, G.; Steffens, G. & Cierny, J.: Man and Mining – Mensch und Bergbau. Studies in honour of Gerd Weisgerber on occasion of his 65th birthday. Bochum, pp. 495-502

Wahl, J. & Wahl-Clerici, R. (1993): Minas Romanas de Três Minas. Vila Pouca de Aguiar.

Wahl-Clerici, R.; Helfert, M & Ramminger, B. (2011): Fenster Europa. Portugal: Mit 3D unter Tage – Römischen Bergbauingenieuren auf der Spur. Archäologie in Deutschland, 2, 2011, pp. 54-55.

Wahl-Clerici, R. & Wiechowski, A.: Untersuchungen zur antiken Prospektion von Erzlagerstätten mit bergbaulichen Beispielen aus dem römischen Goldbergwerksdistrikt von Três Minas / Gralheira und Campo de Jales in Nordportugal. Madrider Mitteilungen 54, 2013 (in press).

Wahl-Clerici, R.; Helfert, R. & Wiechowski, A. (2012): Três Minas – Eine Bergwerkskatastrophe mit Rettungsaktion in der römischen Kaiserzeit. Frankfurter elektronische Rundschau zur Altertumskunde 17, 2012, pp. 12-28.

Wiedemann, A. (2004): Handbuch der Bauvermessung. Geodäsie Photogrammetrie Laserscanning1. Bau-Handbuch, Basel 2004.

From the skies into the underground. Remote sensing, survey and documentation in a medieval mining landscape in the Ore Mountains

Rengert Elburg[1], Fanet Göttlich[1] & Thomas Reuter[1]

[1] Ziel 3-Projekt ArchaeoMontan, Landesamt für Archäologie Sachsen, Dresden, Germany

The Ore Mountains on the border of the German federal state of Saxony and the Czech Republic constitute one of the major sources for polymetallic ores in Central Europe, best known for its rich deposits of silver and tin. The earliest documented mining activities in historical times are the rich finds of silver ore in the region of Freiberg in 1168, which is traditionally seen as the start of the exploitation of mineral deposits in the region. There are some indications for much older mining, probably exploiting placer deposits of tin ore in the Bronze Age, but the evidence is still inconclusive (Bartelheim & Niederschlag, 1998). Two major factors complicate the investigation of medieval and prehistoric mining. Firstly large parts of the mountains are covered in dense, mostly coniferous woods, which make a survey using aerial photographs impossible. Secondly later mining in Early Modern times, made famous by Georg Agricolas handbook 'De re metallica' published in 1556, and afterwards overprinted most mining districts, all but eliminating traces of previous exploitation. With the fortuitous discovery of two large medieval silver mines at Dippoldiswalde and Niederpöbel in recent years it has become clear mining, especially for silver, has been much more widespread than previously documented. With the start of a binational project 'ArchaeoMontan' in March 2012, which unites seven institutions from Saxony and Bohemia and is funded by the European Regional Development Fund (ERDF), investigation into the medieval mining landscape is being carried out in a regional scale for the first time (see also contribution by Burghardt et al., this volume). As it would be clearly impossible to investigate the whole mountain range, covering approx. 6000km^2, neighbouring reference regions were selected at both sides of the mountain crest between Chomutov at the south-eastern margin and Falkenstein/Vogtland at the western edge. Within this still very extensive area an initial inventory of mining relicts is being made and selected zones are investigated in more detail. In the following paper we give a concise overview of the methods used in the exploitation and documentation of these areas on different levels of detail, their advantages and limitations.

Methods

One of the most powerful tools available at the moment for the investigation of ancient mining landscapes is without any doubt Airborne LiDAR scanning (ALS, for a general introduction see Crutchley, 2010). On the German side of the border ALS data is region-wide available, although the resolution of 1m is relatively low; in the Czech reference region a first, high density aerial survey is commissioned and will be conducted in spring 2013. The German ALS are provided

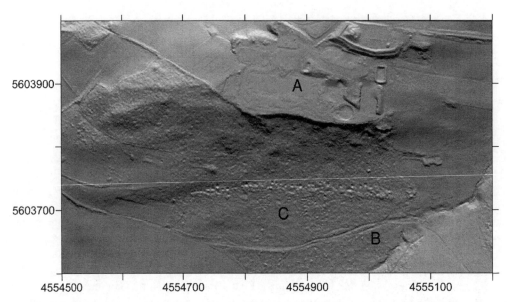

Fig. 1: Hillshade rendering of airborne LiDAR data showing a hitherto unknown, probably medieval mining field in a forest near Beierfeld (Central Ore Mountains). Note the 'erased' buildings (A), sunken road (B) and traces of huts or small houses (C).

by the Saxon Geographical Survey in the form of rasterized hillshades in Tiff-format as well as processed ascii-files which contain the filtered last returns of the laser scanning and can be used for the construction of digital terrain models *(Fig 1)*. After identifying points of interest in the LiDAR scans the individual sites have to be visited for further investigation, as any type of remote sensing can only be a first step in the identification and evaluation of archaeological features. Orientation on the ground is aided by the use of a handheld GPS-receiver in which the coordinates of the features identified in the scans are being fed. Documentation of the features is carried out using differential GPS, often in combination with a reflectorless total station. After classification, and where possible dating, all sites are incorporated in a trans-border GIS.

The complement to the large scale surface surveys is the underground investigation of medieval mines in the eastern part of the Ore Mountains, which gave the impulse to start the whole project. In Dippoldiswalde, a small town ca. 20km south of Dresden, spontaneous collapse of the fills within ancient mining shafts and workings led to several sinkholes opening up within the city, endangering buildings and infrastructure. In cases where sinkholes pose a threat, as in cities and near roads, the underground workings have to be opened up further, emptied and subsequently filled in with a more stable and resilient material like concrete. This gives the archaeologists, working in close cooperation with the Mining Inspectorate a unique chance to enter and record the mines, something which would be otherwise impossible for archaeological institutions due to the prohibitive costs of such an endeavour. The second excavation site was discovered during groundwork in advance of the construction of a flood retention basin near Niederpöbel, 10km south of Dippoldiswalde. Although being a known mining area with exploitation well into the 20th century, the extend and dating of the cavities encountered came as a complete surprise.

In Dippoldiswalde the exploitation started in the second half of the 12th century and seems to follow a regular pattern with shafts giving entrance to the underground workings, which were strictly following the ore veins. As the ore has been completely worked out it is difficult to estimate the original thickness of the veins and their metal content but the few vestiges that could be recovered seem to indicate the veins were very thin, in the magnitude of a few centimetres up to a decimetre. As most veins and lodes are in a vertical to sub-vertical position the mining has resulted in extensive, deep but very narrow stopes, with a width mostly not over 80cm and often considerably less. The depth of the workings regularly surpasses 30m, extending under the level of the valley, which makes draining by adits impossible. In the deeper levels the water must have been lifted by mechanical means, mostly with winches of which several well-preserved stands have been found.

The excavations in Niederpöbel have uncovered a completely different type of site, which even poses the question if the cavities found here represent ore extraction in a strict sense. The geological complexity of the area is at the moment still poorly understood and a thorough interpretation will only be possible after a detailed geological study, which is at the moment still in progress by the Czech Geological Survey. By all appearances the extensive underground workings represent an exploration by medieval miners during a limited period around 1275. Most workings seem to follow contact zones where ores could be expected, but unambiguous extraction of metalliferous ores seems to constitute only a very minor part of the activities that can be recorded here.

Apart from the classical descriptive archaeological documentation assisted by photography and the mostly schematic mining survey which is carried out within the scope of the safety measures, several types of 3D recording are employed. All workings are regularly surveyed using a total station to document the position, direction and approximate volume of the mines, as well as to set out fixed points (*Fig. 2*). The resulting wire frame model gives a good impression of the extend of the workings. It also illustrates the relations between features and finds and bridges the gap between geometry and the written documentation (*Fig. 3*). Where possible and time permitting, laser scanning is used to document the walls and faces. The available equipment, a Riegl LMS Z420i, produces a dense point cloud which can be meshed and mapped with photos for a realistic result and is especially well-suited to record toolmarks.

One of the most remarkable features in the mines is the excellent preservation of wood. Thanks to the waterlogged conditions underground, in combination with local high concentrations of metals and arsenic, technical installations have been preserved either in situ or in secondary positions. All wooden finds are recorded, the level of detail depending on their preservation and if they are still in a primary position or not. After lifting and transport to the conservation department of the Archaeological Heritage Office of Saxony, all timbers are cleaned and assessed. Poorly preserved material or wood without clear context or preserved tool marks is sampled for dendrochronological dating, resulting in a very precise chronological framework for medieval mining on the two major sites.

Fig. 2: Underground survey using a total station (Leica TS02) in a shaft with a medieval ladder in original position.

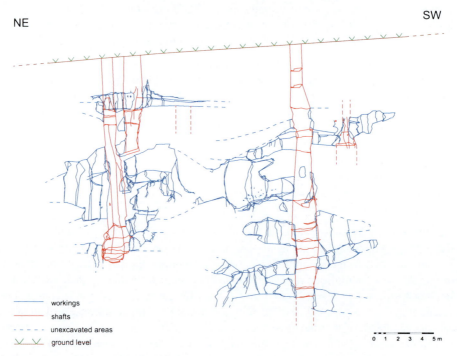

Fig. 3: Typical wire-frame model of a 13th century mining complex in Dippoldiswalde.

The timbers that show relevant archaeological information as well as wooden tools like shovels, scrapers and ore troughs are all documented with a 3D-Scanner. The 3D-laboratory is using two 3D-scanners, a laser scanner Konica Minolta VI-910 and a structured-light scanner Breuckmann smartSCAN 3D-HE. Both are non-intrusive and fast measuring methods. With an optimal resolution of approx. 50μm it is possible to recognize smallest tool marks and use-wear. Analysing 3D models becomes an important step because all original finds will be unavailable for study in the years to come as they will be submersed in large tanks with impregnating agent. With the specially developed software TroveSketch (Lindinger & Hörr, 2008) it is easy to align and measure 3D-Models. The object can be shown from every point of view and different 3D-shaders are available to render standardised images with only a few clicks of the mouse (*Fig. 4*). With the aid of the survey data acquired during the excavations all constructions can be virtually modelled according to their original position. Additionally to the geometry both types of scanner record detailed colour information of every object. In this way it is possible to create photorealistic images and animations in 2D or 3D, which can be used as a means of visual information transfer to a wider audience in publications and presentations.

Discussion

In theory the situation for the documentation of a complete mining landscape in every possible level of detail seems quite ideal, but there are some practical limits to the application of the various methods. The main disadvantage with the 'off-the-shelf' LiDAR-data is the fact that the vegetation cover as well as buildings have been eliminated without clear documentation of the algorithms used. The data are organized in tiles with sides of 2km which contain between 4 and 8 million data points, with the lower limit of one point per square meter being more typical. This resolution is enough to broadly identify even isolated features like the entrances of shafts and adits, and of course mining fields and open cast mining, but is too sparse to differentiate among denser clusters on the level of individual features. A good example is the site seen in Figure 1. The row of sinkholes is clearly visible in the centre of the figure, but it is not really possible to estimate the exact number. On the plateau there are some large buildings that have been completely erased (A), whereas the linear feature of a sunken road (B) is clearly visible. To the south of the mining pits (C) there seem to be some shallower features, which are just discernible in this resolution. From the scan it cannot be determined if they represent real archaeological structures or are just artefacts in the LiDAR. Inspection on the ground revealed them to be possible remains of sunken huts or small houses.

As these as well as all other well-preserved surface relicts lay in wooded area with dense ground cover, dating of the features without invasive methods poses a serious challenge. It is being investigated if metric characteristics of the mining fields can be used for a broad temporal classification. A further complicating factor is the regeneration of the woods in the higher reaches of the Ore Mountains. In the 1980s the forest was heavily damaged, in some places to the point of downright deforestation, by acid rain. After 1990 a dramatic reduction in sulphur emission

Fig. 4: Rendering of 3D-models without colour mapping of three ore scrapers and a miners' pick from Dippoldiswalde.

by the large lignite powered electricity plants at the Czech side of the border was achieved. The subsequent, mostly spontaneous, recovery of the forest locally results in nearly impenetrable brushwood, which makes recording the sites on the ground quite adventurous. Additionally a systematic survey of water courses is being made locate the smelting sites associated with the mines. After a flood catastrophe in 2002 which led to major devastations in the whole mountain range, many of the river beds have been reinforced, severely reducing the possibility to find slag heaps exposed in the banks. In these respects, the project is starting ten years late.

With the subterranean parts of the mines it is especially the very restricted space that complicates the already difficult archaeological documentation underground. The elongated forms of the cavities, be it the near vertical shafts of the horizontal stopes, drifts and adits, result in unfavourable angles during surveying, putting high demands on the precision of the measurements.

The confinement underground also limits the employment of the available laser scanner, which is not only large and heavy, but additionally needs a sensor-to-subject distance of at least two meters, a condition seldom met in the medieval mines. In these cases, the use of freely available software using 'Structure from Motion' for the creation of 3D-models from unsorted digital photos like VisualSfM is becoming an interesting alternative (Hannemann et al., 2012). Even if the resolution of these models is typically in an order of magnitude less than the data provided by high-end scanner systems, the detail in millimetre range is good enough to asses and classify features like tool marks. A particular advantage over laser scanning is the compact and inexpensive equipment, consisting of a digital camera and a light source, which makes it affordable for almost everybody. A major challenge underground is the difficult illumination, which is vital for all methods depending on the processing of photogrammetric data, as well as the dark, reflecting surfaces, which cause numerous artefacts and holes that have to be corrected in the post-processing.

Conclusions

With the wide range of methods, operating on scales varying from kilometres in the initial survey down to the submillimetric resolution of the object scans, we are recording the remnants of medieval mining in all their aspects. Thanks to the close collaboration of numerous specialists from different disciplines and institutes, a comprehensive overview of mining activities at both sides of the border in the Ore Mountains is being obtained for the first time. Also putting to the test different methods of documentation under the often harsh conditions of mining archaeology will be of benefit for other projects facing similar extensive tasks.

Acknowledgements

The Project ArchaeoMontan is being funded by the European Regional Development Fund within the Ziel 3/Cíl 3 Programme for promoting cross-border cooperation between the Free State of Saxony and the Czech Republic. We also would like to thank the anonymous referee for his or her useful comments on an earlier version of this paper.

Bibliography

Bartelheim, M. & Niederschlag, E. (1998): Untersuchungen zur Buntmetallurgie, insbesondere des Kupfers und Zinns, im sächsisch-böhmischen Erzgebirge und dessen Umland. Arbeits- und Forschungsberichte zur sächsischen Bodendenkmalpflege 40, pp. 8-87.

Crutchley, S. (2010). The Light Fantastic. Using airborne lidar in archaeological survey. Swindon.

Hannemann, W.; Brock, T. & Busch, W. (2012): Documentation of conservation state in large-scale subsurface objects. Photogrammetrie - Fernerkundung - Geoinformation 2012(6), pp. 691-700. doi:10.1127/1432-8364/2012/0149

Lindinger, E. & Hörr, C. (2008): Hightech meets handmade - Ein neu entwickeltes 3D-Scanverfahren für archäologische Objekte. Arbeits- und Forschungsberichte zur sächsischen Bodendenkmalpflege, 48/49, pp. 9-18.

Spatial Analysis Techniques for Investigation of Tool Marks on Archaeological Finds

Kristóf Kovács[1,2] & Klaus Hanke[1]

[1] Institute of Basic Sciences in Engineering, Surveying and Geoinformation Unit, University of Innsbruck
[2] Institute of Geography, Georg-August-Universität Göttingen, Germany

Introduction and Related Work

The latest data collection methods provide several tool mark research opportunities in the field of archaeological science. Photographic documentation was used to analyze the tool marks on the surface of archaeological finds in the second half of the 1990s (Sands, 1997). In recent years, the short-range laser scanning offers a unique data acquisition technique in the archaeological researches as well, since these systems can create a digital copy of the find's morphological characteristics for detailed investigations of the tool marks on these objects (Lobb et al., 2010).

Therefore, several entirely preserved patterns of hand tools were surveyed by a FARO® Scan-Arm short-range laser scanner during the accurate documentation of a Bronze Age sluice box from Mitterberg, Austria (Hanke et al., 2011). The aim of our work was the study of these tool marks on the wooden boards of this archaeological object by the collected datasets within the HiMAT (History of Mining Activities in the Tyrol and Adjacent Areas – Impact on Environment and Human Societies) project (Kovacs et al., 2011, Stöllner et al., 2012).

The tool marks have been investigated in several disciplines during the last years and the primary requirements of these researches have been exactly defined in the field of forensic science: The specification of the individual characteristic number, which could offer a positive identification at the evidence investigation; the requirement of an exactly defined evaluation workflow and the results of these exact studies must be repeatable as well (Committee on Identifying the Needs of the Forensic Sciences Community, National Research Council 2009). For these reasons, the research objectives of this tool mark-study can be summarized in the following way:

- Tool mark recognitions by automated methods;
- Implementation of computer-based 3D (three dimensional) techniques for tool marks analysis.

Material and Methods

The basic ideas of the quantitative land-surface studies have been implemented in geomorphometry science (Hengl et al., 2008). The concept of the geomorphometry can be applied in other research fields since the standard landform elements of the Earth's surface such as mountain ridges and valleys can be similar to the micro-relief characteristics of an archaeological object. Therefore, the Geographical Information System-based (GIS-based) surface analysis can offer

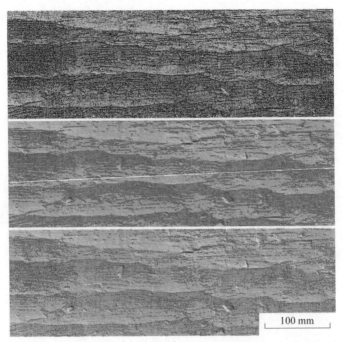

Fig. 1abc: a (top) – The raster grids with null "Flow Accumulation" values indicated by black points; b (middle) – The boundaries of the aspect changes indicated by red shapes; c (bottom) – The exported raster cells indicated by red points after the overlap analysis.

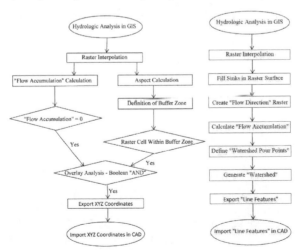

Fig. 2ab: a (left) Flowchart of the first workflow: Combination of "Flow Accumulation" parameters and aspect calculations; b (right) Flowchart of the second workflow: Calculation of watershed boundaries.

novel tool mark-study opportunities in the archaeological science.

In this HiMAT research project, thirty-one wooden objects were documented during three days by the FARO® ScanArm short-range laser scanning system and 440 million points were collected with 0.2mm selected resolution. On grounds of this raw dataset, several hydrologic based tool mark-studies were developed in GIS environment and these workflows will be presented in the next chapters.

Combination of Flow Accumulation parameters and Aspect Calculations

The first workflow was described in detail within a previous publication of the authors (Kovacs et al., 2012). In the first part of this technique, IDW (Inverse Distance Weighted) interpolation was applied during the calculation of raster models in ESRI ArcGIS® Software. The selected raster size was 0.5mm and the "Flow Accumulation" parameters were determined by the "Spatial Analyst Tools". This technique is usually used to recognize the mountain ridges in geosciences since the raster grids with null "Flow Accumulation" values represent the local maxima of the surface model (*Fig. 1a*).

During the second part of the workflow, the edges of the sliding tool marks could be investigated by aspect calculations since the boundaries of the aspect changes can represent the patterns of the hand tools movements (*Fig. 1b*).

In the last part of this method, Boolean operator tools were used to compare the results of the "Flow Accumulation" and the aspect calculations. The requirements were the following: The "Flow Accumulation" values of raster cells are null and these grids must located within the buffer zone of the calculated aspect boundaries as well (*Fig. 1c*). Finally, the raster grids, which also represent the edges of sliding tool marks, were defined by these automated techniques in GIS environment (*Fig. 2a*).

Calculation of Watershed Boundaries

The second workflow is based on the basic watershed calculation techniques in GIS environment and the applied working steps can be summarized in the following way:

1. Based on the point clouds, raster interpolations were accomplished by IDW method and the selected raster size was 0.5mm.
2. Pre-processing of the interpolated raster model, fill small sinks in the raster surface by auto mated techniques.
3. Calculation of "Flow Direction" and "Flow Accumulation" parameters in ESRI ArcGIS® Software, "Spatial Analyst Tools".
4. Definition of the "Watershed Pour Points" in the raster model.
5. Based on the "Flow Direction" parameters and the "Watershed Pour Points", watershed boundaries were generated automatically.
6. Export "Line Features", which represent the edges of the sliding tool marks (*Fig. 2b*).

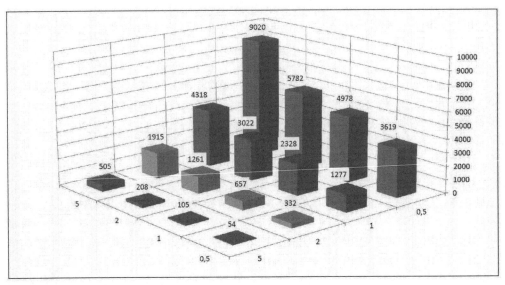

Fig. 3: (Vertical axis) The number of the selected XYZ coordinates; (Horizontal axis – left) Method 2 – Watershed Boundaries with different buffer sizes in mm; (Horizontal axis – right) Method 1 – Surface interpolations with various raster sizes in mm.

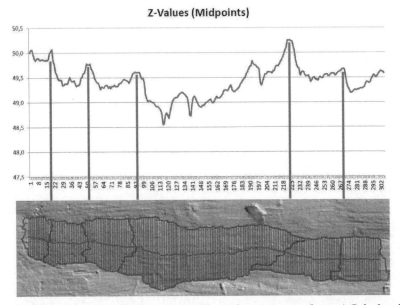

Fig. 4: (top) Visualization of the Z coordinates along the midpoints in mm; (bottom) Calculated watershed boundaries (red lines) and the cross sections (blue lines) within this investigated area.

In summary, the patterns of hand tools were automatically determined in this second workflow. On the other hand, the "Watershed Pour Points" could be only manually defined in the fourth step; however the combination of this working step with the calculated aspect boundaries must improve the selection process of the pour points.

Evaluation and Discussion of the Results

At first, the raster interpolation parameters were investigated and the different raster calculations by various raster sizes (0.5mm, 1mm, 2mm, 5mm) were compared in this study. The research issue was the following: What is the optimal interpolation cell size for the segmentation of the sliding tool marks in GIS environment? After the modification of the grid size, the number of the exported XYZ coordinates which represent the tool marks were efficiently reduced in the first workflow.

The concept was the following:

1. In these workflows, the increase of the interpolated cell size produces significant modifications on the morphological characteristics.
2. After the interpolation in the second workflow, the watershed boundaries could correctly represent the edges of the sliding tool marks.
3. The utilization of various buffer sizes around these watershed boundaries (0.5mm, 1mm; 2mm, 5mm) could be used to determine the optimal interpolation parameters.

The result of this investigation was visualized in a 3D chart. After the comparisons of the two workflows, the approximately 1mm interpolation size could be defined as an optimal grid for the separation of the sliding tool marks in GIS (*Fig. 3*).

In addition the single tool marks (facet) could be defined by automated GIS-based methods since cross sections were created along the sliding tool marks and the Z values of the cross sections midpoints have described the boundaries between these facets (*Fig. 4*).

Conclusion and Future Work

The implementation of spatial analysis techniques in GIS environment provides unique tool mark study opportunities. The comparison of the two presented workflows helped to identify the optimal raster interpolation size for the segmentation of the sliding tool marks and the various facets could be determined by these advanced methods as well. During the future work, the investigation of test tool marks within a scientific experiment must help to improve these applied workflows. Furthermore, this research may have a significant impact on the archaeological interpretations since the shape of the used hand tool and the sizes of the various facets could be exactly analysed by the patterns of the tool marks.

Acknowledgment

The work is generously supported by the Austrian Science Fund (FWF Project F3114) in the framework of the Special Research Program "History of Mining Activities in the Tyrol and Adjacent Areas" (SFB HiMAT) as well as by the Austrian province governments of Tyrol, Vorarlberg and Salzburg, the Autonomous Province Bozen-South Tyrol, Italy, the local authorities of the mining areas concerned, the TransIDEE foundation and the University of Innsbruck, Austria.

Copyright License

We warrant that we own all copyrights in the paper and the paper does not infringe the rights (including without limitation the copyrights) of any other person, company or organization.

References

Committee on Identifying the Needs of the Forensic Sciences Community, National Research Council, 2009: Strengthening Forensic Science in the United States: A Path Forward. National Academies Press.

Hanke, K.; Kovacs, K. & Moser, M. (2011): Virtuelle Rekonstruktion des bronzezeitlichen Waschkastens vom Mitterberg und Untersuchungen der prähistorischen Bearbeitungsspuren des archäologischen Funds. In: Grimm-Pitzinger, A. & Weinold, T. (Hrsg.): 16. Internationale Geodätische Woche Obergurgl 2011. Heidelberg: Wichmann, pp. 195-198.

Hengl, T. & Reuter, H. I. (2008): Geomorphometry: Concepts, Software, Applications. Elsevier Science, pp. 3-6.

Kovács, K.; Hanke, K. & Moser, M. (2011): GIS-based surface analysis of archaeological finds. The International Archives of Photogrammetry, Remote Sensing and Spatial Information Sciences Volume XXXVIII-5/W16.

Kovács, K. & Hanke, K. (2012): Hydrologic and feature-based surface analysis for tool mark investigation on archaeological finds. The International Archives of Photogrammetry, Remote Sensing and Spatial Information Sciences Volume XXXIX-B5, 565-570.

Lobb, M.; Krawiec, K.; Howard, A. J.; Gearey, B. R. & Chapman, H. P. (2010): A new approach to recording and monitoring wet-preserved archaeological wood using three-dimensional laser scanning. Journal of Archaeological Science vol. 37 pp. 2995-2999.

Sands, R. (1997): Prehistoric Woodworking: The analysis and interpretation of Bronze and Iron Age toolmarks. University College London: Archetype Press.

Stöllner, T.; Breitenlechner, E.; Fritzsch, D.; Gontscharov, A.; Hanke, K.; Kirchner D.; Kovács, K.; Moser, M.; Nicolussi, K.; Oeggl, K.; Pichler, T.; Pils, R.; Prange, M.; Thiemeyer, H. & Thomas, P. (2012): Ein Nassaufbereitungskasten vom Troiboden. Interdisziplinäre Erforschung des bronzezeitlichen Montanwesens am Mitterberg (Land Salzburg, Österreich). Jahrbuch des Römisch-Germanischen Zentralmuseums 2010, pp. 1-32.

Airborne laser scans as a tool for historical science? – First methodic considerations using the example of medieval mining in the Saxon Ore Mountains (Erzgebirge/Germany)

Lena Asrih[1]

[1] Bergbaugeschichte, Deutsches Bergbau-Museum Bochum, Bochum, Germany

The project

The PhD project „Analysis of the medieval development of mining laws and settlements in the Saxon Ore Mountains (Erzgebirge/Germany)" (working title) is one of the projects within the Leibniz graduate school RITaK (Raw Materials, Innovation and Technology of ancient Cultures). It is the only historical scientific project amongst nine archaeological studies.

The advantages of multidisciplinarity are often discussed but just as often under-utilised. This short paper will describe the possibilities of combining historical sciences with results of modern survey methods using the example of airborne laser scans in mining history, which is one aspect of the dissertation.

Pictures in historical sciences

Until today, using pictures in historical sciences is not common. A long development started in the 19th century. Medieval studies and studies on the early modern period used pictures, but they were handled different from today. Pictures had been treated as material, not as medium (Lengwiler, 2011:131). They were read like texts without source criticism. In the early the 20th century the Art history became an independent discipline, which had a big influence on methods in historical science in general. Mass media provoked a new handling of sources like posters, films and photography, but the guidelines of interpreting such illustrations still mainly came from the history of art. This changed when in the 1990s debates on the "pictorial/visual turn" came up and "Historische Bildkunde" and "Visual History" constituted own approaches. Around this time, museums and exhibitions boomed (1980s-1990s) and – in addition to that – didactics of history played a role in preparing the "visual turn". Besides this, the "practical turn" helped to clarify, that pictures do not only illustrate knowledge, but simultaneously produce knowledge (Bluma & Nikolow, 2009:52). "Visual History" is still in evolution. It can mean investigation of illustrations as media with all its influence, it includes new possibilities of production and presentation of research results, and technical visualizations like x-ray images or, in this case, LIDAR (light detection and ranging) images, too (in general: Lengwiler, 2011; Paul, 2006).

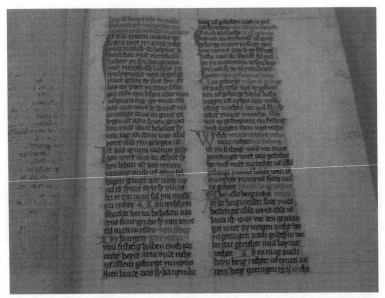

Fig. 1: Freiberger Bergrecht A. Regulations in the mining law of Freiberg from the 14th century are dating back to earlier times of mining.

Fig. 2: Undated mining traces at the Rammelsberg near Freiberg. It is difficult to distinguish the mining traces of different age from one another.

Reading mining traces in the Ore Mountains

In the Saxon Ore Mountains mining traces are distributed all over the region.[1] It is hard to distinguish the different times, in which they were caused. Mining activity in modern times often left written sources or even photos or films. It becomes much more difficult, the older the traces are. The Ore Mountains build a mining landscape since centuries. It probably started with the silver ore findings of Freiberg in the 2nd half of the 12th century and continued until the end of the 20th century (uranium). Apart from economically important resources like silver, tin and copper many other metals and minerals of different importance were mined. All those mining activities changed or destroyed the respectively older mining traces (in general: Wagenbreth & Wächtler, 1990).

Airborne laser scans

Many of the mining traces are in forests and some of them are difficult to find. Their documentation is difficult, too. On photos – for example – it is hard to see heaps or collapsed shafts because of the vegetation and of the perspective. LIDAR images as a result of airborne laser scanning look like aerial images without the carpet of vegetation. A scanner under an airplane sends laser beams to the ground. The reflected laser beams can be measured, and the resulting data build detailed images of the ground, where we can see the asperities of the surface. Archaeologists have been using this survey method effectively in the last 10 years. Some describe this method for archaeological prospection a "revolution" (e.g. Haupt, 2012). This revolution was not experienced by many historians although there are possibilities to use the images for historical research – for example in mining history.

Medieval mining law

For historical science the information from such LIDAR images can be valuable by comparing them to the written sources. In the case of the mining history of the Ore Mountains, the numerous clearly visible mining traces can be adjusted with elements from the detailed mining regulations. Not many written documents are preserved from the early times of mining. The holey historical tradition starts in the middle of the 12th century (monastery of Chemnitz) with a first allusion to mining in the region. The next preserved written sources already concern mining in the wider area of Freiberg (formerly Christiansdorf). Such documents shed light on economic, political, cultural or social circumstances. They deal with privileges, conflicts and peace agreements, payments and other contents. The mining law of Freiberg (Freiberger Bergrecht) is a comprehensive source. It derives from the 14th century and is preserved in two versions (A [after 1307] and B [after 1346]). Although in the 14th century mining already went on for more than 200 years, some regulations can be assumed to be nearly as old as the mining (from 1168 on) itself. (Ermisch, 1887:60-76; Clauß & Kube, 1957) The law texts include a lot of regulations for mining underground and using the surface – amongst others detailed descriptions of how to apply for mining areas. In the 12th and 13th centuries, e.g., the finder of a rich ore vein had to ask the authorities to mark and measure him a mining field. The size of this "claim" is precisely described by law.

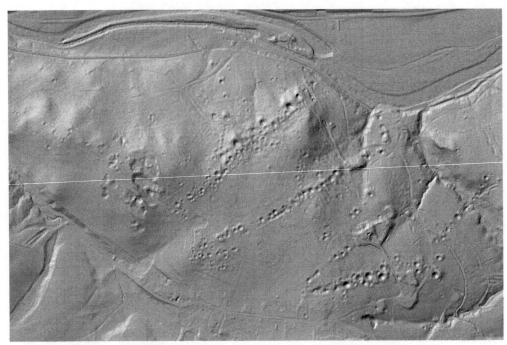

Fig. 3: LIDAR image of Gersdorf near Roßwein. Mining traces of different time periods. (Primärdaten der Laserscanner-Messaufnahme © Staatsbetrieb Geobasisinformation und Vermessung Sachsen 2013)

There are also regulations fixing the number and position of possible shafts or describing how to fix the borderline of two neighbouring mining fields underground. Documents like treaties can be consulted to prove the practical implementation and to get to know about other regulations. A promising assumption is that the varying regulations over time also might be visible in such a way in the area.[2] Next to the dating of mining traces on the basis of their arrangement, the extent of validity of a specific mining law could be investigated. The sporadic reconstructions from literature can be applied and checked.

LIDAR images in combination with other sources

Written information from legends and chronicles can be verified/falsified with the aid of the LIDAR images. The narratives give allusions to past mining and in many cases they include elements of historical truth. On the other hand in many cases a falsification with the help of legends is not possible due to the use of the area by later mining, agriculture or other activities and influences.

Especially in the case of over-stamped mining traces old map material can be consulted. In many cases the maps are showing contemporary already destroyed mining buildings. They show notices on "old mining", "old shafts", "old adits" or "collapsed shafts". Such information can help to reconstruct the older arrangement of the mining site, because many of the later maps are very accurate (esp. since 16th century, cp. Bartels, 2009) and record measurements and physical structures (important to distinguish the traces). It is possible to overlay the LIDAR images with existing maps and to see which traces were known in which times and what vanished over time. Combining those hints again with the written sources and the LIDAR images is very productive.

To get the most possible information out of the LIDAR images it is important to be aware of their weaknesses. If mining traces – for example – lie under a city like in Dippoldiswalde (near Freiberg), LIDAR images show nothing more than the buildings and streets of the city. In rural areas agriculture sometimes has destroyed mining traces (e.g. Rammelsberg near Freiberg). Not at least the technical process of scanning and processing data can influence the result and create for example plane surfaces due to interpolation. Apart from that, not every depression in an area has been caused by mining activities. For this reason, ground checks are necessary and can lead to additional information on environmental and structural questions.

Until now LIDAR images have not been used by historians in this field. The additional benefit deriving from the consideration of such interdisciplinary research methods and results must not be misprized. A historian, who is mostly not familiar with GIS (geographic information system) computer programs, can use the LIDAR images just as a picture, like a satellite or aerial photo. It is not necessary to use all the furthermore available data – like elevation data – to cursory compare the information of the LIDAR image and the written sources or maps. To do the ground check, other specialists like geologists and archaeologists can be consulted to classify specific structures.

Many archaeologists or other mining researchers already work with different archive material to map mining activities of different age. This is multidisciplinarity from the other perspective. It is waste of time if both sides are not including the competences of the respective experts. Historians can support archaeologists in reading archive material, archaeologists are important for historians to read the left material traces of ancient cultures. A successful exchange between both disciplines will help to make multidisciplinarity practicable.

The intensified archaeological research in the Saxon Ore Mountains will provide many new findings in the future, too. Historical research also has to be intensified to get a preferably complete picture of medieval mining history.

Endnotes

[1] Cp. the German-Czech „Ziel 3/Cíl 3" project ArchaeoMontan (www.archaeomontan.eu).

[2] First such analyses were made by Josef Večeřa in the Hrubý Jeseník (eastern Sudetes).

Bibliography

Bartels, C. (2009): Vermessungswesen, Karten und Pläne im Montanwesen an der Wende zwischen Mittelalter und Neuzeit. In: Michalsky, T.; Schmieder, F. & Engel, G.: Aufsicht. Ansicht. Einsicht. Neue Perspektiven auf die Kartographie an der Schwelle zur Frühen Neuzeit. Berlin, pp. 329-350.

Bluma, L. & Nikolow, S. (2009): Die Zirkulation der Bilder zwischen Wissenschaft und Öffentlichkeit. Ein historiographischer Essay. In: Hüppauf, B. & Weingart, P.: Frosch und Frankenstein. Bilder als Medium der Popularisierung von Wissenschaft. Bielefeld, pp. 45-78.

Clauß, H. & Kube, S. (1957): Freier Berg und vermessenes Erbe. Untersuchungen zur Frühgeschichte des Freiberger Bergbaus und zur Entwicklung des Erbbereitens. Berlin (= Freiberger Forschungshefte; D 21).

Ermisch, H. (1887): Das sächsische Bergecht des Mittelalters. Leipzig.

Haupt, P. (2012): Landschaftsarchäologie. Eine Einführung. Aalen.

Lengwiler, M. (2011): Ein Bild sagt mehr…: Visual History und historische Bildanalyse. In: id.: Praxisbuch Geschichte. Einführung in die historischen Methoden. Zürich, pp. 130-152.

Paul, G. (2006): Von der historischen Bildkunde zur Visual History. Eine Einführung. In: id.: Visual History. Ein Studienbuch. Göttingen, pp. 7-36.

Wagenbreth, O. & Wächtler, E. (1990): Bergbau im Erzgebirge. Technische Denkmale und Geschichte. Leipzig.

List of Authors

List of Authors

Lena Asrih 	German Mining-Museum (DBM), Bochum, Germany lena.asrih@bergbaumuseum.de 2008: B.A. at the Ruhr University Bochum in Oriental Studies and History 2011: M.A. at the University of Hamburg in Medieval History since 2011: PhD student within the Leibniz graduate school RITaK (Deutsches Bergbau-Museum and Ruhr University Bochum): Analysis of the medieval development of mining laws and settlements in the Saxon Ore Mountains (Erzgebirge/Germany) (working title)
Lars Bluma 	German Mining-Museum (DBM), Bochum and Ruhr-University Bochum, Germany lars.bluma@rub.de Senior researcher for mining history at the German Mining Museum Bochum. Adjunct Professor at Ruhr University Bochum, Department of History. Main Interests: History of technology, science, and medicine, especially History of mining, Health insurance in German mining (Knappschaft), Body history of mining,
Dirk Brandherm 	School of Geography, Archaeology and Palaeoecology, Queen's University Belfast, UK d.brandherm@qub.ac.uk The author's primary research interests cover a variety of issues from the pre-Roman metal ages of Central and Western Europe as well as the Mediterranean. Specific focus currently lies on the development from Chalcolithic to Bronze Age societies in Iberia, social change in the Later Bronze Age and Early Iron Age contacts.
Ivonne Burghardt 	Archaeological Heritage Office Saxony, Dresden, Germany Ivonne.Burghardt@lfa.sachsen.de She studied medieval history at TU Dresden and Université Marc Bloch in Strasbourg. Her scientific research focuses on high and late medieval economy, law and administration. Since 2012 she is research associate in the ArchaeoMontan-Project. As a postgraduate student at Friedrich Schiller University in Jena she is working on a thesis on the late medieval recession of the silver mining in Freiberg.

Constantin Canavas	Hamburg University of Applied Sciences (HUAS), Faculty of Life Sciences costas.canavas@ls.haw-hamburg.de 1979 Dipl. of Chem. Engineering, National Tech. Univ. of Athens, Greece. 1988 Dr.-Ing. on System Dynamics and Control, Univ. of Stuttgart. 1979-1988 Scientific researcher, Univ. of Stuttgart. 1988-1992 Chem. comp. Henkel (Düsseldorf). Since 1993 Prof. at the HUAS for Automation, Technology Assessment, History and Philosophy of Technology. 1999-2000, 2004 Visiting lecturer for Arab History at the Univ. of Crete, Greece.
Delpech Serge	ERMINA Interdisciplinary research team on ancient mines, France Speleologist – karstic and mining networks, underground topographical surveys.
Diz Ardid Emilio	Ayuntamiento de Orihuela, Spain emiliodiz@orihuela.es Archaeologist; head of Orihuela town council archaeology service and director of the Museo Arqueológico Comarcál. His research interests range from prehistory to the post-medieval period.
Elburg Rengert	Archaeological Heritage Office Saxony, Germany Rengert.Elburg@lfa.sachsen.de Deputy Manager of the project ArchaeoMontan – Medieval mining in Saxony and Bohemia. Field archaeologist specialising on the organisation and managment of large, complicated or otherwise challenging excavations and projects. Special interests: archaeology of mining since the Palaeolithic, prehistoric woodworking and the application of digital 3D-techniques in documentation and analysis of the archaeological record.
Fadin Lionel	French School at Athens (EFA), Greece lionel.fadin@efa.gr Survey engineer, responsible of the topographic surveys of the excavations carried out by EFA.
Feichter-Haid Anita	Institute of History and European Ethnology, University of Innsbruck, Austria anita.b.haid@uibk.ac.at Graduated in History at the University of Innsbruck. Since 2011 doctoral student in History as a recipient of a DOC-team fellowship of the Austrian Academy of Sciences (ÖAW) and member of the research centre HiMAT.

List of Authors

Flor Valeska	Institute of History and European Ethnology, University of Innsbruck, Austria valeska.flor@uibk.ac.at Studies of European Ethnology, American Culture and Literature and Political Science in Bonn, Galway and Innsbruck. Between September 2010 and February 2012 she was a research assistant in Projektpart "Cultural Tendencies and Dominants in Modern Mining" of the SFB HiMAT. Currently she is a lecturer in European Ethnology at University Innsbruck, as well as a scholarship student. She writes her doctoral dissertation on "Living with Lignite. Development Induced resettlements in the Rhenish Lignite Mining Region". Her main research interests focus on mining ethnography, cultural technology studies, football research and narratology.
Giardino Claudio	Department of Cultural Heritage, University of Salento, Lecce, Italy claudiogiardino@hotmail.it Claudio Giardino is researcher at the University of Lecce, where he teaches European proto-history. He focalises his researches in archaeometallurgy.
Göttlich Fanet	Archaeological Heritage Office Saxony, Germany fanet.goettlich@lfa.sachsen.de Surveying Engineer. Her main fields of interest are 3D-documentation, analysis and presentation of archaeological features. Since 2009 she specialises on 3D-documentation of mining archaeology. Currently she is responsible for the underground surveying within the ArchaeoMontan research team.
Gruber Elisabeth	Institute for Languages and Literatures, Department of Linguistics, University of Innsbruck Austria csag9016@student.uibk.ac.at Linguist and Ph. D. student, dissertation on the influence of mining activities on Tyrolean toponymy.
Grutsch Caroline	University of Innsbruck, Institute for Archaeologies, Austria caroline.grutsch@uibk.ac.at Free-lance archaeologist since 2008; Special research interests: prospections, surveys and excavations especially in mining archaeology, (Bronze Age) hoard finds, alpine Bronze Age, rock pictures

Hanke Klaus 	Unit for Surveying and Geoinformation, University of Innsbruck, Austria klaus.hanke@uibk.ac.at Born in 1954, Graduation at Technical University Graz in 1981, Doctor of Engineering Sciences 1984 and Habilitation 1994 at the University of Innsbruck. Since 2010 University Professor and Head of the Surveying and Geoinformation Unit at the Faculty of Technical Sciences of Innsbruck University. Since 1990 scientific engagement in the field of Cultural Heritage Documentation with photogrammetry und laser scanning. Number of scientific papers and international publications, Vice-President of CIPA, the ICOMOS International Scientific Committee on Heritage Documentation since 2006.
Hanning Erica 	Römisch-Germanisches Zentralmuseum, Labor für Experimentelle Archäologie Germany. hanning@rgzm.de Archaeologist at the Laboratory for Experimental Archaeology, RGZM. Research focus on the experimental reconstruction of ancient technologies. Special interests: archaeometallurgy, mining archaeology, experimental archaeology. Since 2008 Phd candidate at the Ruhr-Universität Bochum (topic: Smelting of Sulfidic Ore During the Bronze Age in the Eastern Alpine Region).
Haubner Roland	University of Technology Vienna, Institute of Chemical Technologies and Analytics, Austria rhaubner@mail.zserv.tuwien.ac.at Professor for inorganic technology, specialized on hard CVD coatings like diamond, cubic boron nitride, ceramics, corrosion and failure analysis.
Helfert Markus 	Goethe-University Frankfurt/Main, Institute of Archaeological Sciences m.helfert@em.uni-frankfurt.de Archaeologist; Study of archaeology and history of the Roman provinces, Ancient History, auxiliary sciences of archaeology, classical archaeology, prehistory and early history (MA 2000), PhD (2006), Research Assistant at the Roman-Germanic Commission of the German Archaeological Institute in Frankfurt (2007-08), Research Assistant at the Institute of Archaeology, University of Hamburg (2009), Head of the Research Unit „Ceramics" at the Institute of Archaeological Sciences at the Goethe University Frankfurt (since 2010). Main fields of research: Archaeological and scientific investigation of ceramic, prospecting, 3D laser scanning survey, Landscape Archaeology, Ancient mining.

List of Authors

Hemker Christiane	Archaeological Heritage Office Saxony, Dresden; Germany christianehemker@lfa.sachsen.de Christiane Hemker is an archaeologist and head of the division district of Chemnitz in the department of archaeological heritage in Saxony. Besides organizing excavations in medieval towns, castles and churches, publishing various articles, she gives lectures at the University Freiberg in medieval archaeology and is responsible for the research program "Mining Archaeology" in the heritage office. Since 2012 she is Head of the ArchaeoMontan-Project: Medieval Mining in Saxony and Bohemia.
Herbach Richard	TRACES Lab., CNRS, Toulouse, Université de Technologie de Belfort-Montbéliard, France Richard.herbach@utbm.fr Assistant Professor, fluid mechanist. Mining ventilation.
Herzog Irmela	The Rhineland Commission for Archaeological Monuments and Sites, Bonn, Germany i.herzog@LVR.de Her research interests focus on computer applications in archaeology, especially on stratigraphic computing and spatial analysis. She developed computer programs for these purposes, and this software has been applied to archaeological data from many countries.
Hoffmann Yves	Archaeological Heritage Office Saxony, Dresden, Germany Yves.Hoffmann@lfa.sachsen.de As a trained Site-Technician and with a PhD in medieval and early modern history, he specializes on aspects of mining in Saxony (Dippoldiswalde, Freiberg und Scharfenberg), pottery of Mitteldeutschland and architectural studies of churches and castles (12th to 18th century). In the years 2008-2011 he supervised the archeological surveys and excavation of the high medieval mines in Dippoldiswalde.
Holdermann Claus-Stephan	Context OG, Archäologie – Bauforschung – Kulturraumanalysen office@context-archaeology.info Study of prehistory and Quaternary Ecology, Pre- and Early History, Geology / Palaeontology at Friedrich-Alexander University Erlangen, Nürnberg and Eberhard-Karls University Tübingen, Germany Main fields of research: prehistoric Archaeology, Archaeozoology, prehistorical Archeology, Geology / Paleontology, Museum-Didactics. http://www.context-archaeology.info/

Hornschuch Annette	Deutsches Bergbau-Museum Bochum, Germany annette.hornschuch@bergbaumuseum.de Head of GIS-Laboratory at the German Mining Museum in Bochum.
Jacquemot Denis	ERMINA Interdisciplinary research team on ancient mines, France Speleologist – karstic and mining networks, underground topographical surveys.
Kaiser Marion	German Mining Museum, Bochum, Germany marion.kaiser@bergbaumuseum.de Historian, M.A. PhD student Project: Exploitation and processing of the "Lahn Marble" in the 18th and 19th centuries
Kasper Michael	Montafoner Museen, Schruns, Austria m.kasper@montafoner-museen.at Head of Montafoner Museums, Vorarlberg. Scientific staff Member at the Institute of History and European Ethnology, University of Innsbruck, Austria.
Klemm Susanne	Austrian Academy of Sciences Vienna, Institute of Mediterranean and Prehistoric Archaeology, Austria susanne.klemm@oeaw.ac.at Archaeologist, main fields of research: landscape and mining archaeology in the Eastern Alps (copper and iron production, charcoal production, etc.); periods: metal ages, mediaeval and modern period. Austrian Academy of Sciences Vienna, Institute of Mediterranean and Prehistoric Archaeology.

List of Authors

Knapp A. Bernard	Cyprus American Archaeological Research Institute, Nicosia, Cyprus Bernard.Knapp@glasgow.ac.uk A. Bernard Knapp is Emeritus Professor of Mediterranean Archaeology in the Department of Archaeology at the University of Glasgow, and Honorary Research Fellow at the Cyprus American Archaeological Research Institute. He co-edits the Journal of Mediterranean Archaeology with John F. Cherry and Peter van Dommelen and is the general editor of the series Monographs in Mediterranean Archaeology. He is the author and editor of several books including, most recently, Material Connections in the Ancient Mediterranean: Mobility, Materiality, and Mediterranean Identities, co-edited with Peter van Dommelen (New York: Routledge, 2010)) and Prehistoric and Protohistoric Cyprus: Identity, Insularity, and Connectivity (Cambridge: Cambridge University Press, 2013).
Koch Waldner Thomas	Institute of Archaeology, University of Innsbruck, Austria thomas.koch-waldner@uibk.ac.at Graduated in Archaeoloy at the University of Vienna. Since 2011 doctoral student in Archaeology as a recipient of a DOC-team fellowship of the Austrian Academy of Sciences (ÖAW) and member of the research centre HiMAT.
Kovács Kristóf 	University of Göttingen, Germany kristof.kovacs@uibk.ac.at Born in 1983. MSc degree in Geoinformatics in 2006. Worked at the University of Innsbruck, Surveying and Geoinformation Unit between 2008 and 2012. PhD started in 2009 under the supervision of Univ.-Prof. Dr. techn. Klaus Hanke. The PhD project focuses mainly on the analysis of tool marks on the surface of archaeological finds. Currently he is working at the University of Göttingen as a research assistant.
Krismer Matthias 	Institute of Mineralogy and Petrography, University of Innsbruck, Austria matthias.krismer@uibk.ac.at Main research fields are the chemical- and mineralogical characterization of ore mineralizations and the application of mineralogical and petrographic approachs to prehistoric- and historic metallurgical slags.

Larocca Felice 	Università di Bari "Aldo Moro", Missione di Ricerca speleo-archeologica, Sant'Agata di Esaro (CS), Italy Centro Regionale di Speleologia "Enzo dei Medici", Commissione di Ricerca per l'Archeologia delle Miniere, Roseto Capo Spulico (CS), Italy specus@tin.it He is a speleologist and prehistoric archaeologist. Since the year 2000 he directs the University of Bari archaeological research on Grotta della Monaca site. He is interested on mining archaeology and each aspect of cave archaeology. He co-ordinates speleo-archaeological researches in several cavities of middle-southern Italy.
Lech Jacek 	Cardinal Stefan Wyszyński University in Warsaw, Institute of Archaeology, Warszawa, Poland Polish Academy of Sciences, Institute of Archaeology and Ethnology, Autonomous Unit of Prehistoric Flint Mining, Warszawa, Poland lech@iaepan.edu.pl Jacek Lech is Professor of Prehistoric Archaeology at the Institute of Archaeology of the Cardinal Stefan Wyszyński University in Warsaw and in the Polish Academy of Sciences. His research interests lie in prehistoric mining, flaking industries and distribution of siliceous rocks, as well as in history of archaeology and archaeological thought. He has published many works on the prehistoric flint mining in Poland and Europe. A Corresponding Member of the German Archaeological Institute (Berlin), member of the Executive Committee of the International Union of Prehistoric and Protohistoric Sciences (UISPP) and president of the UISPP Commission "Flint Mining in Pre- and Protohistoric Times".
Levato Chiara 	Università di Bari "Aldo Moro", Missione di Ricerca speleo-archeologica, Sant'Agata di Esaro (CS), Italy Centro Regionale di Speleologia "Enzo dei Medici", Commissione di Ricerca per l'Archeologia delle Miniere, Roseto Capo Spulico (CS), Italy okros@live.it She is speleologist and prehistoric archaeologist. She is a member since the year 2000 of Grotta della Monaca University of Bari Research Mission, studying prehistoric iron hydroxides mining evidence. She is interested in iron oxides prehistoric mining and usage as well as in cave archaeology.
Maass Alexander	Mining Archaeologist Specialities: prehistoric flint, pigment and copper mining, quarries and copper metallurgy oman pigment, copper, silver and gold mining and quarries, medieval silver mining and quarries.

Marshall Peter	Peter David Marshall, English Heritage, Holborn, London, UK
	Peter Marshall studied archaeology and geography at the University of Sheffield undertaking research in Austria on the impact of past metallurgical activities on the environment. Since 1997 he has worked for English Heritage the Government's statutory adviser on the historic environment and also run a scientific dating consultancy (Chronologies). His research interests include the chronology of Late Neolithic Wessex (particularly Stonehenge) and the dating of palaeoenvironmental sequences.
Martinek Klaus-Peter	Independent Researcher, Munich kpmartinek@t-online.de
	Mineralogist with special interest in archaeometallurgy of gold and copper, presently with focus on the beginning of fahlore metallurgy. Contributed to the interdisciplinary and supra-regional research projects "Prehistoric Gold in Bavaria, Bohemia and Moravia" and "Bronze Age Copper in South-Bavaria, Salzburg and North-Tyrol" as well as to several regional studies. More than ten years experience with industrial glass production, refractories and colored glass, especially gold ruby glass.
Mátyás-Rausch Petra	Institute of History, Faculty of Arts, University of Pécs, Hungary stefike.rausch@gmail.com
	2012: defending her PhD thesis and getting a doctorate (qualification: summa cum laude) 2010: PhD candidate 2007-2010: PhD studies, University of Pécs, Faculty of Arts, PhD School of Interdisciplinary, PhD Programme of middle Ages 2002-2007: History and Latin (teacher)
Meyerdirks Uwe	Eberhard-Karls-Universität Tübingen, Germany uwe@meyerdirks.com
Mighall Tim	University of Aberdeen, Department of Geography and Environment, School of Geosciences t.mighall@abdn.ac.uk
	Senior Lecturer in the Dept of Geography & Environment at the University of Aberdeen. His research focuses on using peat bog archives to reconstruct the environmental impact of past mining and metalworking activities

Morin Denis	TRACES Lab., CNRS, Toulouse, University of Lorraine, Nancy, France denis.morin@univ-lorraine.fr Assistant Professor, Industrial history. Mining archaeology – Western Alps, Laurion (Greece), Cornwall (U.K.).
O'Brien William	University College Cork, Department of Archaeology, Ireland W.OBrien@ucc.ie Early metallurgy and metal-using societies in Atlantic Europe; Chalcolithic and Bronze Age in Ireland; early mining and metallurgy in Atlantic Europe, upland archaeology, the study of hillforts and all aspects of monumentality in the later prehistoric period south-west Ireland. Beaker copper mine at Ross Island, Co. Kerry, on early settlement landscapes and upland farming in the Beara Peninsula, first general study of the prehistory of the Cork region
Oeggl Klaus	Institute of Botany, University of Innsbruck klaus.oeggl@uibk.ac.at Speaker of the Research Centre HiMAT. He is palae-oeologist and archaeobotanist and has conducted research on the Neolithic Glacier Mummy "Ötzi". His recent research interests focus on the palaeoecology and subsistence of salt and copper mining in the Alps.
Photiades Adonis	Institute of Geology and Mineral Exploration (IGME), Athens, Greece fotiadis@igme.gr Geologist, Head of the geological map of Greece service. Geological mapping, Alpine orogens, mineral resources.
Reuter Thomas	Archaeological Heritage Office Saxony, Germany thomas.reuter@lfa.sachsen.de Surveying Engineer at the Archaeological Heritage Office in Saxony. He is specialized in 3D-Documentation of archaeological finds with close-range 3D-Scanners. The work is focused on the Ziel3-Project ArchaeoMontan as well as the development of acquisition methods, creating virtual reconstructions and visualisations.
Rosenthal Patrick	Chrono-environment Lab., CNRS, University of Franche-Comté, Besançon, France patrick.rosenthal@univ-fcomte.fr Assistant Professor, geology. Geology and archaeology of ancient mines – Western Alps, Laurion (Greece).

List of Authors

Štefánik Martin	Institute of History of Slovak Academy of Sciences (Historický ústav SAV), Bratislava, Slovakia martin.stefanik@savba.sk Head of Department for Medieval History. Research fields: medieval mining history, medieval towns, commercial relations with italian cities in middle ages. 1998-2003 Fellowships in Padua, Venice, Vienna and Augsburg. 2004-2005 visiting lecturer at Albert-Ludwigs University Freiburg. 2007-2008 Mellon Research Fellowship Florenz: Villa I Tatti – The Harvard University Center for Italian Renaissance Studies.
Steiniger Daniel	Freiburger Institut für Paläowissenschaftliche Studien F.I.P.S., c/o Albert-Ludwigs-Universität, Freiburg, Germany danielsteiniger@yahoo.de Studied Prehistoric Archaeology, Geology and Mineralogy. His Ph.D. thesis focused on Chalcolithic Italy and he created a research project for Early mining in central Italy at the DAI (Dep. Rome). He builds reconstructions of dry stone walls and is engaged in archaeometallurgical experiments. He is a specialist in mining archaeology and has participated in excavations in this field throughout Europe, the Near East and Central Asia with the DBM and the DAI. He has worked in several federal states for the Landesamt für Denkmalpflege. Actually he is engaged in the CeramAlex-Project for X-ray fluorescence analysis in Egypt.
Thomas Stöllner	German Mining-Museum (DBM), Bochum University of Bochum (RUB), Institute of Archaeological Science thomas.stoellner@bergbaumuseum.de His special research interests are based in European Prehistory, especially in Metal Ages and the questions of economic pro-cesses and interactions as well as in economic models based on ethnography and cultural anthropology, in mining archaeology especially in the Eurasian, the European and the oriental cultures but also in South America, in the Iron Age research, especially in Hallstatt- and Latène cultures and in various fields of Archaeometry.
Strobl Susanne	University of Technology Vienna, Institute of Chemical Technologies and Analytics, Austria sstrobl@mail.zserv.tuwien.ac.at Scientific officer, specialized on metallography for characterization of microstructures for metals, slags and ceramics.

Timberlake Simon	University of Cambridge, Department of Archaeology, UK simon.timberlake@btinternet.com Excavations Director of the Early Mines Research Group. Simon is a geologist who has undertaken archaeological excavation and research on ancient mining sites since 1986. Since 1996 he has worked at Bangor, Manchester and Coventry Universities on Leverhulme Trust-unded projects, and now works as a field archaeologist for the Cambridge University Archaeological Unit. Has an interest in experimental archaeology and the reconstruction of prehistoric mining and smelting processes and has published (either singly or jointly) more than 40 papers on early mining related topics. www.earlyminesresearchgroup.org.uk
Trebsche Peter	Lower Austrian Museum of Prehistory, Asparn an der Zaya, Austria peter.trebsche@noel.gv.at Peter Trebsche is an archaeologist working at the Lower Austrian Museum of Prehistory at Asparn an der Zaya. He has directed excavations at the multi-period hillfort of Ansfelden in Upper Austria (1999-2002, 2006-08) and at the Late Bronze Age mining site of Prigglitz-Gasteil in Lower Austria (since 2010). Currently, his research focuses on settlement archaeology, architecture as material culture, and the multi-disciplinary analysis of Iron Age settlements.
Viehweider Barbara	Institute of Botany, University of Innsbruck, Innsbruck, Austria barbara.viehweider@uibk.ac.at Graduated in Biology and Botany (specialization in Geobotany, Population and Vegetation Ecology) at the University of Innsbruck. Since 2011 doctoral student in Palynology and Archaeobotany as a recipient of a DOC-team fellowship of the Austrian Academy of Sciences (ÖAW) and member of the research centre HiMAT.
Wahl-Clerici Regula	Projecto – Três Minas – Projekt, University Hamburg, Germany regulawahl@gmail.com
Windhaber Irina	Institute for Languages and Literatures, Department of Linguistics, University of Innsbruck Austria irina.windhaber@uibk.ac.at Linguist and Ph. D. student. Is involved with the investigation of onomastics in mining within the scope of HiMAT.

Sponsors

Sponsors

Many Thanks to all our Sponsors!

Gefördert von